Challenging Lesbian and Gay Inequalities in Education

OPEN UNIVERSITY PRESS
Gender and Education Series

Editors

ROSEMARY DEEM

Professor of Educational Research, University of Lancaster

GABY WEINER

Professor of Education at South Bank University

TITLES IN THE SERIES

Challenging Lesbian and Gay Inequalities in Education

Edited by Debbie Epstein

Open University Press
Buckingham • *Philadelphia*

Open University Press
Celtic Court
22 Ballmoor
Buckingham
MK18 1XW

and
1900 Frost Road, Suite 101
Bristol, PA 19007, USA

First Published 1994

A catalogue record of this book is available from the British Library.

ISBN 0 335 19130 4 (pb)

Library of Congress Cataloging-in-Publication Data

Challenging lesbian and gay inequalities in education / edited by
  Debbie Epstein.
        p.   cm. — (Gender and education series)
    Includes bibliographical references and index.
    ISBN 0-335-19130-4
    1. Homosexuality and education—England. 2. Educational
  equalization—England.   3. Discrimination in education—England.
  I. Epstein, Debbie, 1945-   . II. Series.
  LC192.6.C43   1994
  371.8'2662—dc20   93-38399
                                                              CIP

Typeset by Colset Private Limited, Singapore
Printed in Great Britain by St Edmundsbury Press,
Bury St Edmunds, Suffolk

*This book is dedicated to lesbians and gays everywhere:
to Pride, fun and the struggle for equality,
in memory of the Stonewall 'Riots'.*

Contents

Series Editor's Introduction

Sexuality *is* an important feature of schooling whatever any government or individual might legislate or wish for. A proportion of children will become lesbian or gay adults, there will be gay and lesbian teachers in our schools and inevitably, school students will want to know more about the sexual options available to them. Also, as the editor, Debbie Epstein points out, lesbian and gay issues are currently receiving a significant amount of attention in the media and in academia. However, Epstein points out also that with notable exceptions (see her introductory chapter) such issues have been bypassed in the world of education. This is partly due to Section 28 of the Local Government Act (1986) and more recent interpretations (e.g. Ofsted 1992) emphasizing the prohibition of the 'promotion' of homosexuality in teaching or resources (though both Stacey and Epstein argue that Section 28 actually advanced rather than diminished lesbian and gay issues); and partly due to individuals working in education wanting to avoid issues which they may find difficult or disturbing.

This timely book seeks to fill the gap in educational thinking about lesbian and gay issues by portraying the complex set of debates, arguments and experiences around sexuality and schooling at the same time as pointing up other points of difference (such as 'race' and ethnicity) as important to the discussion. Thus contributors to the volume tell stories of distress and victimization and also of achievement and support. They make suggestions for challenging prejudice and homophobia through the curriculum and through policy and they reflect on the place of lesbian and gay issues in theoretical debates about equality and 'difference' in education.

Epstein argues that as well as the 'enormous problems' surrounding such issues, 'tremendous progress' has been made in uncovering the experience of being lesbian or gay in British culture as a means of combating prejudice against people with different sexualities from the claimed heterosexual norm (see introductory chapter). In my view, this book deserves to be widely read – by students, teachers, parents and policy-makers – as a testimony to that progress and also as a means by which any future gains may be enhanced and sustained.

Gaby Weiner

Notes on Contributors

Akanke is a black Jamaican, presently studying social policy and social work. She is committed to better education for black children.

Alistair, Dave, Rachel and Teresa have all been active in student and in lesbian and gay politics. They are all now thankful that they are no longer involved in student politics but continue their lesbian and gay activism.

Roy Bartell, pseudonym, affectionate, Shire City man, part-time lecturer, 55, white, non-Brit, able-bodied, loves dancing, seeks warm, open relationship. Honesty and tolerance important. All letters answered with photograph.

Helena Burke has taught in inner-city comprehensives for eight years. She is currently responsible for Personal, Social and Health Education. She is also tutor for initial teacher training and has been actively involved in developing equal opportunities in school for some years.

Debbie Epstein is a lesbian activist of long standing. She taught in schools for many years and currently lectures in Sociology at the University of Central England. She is interested in issues of equality and social justice. Her most recent book is *Changing Classroom Cultures: Anti-Racism, Politics and Schools*.

Richard Johnson, born Hull 1939, married 1963, adoptive father 1971 and 1973, historian 1966–75, Director Centre for Contemporary Cultural Studies 1980–88, widowed 1992. Left University of Birmingham for research and writing September 1993.

KOLA is a growing group of black and Asian gay and lesbian people. It seeks to raise the social and political profile of black and Asian gays and lesbians in the West Midlands and offer practical support in a safe environment.

Máirtín Mac an Ghaill teaches in state schools. He is presently working at the School of Education, Birmingham University. He has recently completed a new book for the Open University Press, *The Making of Men: Masculinities, Sexualities and Schooling.*

Paul Patrick is Head of Year in a London comprehensive school. He has been active in lesbian and gay issues in education since 1974, when he first came out to parents, staff and children.

Peter Redman is a self-confessed practising heterosexual. He currently works for East Birmingham Health Authority doing research on young people and sexual health.

Marigold Rogers teaches Modern Languages in a comprehensive school in Sussex. Her chapter arose out of work done for an MA in Women and Education at the University of Sussex.

Susan A. L. Sanders is 46, white, middle-class and currently able-bodied. She has been teaching in schools, prisons, colleges and community centres in England and Sydney since 1970. She has been totally out in schools since 1988.

Gillian Spraggs is an NUT member and former teacher. She has published a number of articles, reviews and essays on lesbian and gay issues in education.

Acknowledgements

When I began work on this book, I had no idea that editing a collection involved so much toil! There are a number of people who have helped me on the way.

Gaby Weiner, as one of the series editors, has been supportive from the inception of this project. Although she probably does not know it, Gaby was the person who helped give me the courage to start researching lesbian and gay issues in education.

Rosemary Deem, the other series editor, has also been supportive and helpful in discussions about the progress of the book.

Richard Johnson has supported me along every step of the way. Not only did he write the final chapter with me, he also read and commented on all the others. He was always available to advise me when I was not sure how to proceed.

Members of the Politics of Sexuality Group, and particularly Peter Redman, have been supportive of the project. Discussions with this group and with the women in my women's group helped me formulate my ideas on what kind of book was needed.

A number of people have read and commented on particular chapters, in particular Andy Chaffer, Mary Kehily, Máirtín Mac an Ghaill and Diana Paton.

John Skelton and Pat Lee, at the Open University Press, have been patient and helpful beyond the call of duty.

Last, but far from least, all the contributors have worked tremendously hard and have been more than cooperative in responding to my comments and getting their chapters finished.

Debbie Epstein

Introduction: Lesbian and Gay Equality in Education – Problems and Possibilities

DEBBIE EPSTEIN

As I write this introduction[1] (during the first half of 1993) it seems that interest in sexuality, both from within the academy and from the popular media is at frenzy point. Both the BBC and independent television networks have broadcast numerous programmes about (mainly hetero)sexuality recently (for example, *The Good Sex Guide*, *What Should You Tell Your Children*, not to mention Channel 4's Valentine's Day extravaganza, *The Love Weekend*). Academic publishers' catalogues (from both the UK and the USA) on Sociology, Women's Studies, Psychology, Cultural Studies, Literary Criticism and the newly arrived Lesbian and Gay Studies abound with pages of books about sexuality/ies and masculinity/ies. Suddenly, in the late 1980s and early 1990s, an area which had been the preserve of a few brave (usually feminist or gay male) souls has become everybody's key interest.

Repression and resistance

One reason for this is the success of the lesbian and gay movement in putting sexuality on the political and academic agenda. In the United States, Jesse Jackson included lesbians and gays in his 'Rainbow Coalition',[2] as did British 'municipal socialism' in the 1980s (especially in London and Manchester). In the UK, this limited success was one of the themes in the moral panic orchestrated in the popular media about the 'loony left' (see, for example, Cooper 1989 on events in Haringey) which formed part of the campaign to re-elect the Thatcher Government in 1987. In 1988 this moral panic was brought to fruition in Section 28 of the Local Government Act, which prohibited the '*intentional* promotion of homosexuality by Local Authorities' (emphasis added). However, as Stacey (1991: 303) points out:

> The construction of sexuality in Thatcher's Britain must be seen as a constant struggle, where the attempts to control and repress may produce the opposite effects. The challenge to Section 28 and the cultural and political activity which surrounded its opposition took place on an unanticipated scale. Had the initiators of the section had any idea of the extent of the response they would meet, they may have thought twice before proposing a piece of legislation to ban the promotion of homosexuality which achieved just the opposite.

This is a struggle which continues in 'Major's Britain'. The 1993 Education Act seems likely to make it more difficult for schools to address issues related to lesbian and gay sexuality, since parents will now be able to withdraw their children from all sex education which is not about biological reproduction. Furthermore, during April 1993, the Department for Education issued draft guidelines to schools to replace old circulars on sex education (DfE 1993). These guidelines restate Section 28, implying that it applies to schools. The official *Handbook* for the newly privatized inspectors of schools says, in its section on the statutory basis for education, that 'promoting homosexuality through resources or teaching is prohibited' (OFSTED 1992: 13). This restatement of Section 28 is even stronger than that in the draft circular and, indeed, than Section 28 itself. As noted above, the original section prohibited the '*intentional* promotion of homosexuality' by local authorities. According both to legal advice received by Liberty and the Greater London Council and to the Department of Environment's own circular 12/88, it did not apply to schools, teachers or governors. It would be naïve to believe that the restatement of Section 28 in these two places, *in a form which appears to 'make good' the poor drafting of the original clause*, is not deliberate. Whether this renewed attack on the civil liberties of lesbians and gays will lead to a renewed campaign remains to be seen, but it is certainly true that it is harder to mobilize support for a campaign against a paragraph in a couple of documents which hardly anyone sees than against a clause in a bill, with parliamentary debates being reported in the press daily over a long period.

HIV: Moral panic, solidarities and research money

Another reason for the saliency of sexuality as a subject for academic and political debate in the late 1980s and the early 1990s is the epidemic of HIV infection and AIDS, together with their attendant moral panic. From being interesting to a few lesbian and gay theorists (for example, Plummer 1975, 1981, 1992; Weeks 1977, 1981, 1985, 1986, 1991, Foucault 1978; Rich 1980) and the focus of some feminist debate (for example, Brownmiller 1975; Dworkin 1981; Cartledge and Ryan 1983), sexual behaviour has become, potentially, a matter of life and death. There are at least two key agendas in operation in relation to HIV. The first, dominant agenda, as articulated in the popular media, has been that of the 'moral majority', with an emphasis on 'normal' family life and abstinence as a solution for sexual ills. The second, counter-agenda, promoted by voluntary bodies such as the Terrence Higgins Trust and by some statutory groups, such as AIDS Lifelines funded by district health authorities, has celebrated diverse formations of sexuality, considered questions of sexual identity, and has, in the academy, been accompanied by the growth of Lesbian and Gay Studies.[3]

Early homophobic responses to the 'gay plague' have been well documented (see, for example, Watney 1987; Redman 1992). However, this particular response began to change as the potential for white, western heterosexuals to become affected became clearer.[4] In the UK it has been, at least in part, replaced by a less overtly homophobic approach which is, arguably, just as dangerous to gay men. No longer is AIDS the 'gay plague'. It is something which concerns 'us all' (that is, white heterosexuals) with the result that neither government

nor local authorities have been concerned to target HIV pre-
vention or education specifically at gay men (who remain the
largest number of new cases of HIV diagnosed, even though
heterosexuals have a higher rate of increase of the infection).[5]
Instead, we have been treated to a series of television commercials, showing attractive, white, young adults, which carry the
messages that HIV is the result of 'holiday romance', that 'you
can't tell by looking' and that condoms protect with little, if
any, reference to any other form of safer sex (with the under-
lying message that sex equals (heterosexual?) penetration).
Many of these commercials end with messages such as 'This is
a true story. X is 23 and heterosexual'.

This concern with the possible spread of HIV amongst the
heterosexual population has meant that not only has sexuality,
as an issue for concern, been drawn to the attention of heterosexuals, but also that official funding for research on sexuality
and sexual behaviours has been made available in many western
countries, including Britain. This has, undoubtedly, assisted the
increase in academic interest in sexuality. There has, too, been
another effect of the epidemic on the lesbian and gay communities. Many of us (whether lesbian or gay) have suffered the
loss of close friends and, in the case of gay men, lovers. These
losses have resulted in a growth in activism around HIV and
AIDS which has been one of coalition between gay men and
lesbians and members of other groups epidemiologically heavily
affected by the virus. The picture in relation to HIV and AIDS,
then, is not simply one of loss, but a more complex one of
major loss as well as some gain. As Ken Plummer (1992: 149)
puts it:

> No late twentieth-century writing on same-sex experience can
> neglect AIDS and HIV. Both as disease and symbol it has played
> a powerful part in the reshaping of gay and lesbian communities
> throughout the 1980s. The articles [in *Modern Homosexualities*]
> are clearly concerned with the tragic nature of the disease: with
> the death and grief that have touched so many lives. But they
> go well beyond this. For predictions of 'holocausts' and the 'end
> of the homosexual' have been transcended. Instead, these articles
> demonstrate the growth of new communities of support, care,
> and activism.

Sexuality and the academy

The agenda amongst those writing about sexuality within the academy has been largely set by those with a background in lesbian and gay, feminist or AIDS activism (see, for example Weeks 1977, 1981, 1985; Watney and Carter, 1989) and/or influenced by 'new Queer theory' (see, for example, Dollimore 1991; Sedgwick 1991). There is much work among this body which draws upon poststructuralism and postmodernism, and, in particular, on psychoanalytic theory to understand the construction of both lesbian and gay and of heterosexual identities. A considerable and growing body of literature now exists on lesbian and gay studies and on the study of masculinities. Some writers are also beginning to problematize heterosexuality (see, for example, Epstein and Johnson, this volume; Kitzinger *et al.* 1992).

And yet, with a few notable exceptions (in particular, Wolpe 1988; Holly 1989; Jones and Mahony 1989; Harris 1990),[6] the growing interest within the academy in sexuality in general and lesbian and gay studies in particular, seems to have bypassed the world of education.[7] This paucity of books about sexuality and education is illustrated by Ken Plummer's (1992) 'Brief Guide to Further Reading' which, despite a section on 'Young people, coming out and families', does not mention education at all.

Complexity and contradiction

Challenging Lesbian and Gay Inequalities in Education is, then, intended to fill a gap. In focusing upon the experiences of lesbians and gays in relation to the school system in England, it raises issues which are important for all. In this culture we are accustomed to make a split between what we regard as being within the public domain and what we think of as being private. In thinking about this split, it seems like common sense to assume that sexuality falls very clearly within the private domain while schooling falls very clearly within the public. However, schools provide a site for practising heterosexuality within the context of developing conventional gender roles.

This is a process which is present in the early years – in, for example, the ways in which children play at different roles – and which continues throughout school life. The interconnections between gender and sexuality may be more obvious in the secondary school, where there is an expectation that girls will start to have 'boyfriends' and vice versa. This presumption of developing heterosexual relationships may well cause considerable discomfort for those whose identities do not fit: for example, the 'academic' girl (see Alistair *et al.*, this volume); the boy who finds it difficult to initiate heterosexual interactions; the girl who identifies as lesbian; the boy who identifies as gay.

The experiences of black lesbians and gay men bear both similarities to and differences from those of white lesbians and gays as they are revealed in this volume. The experience of racism is, clearly, common to Mac an Ghaill's research subjects, to those taking part in the KOLA discussion and to Akanke. However, the decisions which members of KOLA have taken to become members of a black lesbian and gay group and, in general, be out about their sexuality have different consequences in their lives to the consequences for Akanke of her decision to remain, as she says, 'semi-closeted'. Thus, no individual testimony should be made to bear the burden of representation for all black lesbians and gay men, any more than the experience of a white lesbian or gay man can stand for the experiences of all. The commonalities are important, but so are the specificities.

The picture built up through the book as a whole is, then, one of complexity and contradiction. In the personal accounts in Part I, all the contributors tell stories of distress and victimization, and of achievement, support and solidarity. Part II traces both enormous problems and tremendous progress in combating lesbian and gay inequalities in education. Indeed, the appearance of this book, as part of a major series produced by a mainstream publisher is, in itself, evidence of new possibilities. It is inconceivable that this would have happened before Section 28.[8] It is, however, relevant to note here that this is an area of constant struggle. One chapter, commissioned and written, has not appeared because of concern by the author's headteacher about the 'marketability' of the school (see p. 117). This is symptomatic of some of the inroads which have been made by the New Right into previous gains in education for social justice. In a world dominated by the market, it is sometimes difficult to be brave. The 'market', however, may be mythically constructed, with headteachers being worried about the loss of pupils because of supposedly unpopular policies for equality and social justice, while a significant number of parents may make positive choices to send their children to schools retaining these ideals (see Gerwirtz *et al.* 1993).

It seems that education is a particularly difficult site in which to challenge lesbian and gay inequalities. Part III of this book traces some of the historical and theoretical reasons for this difficulty. I argued above that Section 28 has had contradictory effects, agreeing with Stacey's claim that it actually succeeded in promoting homosexuality. However, within schools, there has undoubtedly been an enormous amount of self-censorship. Some teachers believe that Section 28 does apply directly to their work and are, therefore, afraid of tackling issues of sexuality. Others have used it as a way of avoiding approaching issues which they find uncomfortable and difficult to deal with. Yet others have, no doubt, welcomed it because it legitimated their own homophobia.

Nevertheless, we are living through a time and in a society which is not homogeneously homophobic. The contradictions, and even polarizations, mentioned above are manifold, in public policy, between different people and even within the same person. For example, the government is currently restating Section 28 in a variety of ways, but John Major has entertained gay activist and actor, Ian McKellan, at 10 Downing Street. The same police force may be simultaneously engaged in harassing gay men and appointing community liaison officers to work with the lesbian and gay community and actually increasing police presence in areas near gay pubs and clubs officially to protect lesbians and gays from 'queer-bashing'.[9] *British Social Attitudes* (1992/3) shows that the majority of those surveyed both favoured a lowering of the age of consent for gay men and found the sight of two men kissing in the street offensive (but not the sight of a man and a woman kissing). It is, of course, likely that such contradictions would always exist. However, the extent to which they are apparent at present can be taken as an indication that this is a critical time at which to challenge lesbian and gay inequalities in education.

Notes

1 An earlier version of part of this chapter appeared in *Curriculum Studies* (Epstein 1993).

2 It is, perhaps, important to note that the course of events in the USA and Britain has been very different, with Clinton appealing deliberately and directly to a lesbian and gay constituency in his presidential campaign in 1992, while in Britain the Labour Party has never attempted to appeal specifically to lesbians and gays and the Conservative Government remains obdurately homophobic.

3 It is interesting to note that, over the last three years, there have been at least three major academic conferences held in the UK alone on Lesbian and Gay Studies; there is an ERASMUS (European universities) network for Lesbian and Gay Studies; and the 1994 British Sociological Association Conference is on the theme of sexuality.

4 On a global scale, HIV does not primarily affect gay men, though it does primarily affect people who are discriminated against and/or poor and dispossessed in both Western and 'developing' countries. Thus, for example, in Uganda between 1.5 and 2 million people out of a total population of 17 million are known to be HIV positive (Sussex AIDS Centre *Newsletter*, May 1992).

5 See Simon Watney's regular column in *Gay Times* for development of the argument about the irresponsibility of the 'degaying of AIDS', and the threat to young gay men arising from it.

6 These are books published by mainstream publishers in the UK. There have been others which have been privately published, e.g. Leicester NUT (1987). Another volume, which deals with the situation in the United States, is Sears (1992).

7 Of the books referred to here, only Harris is specifically about lesbian and gay issues in education. Harris' concern is, however, not the broader canvas of education, but the secondary English curriculum in particular.

8 In saying that it is 'inconceivable', I do not intend to suggest that no mainstream publisher would even consider publishing such a book – indeed, the editors of this particular series have had the publication of a book on lesbian and gay issues on their agenda since the mid-1980s. What is inconceivable is that there would, simultaneously, have existed both the publisher's interest and a sufficient number of appropriate contributors with the confidence to publish in this area. The fact is that it took Open University Press eight years from first conceiving the idea of a book like this one to finding an editor willing and able to put it together.

9 This is certainly the case in Birmingham, where I am involved in lesbian and gay activism.

References

British Social Attitudes (1992/3) 9. London: Gower Publishing Company.

Brownmiller, S. (1975) *Against Our Will: Men, Women and Rape*. New York: Simon and Schuster.

Cartledge, S. and Ryan, J. (eds) (1983) *Sex and Love: New Thoughts on Old Contradictions*. London: Women's Press.

Cooper, D. (1989) Positive images in Haringey: a struggle for identity. In C. Jones and P. Mahony (eds) *Learning Our Lines: Sexuality and Social Control in Education*. London: Women's Press.

Department for Education (1993) Draft circular to replace Circular 11/87: *Sex Education in Maintained Schools*. London: DfE.

Dollimore, J. (1991) *Sexual Dissidence: Augustine to Wilde, Freud to Foucault*. Oxford: Oxford University Press.

Dworkin, A. (1981) *Pornography: Men Possessing Women*. London: Women's Press.

Epstein, D. (1993) Practising heterosexuality, *Curriculum Studies*, 1(2), 275–85.

Foucault, M. (1978) *The History of Sexuality, Volume 1, an Introduction* (trans. R. Hurley). Harmondsworth: Penguin (first published 1976 as *La Volonté de Savoir*).

Gerwirtz, S., Ball, S. J. and Bowe, R. (1993) Values and ethics in the education market place: the case of Northwork Park, *International Journal of the Sociology of Education*, 3(2), 233–54.

Harris, S. (1990) *Lesbian and Gay Issues in the English Classroom*. Milton Keynes: Open University Press.

Holly, L. (ed.) (1989) *Girls and Sexuality: Teaching and Learning*. Milton Keynes: Open University Press.

Jones, C. and Mahony, P. (eds) (1989) *Learning Our Lines: Sexuality and Social Control in Education*. London: Women's Press.

Kitzinger, C., Wilkinson, S. and Perkins, R. (1992) Theorizing heterosexuality, *Feminism and Psychology, Special Issue on Heterosexuality*, 2(3), 293–324.

Leicester NUT (1987) *Outlaws in the Classroom: Lesbians and Gays in the School System*. Leicester: City of Leicester Teachers' Association (NUT).

OFSTED (1992) *The Handbook for the Inspection of Schools*. London: Office for Standards in Education.

Plummer, K. (1975) *Sexual Stigma: An Interactionist Account*. London: Routledge & Kegan Paul.

Plummer, K. (ed.) (1981) *The Making of the Modern Homosexual*. London: Hutchinson.

Plummer, K. (ed.) (1992) *Modern Homosexualities: Fragments of Lesbian and Gay Existence*. London: Routledge.

Redman, P. (1992) Invasion of the monstrous others: identity, genre and HIV, *Cultural Studies from Birmingham*, 1, 8–28.

Rich, A. (1980) Compulsory heterosexuality and lesbian existence, *Signs*, 5(4), 631–60 (reprinted in Snitow, A., Stansell, C. and Thompson, S. (eds) (1984) *Desire: The Politics of Sexuality*. London: Virago).

Sears, J. T. (ed.) (1992) *Sexuality and the Curriculum: The Politics and Practices of Sexuality Education*. New York and London: Teachers College Press.

Sedgwick, E. K. (1991) *Epistemology of the Closet*. London: Harvester Wheatsheaf.

Stacey, J. (1991) Promoting normality: Section 28 and the regulation of sexuality. In S. Franklin, C. Lury and J. Stacey (eds) *Off-Centre: Feminism and Cultural Studies*. London: Harper Collins Academic.

Sussex AIDS Centre (1992) *Newsletter*, May.

Watney, S. (1987) *Policing Desires: Pornography, AIDS and the Media*. London: Methuen.

Watney, S. and Carter, E. (eds) (1989) *Taking Liberties: AIDS and Cultural Politics*. London: Serpent's Tail.

Weeks, J. (1977) *Coming Out: Homosexual Politics in Britain, from the Nineteenth Century to the Present*. London: Quartet.

Weeks, J. (1981) *Sex, Politics and Society: The Regulation of Sexuality since 1800*. London: Longman.

Weeks, J. (1985) *Sexuality and its Discontents: Meaning, Myths and Modern Sexualities*. London: Routledge.

Weeks, J. (1986) *Sexuality*. London: Tavistock.

Weeks, J. (1991) *Against Nature: Essays on History, Sexuality and Identity*. London: Rivers Oram Press.

Wolpe, A. M. (1988) *Within School Walls: The Role of Discipline, Sexuality and the Curriculum*. London: Routledge.

PART I

Personal Issues

CHAPTER 2

So the Theory Was Fine

ALISTAIR, DAVE, RACHEL and TERESA

Introductory note (by Debbie Epstein)

This chapter is an edited transcript of a group discussion which I had (way back in January 1992) with a group organized by Alistair. The transcript was subsequently edited by Alistair and myself. All the participants were his friends and shared with him an involvement in lesbian and gay politics and either past or present involvement in student politics. Although members of the group did not necessarily know each other well, there were shared assumptions and understandings which made the undertaking possible, even though the transcript reveals very many differences as well.

Early experiences

Dave: I grew up in an Irish, Catholic, working-class family in the north of England and all of those things affected my whole development, including my sexuality. I remember being six or seven and playing with boys; having some physical feeling towards them as early as that. But I gave my memory significance once I understood what the 'trouble' was. When I was in my early adolescence I started to realize there was something 'wrong'. What was happening to me was different. I was looking at girls and they just looked exactly the same as they'd always done. But I was expecting that, once I got to sexual maturity, somehow the feelings I was having would go away because I'd be a man. And they didn't.

It took me a while to work out what the 'problem' was – and I perceived it as a problem. I reacted in a really common, typical way. I went through [a stage of] being really outwardly homophobic, which is quite easy if you're a Catholic, because you can dress up your homophobia in a religious sensibility and you can use the language of your religion to defend it.

Alistair: Between about 14 or 15 and about 19, I suppose what I did was to come out, tiptoe by tiptoe, in different places. I flirted with ideas about homosexuality with different friends; I had a girlfriend at school; and I had a whole set of different identities. What you said reminded me of an older memory – of thinking, 'When I get with girls, I won't fancy boys anymore. It just depends on becoming a "man"'.

Rachel: My family is middle-class, trendy lefty so I've always had an awareness of these things and when I was 13 or 14 I was in the Anti-Nazi League and thought Tom Robinson's Band were great. So the *theory* of everything was fine. My school friends and I used to have long discussions about whether or not we thought we were gay and then suddenly, around the age of 16, they all started going to parties and getting off with boys. So I had the *awareness* but thought it was a phase and didn't really apply to me.

The other thing, for me, was that the idea of gay *men* was never any problem. I could cope with that, but the idea of lesbians was a very different matter. I went to an all girls' school with all the jokes about the games teachers being lesbians, so lesbianism was a totally different matter. There was the word 'lesbian', which I found a very ugly word for a long time as well. I suppose that was because gayness was much more of a real thing, which you came into contact with and we thought it was fine. We also had friends who were gay men because they were no threat. But anything to do with *women* being gay was not on at all really.

Teresa: I had a similar Catholic, working-class background to Dave. But I don't remember knowing any lesbians or gay men when I was younger. We never talked about being lesbian or gay or asked ourselves whether we were lesbian. We just fell into line with what our parents were teaching us. The Catholic religion was very strong, so certainly when you got into your teenage years, all you talked about was boys. You just fell into it without thinking.

It wasn't until I left school and was about 17 or 18, when I started to think for myself, that I began to realize that I didn't really want to settle down and get married. My friends were beginning to have steady boyfriends and getting engaged and married, and I started to panic then, because I thought, 'Oh God, I don't really want this'. But I couldn't explain why not then. I didn't know that I was a lesbian at that stage, though I knew that settling down and getting married wasn't what I wanted. So I thought, 'Well, I'm not going to, but if I stay here it's what's going to happen to me'. That's when I left home.

I didn't realize at the time it was because I was a lesbian. Those ideas just never arose. When I look back at it, I realize that if there was something on the TV or in the paper about lesbians or gay men, my parents were *so* homophobic and when I go home now it's really frightening because they still say really homophobic, really racist things and to think you were brought up in that environment, is quite scary, really.

Relationships with parents

Dave: Everything you say rings really true with me. I came out before I left home and then I left home because I came out. But leaving Sunderland, *the moment* of getting on the A1(M), was incredible. When I came away to university I said good-bye to my parents; and knowing that I was *never* going to have to explain where I'd been again and never going to have to lie about it in such a clear way was such a relief. Leaving home was the moment when I was able to get together all the problems that I'd had when I was growing up and to make them all something positive: my religion; my ethnicity; my clumsiness; my disability; not having any money.

Alistair: I came out to my parents about a year and a half or two years ago and started to remember all those things about when I was younger that I deliberately tried to forget before. But I never had that kind of confrontational relationship with my parents. I can only remember one confrontation, when

I was rushing to catch a train to London for the day and my mum chased me down the road in the car and was shouting out of the window saying that I was going to give the whole family AIDS because I had an ingrowing toenail and there was blood in the bathroom! I nearly didn't go home and it was never mentioned again.

DE: When was this?

Alistair: It was, say, seven years ago.

DE: So did she know you were gay even though you hadn't come out?

Alistair: Well she made quite a lot of comments suggesting she did know. On the one hand, they were putting pressure on me to talk about it, but on the other, they were completely undermining me. She'd say things like 'Oh, you mix with a lot of funny people' or, 'How did you get a hole in the seat of your trousers?' and that kind of thing, which didn't really make me feel very much like talking about it. Now that I've come out to them, the whole thing's turned on its head and it's made me very powerful.

I suppose that's why, in a way, I wish I'd had to confront them much more directly, because I think it would have made the process much quicker and it would have made me feel much more positive much earlier. I think I must have upset myself and a lot of people in my family as well.

Rachel: I was sensible about school, you see. I was sensible and I was hard working and I always thought I was the sensible student who got on with my work and that's why I wasn't madly bothered. All my friends had sisters, so they didn't know what boys were like. I didn't see that boys were that wonderful. I had a brother and I was 'sensible' about boys.

I'm sure that my dad's coming out was tied up with that as well. Although he hadn't said or done anything at the time, I think he must have been feeling his way around things as well. Just after I'd finished my upper sixth, my brother opened a letter of my dad's by accident and it was about a gay teachers' group. It turned out that he'd had relationships with men before he was married. He got married very late and he told my mother he'd made a conscious effort to suppress that side of his nature. And now he was starting to think about it again. There was at least a year when he was thinking about it – talking to his friends and sorting things out.

Meanwhile, my mum was left feeling she couldn't talk to anyone. So, I was very much on my mum's side. She didn't feel she could talk to anyone. He was going around being what I think of as a 'pretended family': he was happy; he was coming to the parents' evenings; he was very concerned about our education; and in between times he was meeting up with blokes. And my mum felt she couldn't talk about anything.

She's sorted it out now. She's very clear about what was the deception (which she was unhappy about) and what was the business of him being gay (which she can cope with). But it was also a point when I was thinking, 'Supposing I got involved with a woman, what would my mum think? Would she understand?' Not because she's homophobic, but because of having been through all that with my dad. Would it have got all her sensibilities confused? So it's all very mixed up. He came out before I did. I think that, when I was in my late teens, he was probably going through the kind of thing that you two were talking about – being homophobic or not discussing things because he was so uncertain who he was then. I'm sure that a lot of things are the same and a lot of things are different when you're 60 and have gone through a lot more years of hating yourself.

Homophobic abuse

DE: Do you want to say something about the kind of things that happened in school – in class, in the playground, or whatever, and what impact that had on you and your own role in it?

Dave: I think that at school words like 'queer' and 'poof' and all that stuff were just insults, like everything else. In my mid-teens there was no real connection made between what those words meant and what being queer involved. There were two boys who spent a lot of time together and people might have said, 'Oh they're queer,' but that was just part and parcel of a whole other set of insults which were quite commonplace. It wasn't until two or three years later, when they were in their late middle teens that people began to make a clear association between those words and being gay and that seems tied to the outbreak of the AIDS panic. At that time a lot of people were talking about AIDS and I remember quite a clear change in tone. I'm not sure whether that was an objectively observed thing or whether it was because I was starting to identify myself with words like queer and poof.

Teresa: We used to have one boy that we used to call names and abuse. I was horrible. I was part of a horrible gang of girls that used to bully everyone. Some of the terms of abuse we used, like 'poof' and 'queer' – I don't really know if I knew what they meant. They were just a form of abuse that we used. But we did use them and they were directed specifically at this one boy, so whoever originally thought up the term of abuse for him must have known what it meant or associated it with him. We just followed on whatever was being said and used it as a way of insulting him.

DE: What was he like?

Teresa: He was really quiet and he always used to get his homework done, used to have his school uniform on and then, none of us had a school uniform. He did. So he was just different and attracted abuse.

Alistair: I remember, when I was about 15 or so, people at school who were singled out as queer. There were a couple of camp men that spring to mind, whom I befriended in a detached kind of way. I was quite friendly with them. I did call people queer and that kind of stuff, but I didn't do it to *them*. I'm not sure why I did it – perhaps to protect myself from abuse. So, if somebody was saying something about a bloke I'd say 'queer', in order to protect myself, whereas I could be nice to these 'nellies' in the woodwork and keep my masculinity intact.

Teresa: I think when you're at school, you go along with whatever your friends do really. You tend to do things without thinking, 'What does this mean? What am I actually doing? What effect am I having on this person that I'm abusing?' It's just like another game you play in the playground and if you don't play it then you're the one who gets abused. When I think back to it, I've been quite horrible and some of the homophobic things that I did and said make me feel quite horrible, thinking about it.

Dave: In my school – I can't remember exactly when it was – there was someone who was gay. He'd come out and he was outrageously camp and he would have been called queer whether he was or not anyway. But when I came out there was quite a lot of surprise because I was quite 'normal'.

I ask because my bad experiences at school were more to do with my disability. (I was both colour blind and dyslexic and also had a dexterity problem. I can't manipulate physical things very well). They were also to do with being a Catholic. You might have expected that the most painful memories from my adolescence would be explained through sexuality. But if someone called me a queer, it was quite a nice change from someone blaming me for Enniskillen, or saying that I was stupid because I couldn't spell. I was wondering how significant homophobia was over and above other forms of abuse.

Rachel: At my school people just could not imagine lesbians and gays could exist. I can remember one particularly awful teenage party – one of many millions of awful parties. It was when I was in the sixth form. I was spending a long time talking to this bloke whom I knew was gay about someone else, a bloke whom I had a crush on at the time. I was just sitting in the garden talking to this one bloke about the other one and about their experiences in a phone box in Berlin, getting more and more drunk and going on about how we both quite liked this bloke. I was so cross afterwards because I was accused of trying to 'steal' this bloke that somebody else liked. Now I was never someone who stole anybody's blokes when I was at school because I was little and quite dumpy and I was a dirty swot. It had never crossed her mind that this bloke – any of you would have known was gay – was gay. It was sexist as well. It couldn't occur to her that *he* could have been doing anything 'wrong'.

Dave: There's this great reality gap between whatever the real situation is and what people imagine it to be. I remember when I was coming out, I had a very good friend who was a woman and I spent so much *time* talking to her about it. She was the first person I came out to. I was going through this great trauma, so when we were out with a group of people, we would disappear. I wanted to hit my head against a brick wall because I *couldn't* tell them about what we were doing, until we'd talked a bit more. It was *awful. It was awful.* You have to laugh about it, really.

Alistair: When I was still at school, I was partially out to myself; out in some environments. My relationship with school changed from being the centre of my existence to me not really worrying about it. I didn't really care about it at all. A lot of people who used to be my friends before, I only saw if I happened to bump into them. At the time I felt like I had this great burden, of going to this shitty school which I didn't like at all. But in some ways being gay made me a kind of member – it was somewhere else I had that was important to me. So I didn't care about what [people at school] thought, I could exist. I could exist and just go through coming out like school wasn't there. And so I didn't go through those coming out traumas at all, because what I did was to try and get away from school in my mind.

Teresa: I've just been thinking about what Dave was saying about the way in which being called queer was just another name. But now, when I think back about this particular boy, I think the reason why we took a great deal of delight in calling him queer was that we'd get a reaction when we called him that. He would burst into tears and so we knew that this was a horrible thing to say. And because it was a horrible thing to say, we kept saying it because he was going to burst into tears. I still don't think I knew what it really meant. I just knew he didn't like it, and so it was another form of abuse, it was one where we had success.

DE: But you didn't use it to other people?

Teresa: No, because, it depended on the people we were abusing at the time. Some people would obviously be sensitive to some issues more than others.

DE: So you were quite choosy about your abuse?

Teresa: We used to abuse everybody, but used different forms of abuse on them, depending on where you got a result. If you got a result one time by using some abuse, you'd use it again and again and again. This particular boy was probably singled out for this particular type of abuse because he always used to burst into tears whenever he was called 'poof' or a 'queer'.

Dave: Which meant of course that he was.

Teresa: Of course! He wasn't one of the lads. He always did his homework, he was very much on his own a lot of the time and he always had his own neat satchel, neat books, school uniform and was neatly dressed. He was singled out from the rest of the lads because he didn't play football or anything like that.

Academic girls

Rachel: Everything in my mind is tied up with being good, and being good at work. You can also make the same distinction in your mind between being either academic or doing your sporty things – except of course at the 'better' schools, where it's an all-rounded person who does everything. There is this feeling of it not mattering so much whether you're going out with boys and all those kind of things if you've made it quite clear that your priorities were getting on with your work. Work was somewhere to hide, and the fact that I was no good at games was also a reason for getting on with my work.

DE: So what you're saying is, you had a choice.

Rachel: Yes.

DE: You could choose to be the academic girl and avoid the compulsory heterosexuality?

Rachel: Yes. I don't know how much it was a choice and how much my friends very much steered me into it, because I *was* good at my work. I don't think I had very high self-esteem; I think I got labelled, but they might think I labelled myself. I remember the conversations on the Monday mornings after the parties – 'and so-and-so got off with so-and-so and so-and-so got off with so-and-so and Rachel got A in her maths tests'.

It's really funny now, but it wasn't, it was horrible. I used to spend my whole Sundays, when they were out walking round the park with their boyfriends, at home doing my maths. I would have given anything to have gone to bloody Forest Hill with some awful boy with zits – but given that I didn't think I was any good at playing that particular game and I was very shy as well, it was much easier.

Dave: I think that might have something to do with single sex education. I think it was because of my disability, but up to 16 I was a complete write-off. All of the boys in my school were a complete write-off. We used to just riot and really hassle the student teachers. The girls used to be the ones who got ten O levels or As, and the boys got half a dozen. Then at A level everything changed. The boys got As, Bs and Cs and went to university. The girls didn't; it was definitely, clearly, a gender thing. It's to do with streaming as well. There was the odd boy who *was* a bit odd, who used to work all the time, but no one used to talk to him anyway.

Role models?

DE: It wasn't made easy, for any of you, in terms of either role models, or people you knew, or profiles of public persons?

Teresa: But this was why it was interesting with Section 28 – the way people get really panicked about what you shouldn't teach children about homosexuality. Because when I think about it no one was teaching us about homosexuality, but, here I am, I'm a lesbian. My brother's gay as well and there's just the two of us, [coming from] that environment. We had no role models. What happened?

Rachel: I had one friend whose parents divorced because her mother started having a lesbian relationship. I think originally she got involved in women's lib, and then she went off to the meetings and met all these women. My friend had all these great stories about women coming round the house and one of them pouring tea all over her dad. So it tied in with all kinds of other things, including the fact that he then got custody of the kids and she only went to see her mum over weekends. I remember her attitude, and the way she felt about her mum. But when she had parties, her mum was great. She'd always let us have parties, and we'd see her mum and we'd see her mum's lover and we'd all scuttle away. We knew she was there but it was a world apart and it wasn't even very much to do with my friend's family, because she lived with her dad. So she wasn't a role model.

Dave: There was a lesbian lived on our street. She was the age I am now, when she was with her husband. And she'd go and get the ice cream in her slippers – really awful things – she didn't have net curtains when she was married, and then she became a lesbian. It was just all part of it. The reason she became a lesbian was because she didn't have net curtains!

DE: I remember I had a woman friend, who wasn't a lover of mine. Her husband, who didn't like her being my friend at all, decided that I was a lesbian because I had red boots, which was quite scary because I wasn't out at the time.

Teresa: I think my parents look for excuses. They can excuse the fact that I'm not married now. They can put it down to the fact that I've moved away to London and I've been influenced by people in London. They don't like to admit that lesbians and gay men can actually exist on their own doorstep. They always look for an excuse, maybe that's why, if you haven't got the net curtains, you're a lesbian.

Alistair: When Rachel said about scuttling away from this woman's mother I thought of a few connections. One of them is about the time when *Gay's the Word* was raided at the beginning of the '80s. I remember being at a YS [Young Socialist] event and somebody asked me to sign a petition about *Gay's the Word*. Although being gay was on my mind, when there was a gay man asking me to sign this thing, suddenly I was really terrified, really scared. I felt quite guilty about being scared about things for a long time. I went to a lesbian and gay Young Socialist fringe meeting at this conference and sat at the back. It wasn't really a 'backs to the wall' situation, but I was asking myself 'are all these people really gay'?

The other experience was with this friend who used to teach me to play the guitar. He was a teacher in my primary school, who was a really close friend of my mother. When I was about 14 my mum told me he was gay. So what I remember is my being partly completely surprised and partly intrigued and partly disgusted by it. Occasionally I still feel like that – this little voice at the back of my mind which says 'he is really too nelly' – although the larger part of me likes nellies.

Coming out and seeking support

Dave: I contacted the local 'Friend' in Newcastle and I was
befriended and taken to a gay youth group. I rang up and
it was pretty awful – complete horror, including ringing and
talking for hours. And then meeting this person. I remember
waiting at Albert Square, a big public area in Newcastle, and
I think we'd agreed some sign. I was looking out while I was
waiting and I was a bit early. I was looking at all the men
that were there and I was thinking, 'is it him, is it him, is it
him, is it him?' Then suddenly, when I saw this recognition
that we'd agreed, he came towards me and I was thinking '*Oh
my god*'. This was the first stranger that I was going to have
to talk to about my sexuality, face to face. I was really, really
frightened. We went for a cup of tea and we talked for quite
a while – it all reminded me of confession: head down you
know, you just mumble a lot, say what you'd got to say and
then go. Then after we'd had that meeting, which was quite
all right in itself, I came away and really shat myself for
about 24 hours. Then I went to this great youth group, which
met in Newcastle. I remember walking up the stairs. I can
picture an image for every single point and every point was
absolute agony: buying the ticket; getting on the train; getting off the train; going to the street; every single step. It's
not a positive experience at all, none of it, including the
meeting. It was a young gay men's group and all of the men
there were in their early twenties. We went to a big fair that
takes place every year in Newcastle, and *now*, if I went I
would enjoy myself, but at that point every single moment
I was just looking at someone and I was thinking, 'you *can't*
be gay', because he was normal. During that evening I went
through all of the homophobia and all of that heterosexism
that I'd been brought up with. There was loads of them that
were complete queens [with limp wrists] which now I can find
quite charming and funny. But at that point I thought 'Oh
he's a poof and I'm not like that'. In terms of role models,
I was looking for someone who was like me and then I could
say, 'yes, it's not just these horrible effeminate men', someone
whom I could identify with.

Alistair: Is there an event when you think you came out? I
remember the first man that I got off with. It was really

awful; it just didn't work at all. It was a disaster from beginning to end. I was glad when the next morning came. It was
actually set up, because I was with all these political friends
who were saying 'Go on, go on, get off with Alistair' and 'Oh
Alistair's going to get off with a boy and isn't it exciting and
aren't we right on and we can sleep with anybody'. At that
point, being political meant that my sex life actually got
submerged and I was patronized rather than being able to
assert my sexuality. But because it was a disaster getting off
with him, it meant that I became unsure. I'd gone through
all this trauma and had sleepless nights, working myself up
to get off with a man and when I got off with him, it was
dreadful. At the same time, there was this woman who was
pursuing me very, very heavily and so I was confused for
months after that. Although, *now* that's my dramatic turning
point, at the time, it actually just made things a lot worse and
a lot less clear.

Dave: Alistair's talking about politics. For me, the process
was the other way round. You were political and then you
came out, didn't you, while I came out and then became
political.

There was a point when I wanted to kill myself and tried
as well. I was under a psychiatrist for a while and all that
horrible, horrible, horrible, disgusting stuff, when I was still
trying to be a Catholic. And then I left the church and I discovered, I discovered that people genuinely supported what
I was. That really helped, but it wasn't until I was 18 and
doing my A levels in an FE college. Thank god for the relief.
I realized that what I was doing was right. It was my politics
that got me through that last hurdle.

Rachel: But, you know, one Saturday you met this guy in this
square in Newcastle. The next Monday you're still back sitting just the same, sitting in your school.

Dave: Yes I know what you mean. My experience of school is
a completely horrible, negative one and not to do with being
gay. It's to do with being poor and to do with the comments
I had to deal with, about being like Catholic and Irish, and
being in the north of England and having teachers who were
paid shit wages and all of that. My problems from school
were nothing to do with my sexuality, I don't think. They
were to do with all of those other things.

Rachel: So it was a compartmentalized thing? When you were at school everything to do with school's horrible anyway?

Dave: Yes.

Coming out dramas/liberal homophobia

Teresa: There's a pressure to have a coming out drama. It's expected that you tell your parents and have a big crisis.

Rachel: I don't know about the crisis. I want to make a big thing of it and I want people to be just a little bit shocked so that I can acknowledge it. You don't want it to pass without comment. They should acknowledge it in some way or other and if people just say 'Oh yes' and they're so incredibly right on that they don't comment at all then they are denying what is important to you.

Dave: I think people, especially in higher education, do generally think that they're 'right on'. People think that they can cope with it when you come out to them. When men come out to women (and perhaps, lesbians come out to men), when it's across gender, it's all very different; they want not to be shocked and so they try not to be. So you say, 'well I'm gay', and they go 'Hey man, that's all right [gesturing 'hippie style'] and they don't say anything. Then, when something actually happens, you start kissing someone or they meet up with someone you got off with, or they see you with *The Pink* or *Gay Times* or something like that, when something that actually confronts them, then they have a problem. I think there's a real tendency amongst students to try not to be offended and to work very hard not to be offended and that's really annoying.

Rachel: Yes! One of my best friends at university, we were both in the Women's Group, would go around talking to the Rugby Club. They'd say 'Oh, Women's Group, Women's Committee, Labour Lesbians' and she'd say, 'Yes, that's right. They're all lesbians.' And you *might* think it was marvellous, but she was straight. I always used to get furious and I didn't know why, but it was easy for her to say. Now, two years later, she still hasn't met my partner. She goes 'Oh, how lovely!', but she hasn't taken it on and it was always just the shock value that she was interested in. She hasn't accepted it at all. I want to go and shake her and say 'Look, you know, it's not what you were talking about! It's *me*. I mean it.'

Taking power/'stroppy poofs'

DE: Is there something powerful in being out?

Alistair: Yes. I found being a 'stroppy poof' intimidated the Rugby Club at college, or the managers in my old office, where the union was run by the 'lavender mafia'.

Teresa: I notice that a lot of lesbians are beginning to get like that as well, and not only coming to terms with being a lesbian but beginning to use it in a positive way: taking the power away from everybody else. First of all, by telling them that you're lesbian or gay takes the power away from them completely. They always imagine, that, certainly, for gay men, that you're just a pansy. And when they see that you're out there doing things just the same as everybody else, if not doing it better than anyone else they're really shocked.

Alistair: My favourite phrase from my old regional manager was 'Oh god, it's those stroppy poofs from Brighton' when we went on strike. And he was right as well.

Teresa: I think there's a lot in taking terms of abuse and using them yourself. It takes the power away from the people who are homophobic. Well, when I think about it, looking back at being at school, if that boy had stood up and said, 'Yes, I'm a queer, so what' we would have all just run away. And the same thing that happens now. If someone says, well, 'you, you lesbian' you just say 'yes, so what'. They just say 'oh, right, OK'.

Being a teacher

Rachel: It depends on the situation. I can't imagine many situations when people have said things like 'yes, so what' as a teacher. At the school I was working at, I was aware of mutterings, about this time last year, as I was walking around the school. I thought, 'What is it? What have I done? I haven't changed.' I hadn't changed from what I was wearing the

previous term. My friend, another teacher, told me that I'd
recently been seen snogging a woman at a bus stop. 'Oh
shit!' I said, 'what shall I do?' I'd only been teaching a year
and a half in this school that's not very supportive generally. For my department lesbians and gays don't exist and
the rest of the school was worse. Well, what on earth was
I going to do? I worked out that it wouldn't be good to get
in a great state about it and talk to lots of people, so I
thought, 'Well, maybe I'll only talk to the head' – the last
thing I wanted to do. I talked to the union rep and she said
the only thing to do was talk to the head who wouldn't mind
what happened so long as I'd been honest with her. So I went
to talk to this head. We talked about policies and she admired
me for coming to talk to her. She said 'I think you'll find
that the girls are better about this than you think. There's a
girl who was in the fifth year last year and she's of mixed
race as well, which doesn't help' – I quote – 'and she calls a
woman daddy'. I doubt very much the girl does that, but
that's what the head said.

So the crisis came and went. A couple of months later, one
of my form, a first year, came and found me, and I *knew*
what she was going to say. She said, 'I've got to ask you
something. Oh no I can't. Oh I've got to ask, oh no I can't,
but someone told me that, oh, I can't say it, can't say it,
someone told me that you're a lesbian'.

I didn't know what to do. I know what everyone says you
should do in these situations, but I thought, 'Well this girl is
one of these people who's always set up to go around saying
everything and getting into trouble. She's not really thick, but
she's so insensitive and she's been set up in this way to be
everyone's fall girl all the way through school. If you say
something she's going to distort it.' So I just said 'Listen, if
someone said something, if you heard someone was spreading rumours about you, what would you do? You'd be very
cross wouldn't you? You'd say, "You shouldn't listen to gossip
from other people. You should go and talk to the immediate
person. You wouldn't like anyone spreading stories about
you." ' So she said 'Oh I knew it wasn't true!'

You think, 'Well probably I've managed that one', but I'm
sure that's not the right thing to do and I'm sure it [doesn't
take back the power]. But I still think that it was the right

thing to do in that particular situation because if I'd tried to say anything more detailed that particular child wouldn't have got the gist of what I was saying.

Rachel: The thing is at work, or in other situations, a lot of the time your first identity – once you get caught up in the education business – is as an educationalist. Certainly at work I think of myself first and foremost as a teacher.

As a teacher I went through all that stuff about coming out, or not, to pupils and also wondering 'how do you go about it?'. I think when I talk to the staff at where I am now, I'm a lot more confident than I was in a school. I think you can be a lot more open in an FE college anyway.

In my particular building there are five students, as well as the senior management, who are lesbian or gay. What I've said to myself about that is 'If someone asks about my sexuality, or if they say anything where there's only one way of answering *and* being honest then I'll be honest'. But I don't know the people very well, they're not friends [yet], they're just colleagues. I don't want to come out just for the sake of it. In terms of the teachers I can judge when it's going to be the right time to say something. In terms of the kids they're the age that we've all talked about – 16. It doesn't come into their conception of how the world can be.

We never thought to ask our teachers when we were 16 if they were lesbian or gay. Except your PE teachers that we all knew about. They're women and they had to touch people, they had to touch people's ankles when they sprained them so they must be – all those kinds of views that we had. But what do you do? I still don't know, with the best will in the world and more confidence – and if I taught for 40 years I still don't think I'd know – how do you come out it in a way that it's going to be meaningful for the kids. I don't want either 'Oh that's great, let's set her up with someone we can take the piss out of' or 'Why on earth did she bother to tell us that?' as a response. I can imagine they'll either tell me I'm gonna be flayed and boiled in boiling oil or some such thing or 'why do you need to bring that up then?'

Teresa: You make it seem like it's an issue that teachers are thinking about, whether to tell children. But I know someone who is involved with teacher training and she said that sexuality is an issue that's a 'no-no', and that they still don't talk about it. They talk about every other form of oppression but its almost obvious that they avoid sexuality.

Dave: When looking through job advertisements and equal opportunities statements I purposely, every single time, even if I'm not looking for a job, look at the equal opportunities statement. [assumes 'official' voice] 'Yes, we strive towards equality'. My university in fact has this terrible equal opportunities statement which talks about, any opinion or preference legally held – or something like that. But if you're a gay man, particularly, and explicitly, most of your sexual activities are illegal, even if you are over 21. They go on about we accept applications from people from ethnic minorities, people with disabilities, open to job share, and no mention of sexuality or sexual orientation. Whenever a council changes hands the first thing that always goes from the equal opportunities statement is sexual orientation. It's accepted to actively discriminate.

Positives

Dave: Looking back on my whole experience of my whole sexual life, although there are moments which I just remember with such horror, and trepidation, the best thing I ever did was coming out. The *positive* ways I feel about how much more secure and sorted out and confident I am now, are due to coming out. It sounds a bit naff to say it, but I'm a much better and happier person now that I've gone through all of those horrible things. What overwhelms and overtakes any of these horrible experiences, which I can have or ever have had about being a gay man, is that I know that what I'm doing is such a positive choice for me to make. It's not a choice that I'm gay but it is a choice about the way I deal with it. What I've learnt about myself, and about everything else, from coming out is just amazing. I am a much happier person now that I've come out. And no matter what might happen to me from this point on, whether I get the shit kicked out of me or anything else, I'll always know that what I've done has been the right thing.

CHAPTER 3

Growing Up Lesbian: The Role of the School[1]

MARIGOLD ROGERS

As the mother of a daughter who had identified as lesbian during her time in a mixed comprehensive school, I have long realized how little help or support a pupil in this situation could expect. Schools are a microcosm of society at large and pupils who do not conform to the expected norm, for whatever reason, often find themselves discriminated against. My experience of 17 years as a teacher in mixed comprehensive schools has also led me to believe that it is unusual for a school to deal openly with sexuality (even heterosexuality) and therefore it is hardly surprising that any mention of homosexuality is taboo and that little material exists on the subject of young gays in full-time education and even less on young lesbians.

The case study

As increasingly I became aware of the silence, invisibility and misrepresentation which surrounds the lives of many young lesbians, I decided to study women who had identified as lesbian while they were still at school. This was not easy, for, as Trenchard comments: '[L]esbians don't grow horns or flashing neon signs, it is often difficult to find someone who is lesbian and will be able to tell you what it means to them' (1984: 8).

I found my respondents through a combination of networking and appeals in the gay press. I questioned 21 women between the ages of 17 and 35, most of them white.[2] It should, therefore, be noted that their experience is not necessarily

Personal Issues

representative of that of *all* young lesbians, and that, in particular, the biographies of young black lesbians are likely to
include experiences of racism as well as those of heterosexism.
My respondents had attended a variety of schools, the majority
being from mixed comprehensives. The interviews were relaxed
and not highly structured although I always began by giving
some guidelines or headings. As I was asking women to talk to
me about a personal and sensitive area of their lives, I explained
that I too was a lesbian, albeit a late-bloomer! This openness
increased the feeling of cooperation and solidarity which was
present during the interviews.[3]

Research in this area presents specific problems. Although,
increasingly, lesbian and gay issues are being discussed and
studies are being carried out, difficulties can occur for the writer
or researcher. Jeffrey Weeks writes of the dangers of discussing
sexuality because:

> writing about sexuality outside the acceptable discourses has
> carried with it the touch of scandal that inhibits the conventional
> career; though today you are not so much regarded as subversive
> as eccentric and obsessive.
>
> (1991: 2)

These difficulties are magnified when lesbian and gay issues are
linked with education and young people, as this immediately
brings to the surface the multitude of myths and preconceptions which often find expression in the tabloid press: the predatory lesbian; the man-hater; the corrupting gay man or child
abuser.

The effects of Section 28

As I have pointed out above, schools tend not to deal openly
with issues of sexuality (see also chapters in this book by
Redman and by Epstein and Johnson) and even less with lesbian
and gay sexuality. This tendency has been exacerbated by
legislation. The Education Act (No 2) 1986 gives school governors the duty of laying down sex education policies. Deem *et al.*
(1992) have pointed out that school governors are generally not
likely to be well informed about or strongly committed to equal
opportunities policies and practices. This means that they are

unlikely to adopt sex education policies which challenge the prevailing heterosexism of schools. Nevertheless, there are some schools where the governing bodies have adopted equal opportunities and sex education policies which cover lesbian and gay sexuality positively (see, for example, Patrick and Sanders in this volume).

Section 28 of the Local Government Act 1988 prohibited LEAs from 'intentionally promoting homosexuality' and from 'promot[ing] the teaching in any maintained school of the acceptability of homosexuality as a pretended family relationship'. However, these prohibitions apply only to LEAs (which, in any case, have less and less power as a result of the Education Reform Act 1988 and subsequent government action). *They do not apply to individual schools* (see Colvin with Hawksley 1989). The NUT's (1991) advice to schools on Section 28 is that 'it should not be interpreted as a prohibition on objective, factual teaching about homosexuality.'

Nevertheless, Section 28 legitimated and produced both a narrowness of focus in schools' curricula and personal bigotry and prejudice against lesbians and gays. At the same time, however, as Helen commented:

> One good thing I see as having come out of the Clause 28 business was that it raised the profile of gays and lesbians. A lot of the publicity was bad, but at the same time, it gave the message that we are present in sufficient numbers to be worth legislating about, even if it was legislating against.

This publicity could even be helpful to lesbian and gay pupils in perhaps going some way to counteract their isolation in an overwhelmingly heterosexual environment. Others have also commented on the contradictory effects of Section 28. Jackie Stacey, for example, argues that:

> The effects of the introduction of Section 28 . . . contradicted its aims and produced an inadvertent promotion of homosexuality. Rather than silencing and marginalizing lesbians and gays, the introduction of Section 28 set in motion an unprecedented proliferation of activities which put homosexuality firmly on the agenda in Britain in 1988–9.
>
> (1991: 302)

Compulsory heterosexuality in schools

Adrienne Rich (1980), writing in the US context, coined the term 'compulsory heterosexuality' to describe the ways in which heterosexuality in reinforced and 'promoted' while lesbian (and, I would add, gay) sexuality is punished. For the majority of pupils in our schools, heterosexuality is as compulsory as maths and English. Compulsory heterosexuality is implicit in the gender roles which students are expected and encouraged to adopt and within the sexist norms which prevail in our society. Consequently, attempts by schools to adopt anti-sexist practices are likely to fail if they are not integrated with anti-heterosexist approaches.

The 'macho' stereotype is often seen as the ideal for boys and when they fail to live up to this then homophobic insults are common currency (see also Mac an Ghaill in this volume). As Paula pointed out:

> On occasions we had to share halls in PE and I remember one of the teachers saying to one of the boys who wasn't very good at what they were playing, 'What are you, some sort of pansy? Come on, get your finger out, are you a nancy-boy?' It's an insult to their masculinity, or that's how it's perceived.

This boy's masculinity was being called into question because of his lack of ability in sport and by using the words 'pansy' and 'nancy-boy', the teacher was reinforcing the idea that a gay boy is not a 'proper' boy and that sensitivity in men is unacceptable. While pre-pubertal girls are often allowed some latitude in transgressing gender roles by behaving like 'tomboys', boys, of any age, are punished for 'feminine' behaviour. What is significant is the way in which this is so frequently done by derogatory references to gay sexuality – insults which carry implications for girls identifying as lesbians, just as much as they do for boys. Hence Paula's concern to make her point.

In schools heterosexuality is considered to be the norm and any variation from it is seen as being in some way deviant, abnormal and usually unacceptable. Sue Lees (1987) details a number of male insults which define girls' sexuality – for example, 'slags' and 'drags'. She found that of all these, 'lezzie' was seen as the worst insult. Just as the use of 'nancy-boy' or 'pansy' is seen by the boys as a slur on their own masculinity, so 'lezzie' is used to make sure that girls do not wander from the hetero-sexual path. April commented on her experience of this:

> Slag and slut were quite tame really, it could be a joke whereas lezzie or lesbian could never be a joke, it was always really barbed, really an insult.

Most of my respondents, therefore, kept very quiet about their sexuality during their schooldays. Of the few who were open, the majority experienced hostility. Diane, for example, told me the following story:

> My form tutor (who was a woman) once took me out of the classroom after registration and asked me if I could stop talking about my sexuality in front of the other girls because apparently it was upsetting some of them! I feel that this was a bit of a one-sided request because I had to put up with *them* going on about their boyfriends all day and no one asked *me* if I found that offensive.

In this incident, Diane was challenging the prevailing invisi-bility of lesbians by talking about her own sexuality. However, her teacher effectively demanded invisibility of her.

The three-fold invisibility of young lesbians

Young lesbians are subject to a triple invisibility: as children, they are invisible in the adult world; as women, they are invisi-ble in a male-dominated world; and as lesbians they are invisi-ble in a gay world.

Children in an adult world

Like all young people, young lesbians are rendered invisible by their age and thus by a lack of economic power and finan-cial independence. Young women (and men) who come out to their parents as lesbian (or gay) may risk rejection and find that they are disabled by lack of support. On identifying as lesbian many girls do not tell their parents because they fear a hostile reaction and, unfortunately, this fear is often well-grounded. Amongst my respondents there was a variety of parental reactions. Some parents discounted lesbianism as a phase of development which their daughter was going through. For example, Kate said:

> I first started to fancy women when I was about a first year in high school and I did actually talk to my mum about it in those years but she would always say to me, 'Oh, it's just a phase you're going through.'

Rose spoke to her father who said that 'he didn't think I was [lesbian].' Although neither of these reactions was totally negative, both were dismissive and patronizing.

Some parents had adverse reactions at first because they feared that the negative stereotypes so often applied to lesbians would be applied to their own child. Debbie's mother, for example, was afraid that the rest of the family might see a lesbian as a corrupting influence. She feared that, if the family found out about Debbie's lesbianism, 'they wouldn't let me near the children'.

Some of the women have never felt able to 'come out' to their parents and this undoubtedly gives rise to tension in this relationship. Some of them would have liked to tell their parents but did not feel able to do so. As Sue said, 'My parents don't know and that's the only hang-up I have'. Sometimes parents had some idea about their daughter's sexuality but chose not to acknowledge it and this was a difficult and uncomfortable situation for the young lesbian. Joy felt that her

> parents . . . kind of suspect, know, don't want it to be true. I had a really bad experience in the summer because they were aware I was seeing a woman but they weren't aware, being incredibly vague and hinting at things and that was a hellish experience.

She felt that if she forced her parents to face up to the situation:

> [I]t would be a big embarrassment. I can see that if I took someone home and said, 'This is my lover', that would make them totally eliminate me.

Such fear and doubt about parental reactions places great stress on a young lesbian, particularly if she is not financially independent. This is increasingly likely to be the case; jobs are not readily available; income support for young people under the age of 18 has been severely cut, as has housing benefit;

student grants are disappearing and being replaced by loans and students can no longer claim any other benefits. Given this situation many young lesbians may feel that keeping their sexuality invisible to their parents is the best (perhaps the only viable) choice for them, despite the pressures associated with living a double life.

Happily there are parents and families who do respond in a positive manner, as Rachel said, 'My family totally accepted me when they finally found out . . . age 18.'

Women in a man's world/schoolgirls in a boy's world

As women, lesbians disappear in the world of 'mankind', 'the rights of man' and the definition of human in for example the *Concise Oxford Dictionary* as 'of or belonging to man'. This has been well documented in feminist writing both in terms of the general experience of (western) women and in terms of the specific experiences of girls in the context of British and US schools (see, for example, Rich 1979; Spender 1985).

Notwithstanding the development of anti-sexist initiatives during the 1980s, it remains true that many girls will use material in many subjects that renders them invisible.[4] Both in the classroom and the playground boys demand and obtain more space and time, relegating girls to the periphery where many of them feel coerced into silence. Even when a teacher is aware of the machinations of gender it can be difficult to change the balance (see, for example, Spender 1982; Mahony 1985).

Where sexuality is concerned, girls and women are expected to remain invisible and 'barely sexual at least in public' (Jackson, 1982: 170). For girls in schools there is no celebration of female sexuality *per se*; it is seen only as a mere counterpart to male sexuality, and then invariably in a heterosexual setting.

Lesbians in a gay world

Young lesbians experience an additional form of invisibility: as lesbians in the gay world. Although the sexuality of gay male school students is often made invisible in the school context, outside the school young gay men are more likely to find reference to their sexuality than young lesbians. This is partly for negative reasons: the illegality of sex for young gay men is, in itself, a form of visibility. It is also because gay men tend to be richer than lesbians. Simply because they are men, they are likely to earn more and they are also considerably less likely to have dependants than are lesbians. This means that the 'scene' is largely male, a fact which has consequences for the avail-ability of support. For example, a perusal of the *Pink Paper* will reveal that, in most towns, lesbian and gay switchboards (which tend to be staffed by gay men) operate every night, while lesbian lines may operate for only two hours a week. Similarly, other sources of support may well be male oriented. Many young lesbians share the experience of Annie who told me that, when she was referred to a gay youth group, she found that 'it wasn't very useful as it was only men'. My own experience of a support group for parents of gay children followed a similar pattern.

The experience of lesbian pupils

Many of my respondents described how, within the school context, they felt ignored and isolated. Helen, for example, said:

> I think the worst aspect of my schooldays was the complete and utter absence of any mention – at school, at home, in literature, in the media – of lesbians and gay men. I felt, to use the cliché, as if I was the only person in the world to love other women. This is not to say that there was no mention of lesbian and gay issues anywhere in the media but there wasn't any in what I read, listened to, watched.

During their time at school all pupils are bombarded with learning experiences. There is the formal curriculum in a multi-plicity of subjects and the hidden curriculum with its equally powerful messages.

The formal curriculum

Ann's response to my question, 'Was lesbianism or homosex-uality mentioned in any lessons?' was a terse, 'Oh! don't be silly!' Several of my respondents spoke of a complete lack of information in any lesson. As Jill, commenting on her 'fairly liberal' school, said, 'There was no information about homosexuality at all in any class at school, at any age'.

Four of my respondents remembered homosexuality, but not lesbianism, being discussed during English lessons. However, three of these examples come from one school and from one teacher's lessons. These mentions of homosexuality had little relevance to the lesbian pupils, first because these references were male oriented and also because, as Nina commented, they were dealt with in a 'theoretical' and 'detached' way which distanced them from the class. Oscar Wilde, in his role as 'famous gay person',[5] was responsible for two of my respondents' memories of reference to homosexuality – a mention made safe by the distance time lends and, perhaps, the fact that Wilde is well-known not only for being gay, but also for being punished for this.

All my respondents found that any mention of homosexuality within the formal curriculum was minimal and almost invariably negative. For example, Sue recounted the following incident from Religious Education:

> We could ask questions anonymously and someone asked if love between people of the same sex was wrong. The teacher answered that he did not want to condemn anyone but on the other hand 'a plug and a plug and a socket and a socket'. It was never mentioned again.

This brief, dismissive answer reveals a good deal about the teacher's attitudes to sexuality. First, his failure to deal with the question of love illustrates the common-sense equation of lesbian and gay relationships with sex. Second, by using the plug/socket metaphor, he discounts any form of sex apart from heterosexual intercourse. The teacher equates sex with penetration, relationships with sex with penetration, therefore lesbianism with sex with what? His claim to wish to refrain from condemnation, is, at the very least, dubious. In any case, an opportunity for a serious and useful discussion about relationships was lost here.

Sex education, either as a discrete subject or as part of a programme of Personal and Social Education, is one area of the curriculum where homosexuality might be expected to appear.

However, as AnneMarie Wolpe has stated, 'homosexuality and lesbianism are generally avoided and attempts to introduce such elements to sex education are likely to be met by strong protests' (Wolpe 1988: 114). The women who took part in my research found little to engage them in sex education. Most of them could remember nothing of any significance being taught, despite some references to condoms and contraception (see Redman in this volume for further discussion of sex education). Joy did remember one reference to homosexuality during the topic of reproduction when the teacher said:

> '. . . and there is a theory that homosexuality', and I perked up and listened, 'has something to do with the imbalance of hormones.' Then she moved on and I thought, 'Wow! I've been mentioned.'

This passing reference to homosexuality highlights the heterosexism present in the curriculum. As Joy remarked, 'I didn't take it seriously but when I think about it now, it makes me really angry.'

It is hardly surprising, with so few mentions during lessons, that, when it comes to the school library, lesbian pupils fare no better! Several of my respondents made comments similar to June's, 'Our school library had absolutely nothing about sexuality'. Few school libraries have much in the way of feminist writing (see Spender 1987) and even fewer have anything pertaining to lesbianism. A feminist paradigm of education which validates women's experiences and places little reliance on hierarchical power structures is threat enough to male-dominated education. Lesbianism, which represents a way of life where men are largely unnecessary, presents an even greater threat. Small wonder, then, that the school library has nothing to offer and that if something of use should appear, its existence may be short lived. Jill tried to take direct action:

> There was no information in the school library. I actually took some gay fiction books into the library and planted them on the shelves for other people when I was about 12. They disappeared immediately.

It can be seen, then, that there is little of relevance to the situation of young lesbians within the formal curriculum. With so little validation of their sexuality, it is not surprising that some young lesbians go through moments of despair, since, as April said:

> for a lot of young lesbians and gays at school they just can't imagine how they are going to cope with it and there's no one saying, 'Look, I can do it, you'll grow up, you'll find ways to be yourself.'

The hidden curriculum

When it comes to the hidden curriculum, the message that comes out to all pupils, whatever their sexual orientation, is that 'heterosexuality rules OK!' This message can come from overtly homophobic language used by teachers as well as other pupils; from the silence surrounding the whole topic of lesbian and gay existence; and/or from the general heterosexist assumption of heterosexuality. Furthermore, teachers who fail to challenge homophobic comments implicitly condone them. Such failures can easily take place within a context of 'liberal' or even 'progressive' educational discourse. The idea held by some liberal/radical teachers that students should be allowed to work out their own ideas in free discussion may result in reinforcement of homophobic attitudes. Thus, for example, April described a class discussion in which:

> two boys in particular . . . [said] that '[lesbians and gays] should be put on [an island] and then the place should be bombed . . . they're sick and disgusting'. [The teacher] didn't interfere, wanted us to argue with each other . . . but she could have said, 'Let's keep our comments sensible'.

April pointed out that she felt unable to counter such homophobic comments herself because of her own vulnerable position. It is likely that any other lesbian or gay pupils would feel similarly vulnerable, while heterosexual students would wish to avoid the stigma attached to challenging homophobia. In this way, the progressive discourse may, in itself, be oppressive (see, also, Walkerdine 1981 on child-centred pedagogy and young children's sexism).

I found many examples of other pupils (and sometimes teachers) behaving in a homophobic way to the lesbian pupils. Teachers rarely intervened – a fact which my respondents resented. As Meg said:

I cannot believe that none of the teachers heard the name-calling I was subjected to or the gossip about me, yet they did nothing to my knowledge and certainly offered no support.

This type of behaviour often happened outside the classroom. The word 'lezzie' was often used as an insult and as Sally said it was 'a bad insult'. She went on to say:

If you said the wrong thing they'd say 'lezzie, lezzie', and you'd be left wondering what you'd done. You couldn't suggest that a woman was someone to be admired without 'lezzie, lezzie'.

She said of the teachers that, 'if they heard they certainly didn't do anything about it'. Sally's experience illustrates clearly how anti-lesbianism places limitations on girls and women because the only safe person to admire in these circumstances is a man.

Similarly, homophobic gender stereotyping places a constraint on young lesbians. For example, Mary recounted being:

taken aside by the headmaster and he talked to me. He told me to try to act a bit more feminine, to have a 'proper girl's' haircut. He told me to put a grip in my hair!

Mary had transgressed, not by producing poor work, nor by disrupting classes, but by her decision not to follow a stereotypical pattern of femininity. This had a profound effect on Mary's school life and she 'decided to leave school as soon as I possibly could, and once I'd left school I started feeling more positive towards myself.' Pat too was a threat to the heterosexual status quo. Her parents were called into school and interviewed by the headteacher and deputy.

They didn't say anything to me . . . they went on about the clothes I wore, my bad attitudes and that I wasn't friendly enough. They actually said to my parents, 'Is she a lesbian?' . . . It was devastating, it was really awful, it was grossly unfair.

Notwithstanding a common rhetoric within the education system about the importance of students developing a 'positive self-image', when this image contravenes the 'rules' of heterosexist society then it is unacceptable. The choices open to young women within our schools are limited by these 'rules'.

All my respondents had either encountered directly or been aware of homophobia during their school years. Some had been the butt of barbed jokes and insults or the victims of prurient gossip. Sometimes teachers were unaware of what was happening, but only too often it seemed to the women that teachers were aware but they chose to ignore it. Helen recounted an incident which happened when she was about 13 or 14 years old. She was in love with a girl from another class and one day, while she was stroking her friend's head (because her friend had a headache), she was seen by some of the other girls. Later, they were waiting for her in the changing room where they lined the lockers and shouted, 'lesbian, lesbian' until the teacher came in and stopped them. Helen said of the incident, 'I felt terribly ashamed and shrank into myself', and she made the point that although the teacher intervened to stop the shouting, she did not investigate the incident in any other way.

Other than in the form of homophobic harassment, my respondents reported little occasion for discussion about lesbianism between themselves and their peers. The general assumption was that everyone was heterosexual and several women reported pretending to have boyfriends in order to fulfil the expected norm. However, there were some interesting exceptions, which seem to be related to the specific politics and culture of their friendship groups. All these exceptions took place within the context of the smaller friendship group, rather than within the wider school context.

Nina and April were in the same group of friends and they recalled a number of discussions. April remembered how:

> we used to talk about sexuality and society because we were quite academic, top-band, middle-class and I think they usually do talk about those things. Very much in the abstract, nothing you would relate to yourself or to another person you knew.

Nina made similar comments:

> Our group was trying to be quite open and liberal in its views . . . [They were saying] 'we're right-on lefties and we can cope with you being bisexual' because that's what they thought, but it was in a theoretical way.

This theoretical and abstract discussion was being held without reference to the lesbian identities of either April or Nina who, significantly, had not come out to their friends. There was no actual acceptance of either of them as lesbian with all that implies, but a limited acceptance of homosexuality in the abstract. Being 'coped with' by her 'right on', 'lefty' friends was not experienced as positive by Nina, but, rather, as patronizing.

My research seems to indicate differences between mixed and single sex girls' schools. All those who had been at single sex schools reported discussion, albeit on the level of gossip, about lesbianism. In these schools there also seemed to be more speculation about the possibility of teachers being lesbian. Helen, for example, said that her headmistress was reported to be a lesbian because:

> on a school skiing trip, she offered to carry out the application of ointment to someone's leg following injury. They thought she seemed keen to do this nightly and therefore she was a lesbian!

The other examples were similar, being based on supposition and rumour.

Glad to be gay'[6]

Although many of the experiences of young lesbians in school are negative, I was impressed by the strength of the women in my sample. I would not want to portray them in any way as victims as they certainly do not see themselves as such. Yet they have often been through times in their lives when they have felt isolated because of homophobia and heterosexism as detailed in this chapter. Trenchard and Warren, in their survey of lesbian and gay teenagers in London, found that '80 respondents (19 per cent) said they had attempted suicide as a direct result of being lesbian or gay' (1984: 145). If, in most areas of life, your sexuality is denied or ignored, then feelings of anxiety and confusion are likely to be experienced. Thus, for example, Kate commented:

> You think 'How can I feel so good when it's meant to be something that's so evil and not right . . . It made me so depressed.

These feelings are not a result of identification as lesbian but of hostile and inappropriate responses to that identification.

Schools, with their responsibility to all pupils, are failing the lesbian and gay members of their communities if they do not challenge lesbian and gay inequalities in education.

Despite some moments of despair, the majority of my respondents appear to have thought through the whole question of sexuality more carefully than many of their heterosexual peers.[7] They had little to go on, few role models and often no one to talk it over with. However, as Paula said:

> It made me question myself more heavily than I think my heterosexual friends did . . . I've thought more deeply about sexuality than they have and I came to the conclusion all along that I was right and they were wrong.

Pat felt that as a lesbian she had had to take more responsibility for establishing a way of life for herself:

> We have to find our own way, we have to make our own ground rules up about things because we don't get any proper guidance, information or images.

Similarly, Jill said, 'I did it all for myself . . . I didn't know any other lesbians at school'.

The way forward

Schools provide education for a vast and varied school population. It is the task of teachers to ensure that this education is made available and relevant to all pupils. Many writers have addressed the issues of race and sex discrimination in schools but few have considered discrimination on the grounds of sexuality. Thus young lesbians (and gays) remain an ignored minority. They need to be accepted as part of the school community. They know what they want. As Julia Melia has said, 'These young people are quite clear about what they want from education: an acknowledgement of their existence and a right to a self-defined identity' (1989: 217).

My respondents thought that schools should consider lesbian and gay sexuality openly, ranking it alongside heterosexuality; challenge homophobia along with racism and sexism; provide positive images of lesbians and gay men; and, where possible, form links with, or at least provide information about, lesbian and gay youth groups. Although they realized how difficult it would be for a lesbian teacher to be out at school they felt that it would be, as Helen said 'unimaginably wonderful'. June also felt that:

> Lesbian and gay teachers should be out . . . talk about partners, home set-ups, etc. that the reality of the daily life of lesbians and gays is visible, not just something exotic that happens on scatter cushions in boudoirs.

I shall finish this chapter with Jill's list of 'Things that could have made a difference'.

open discussion of homosexuality in class (not addressed as a problem);
open discussion of the oppression of lesbians and gays;
role models;
talks by ex-students;
plays;
books;
teachers standing up for you;
being taken seriously.

This list forms good, realistic advice for any school which aims at providing an education for all its pupils whether lesbian, gay or heterosexual. I did not compile this list, it was written by a young woman who has recently spent several years in a school as a lesbian pupil; she is an expert, I am not. As a teacher, I would like to think that every item on this list could be achieved and that by its application to the everyday life of a school, teachers could attempt to make changes of their own and their pupils' attitudes and behaviour.

Notes

1 Although I have never met them, I would like to thank Lorraine Trenchard and Hugh Warren for their pioneering work with lesbian and gay teenagers. Without their example, I do not think that I would have attempted this research. I would also like to thank all the women who took part in my research. The article has benefited from the comments of a number of people, in particular: Debbie Epstein, Richard Johnson, Máirtín Mac an Ghaill, Jenn Price and

Allie Rogers. I would also like to thank Carol Dyhouse and Jenny Shaw for their support and encouragement when I was doing this research for my MA dissertation.

2 All names have been changed to preserve confidentiality.

3 For discussion of problems around interviewing see, for example, Oakley (1981). A number of feminist researchers have also discussed the ethical and methodological issues which arise when, for instance, white researchers interview black respondents. Amina Mama (1989), for example, went to considerable lengths to match the ethnicity of interviewers and interviewees in her project on domestic violence against black women on the grounds that women would feel more comfortable talking to someone with whom they felt they had a shared experience.

4 The centralizing effect of the National Curriculum and its conservatism combine to make women's invisibility (as well as that of black people) an increasing rather than decreasing problem.

5 It should be noted, here, that the word 'gay' did not connote sexuality during Wilde's lifetime. Wilde himself would, therefore, not have use the word.

6 This phrase is taken from Tom Robinson's song, which has become an 'anthem' of the lesbian and gay movement.

7 This finding is similar to that of Mac an Ghaill (in this volume) with respect to boys who identify as gay.

References

Colvin, M. with Hawksley, J. (1989) *Section 28: A Practical Guide to the Law and Its Implications*. London: National Council for Civil Liberties.

Deem, R., Brehony, K. J. and Hemmings, S. (1992) Social justice, social divisions and the governing of schools. In D. Gill, B. Mayor and M. Blair (eds) *Racism and Education. Structures and Strategies*. London: Sage in association with the Open University.

Jackson, S. (1982) *Childhood and Sexuality*. Basil Blackwell: Oxford.

Lees, S. (1987) The structure of sexual relations in schools. In M. Arnot and G. Weiner (eds) *Gender and the Politics of Schooling*. London: Hutchinson in association with the Open University.

Mahony, P. (1985) *Schools for the Boys. Co-education Re-assessed*. Hutchinson: London.

Mama, A. (1989) *The Hidden Struggle: Statutory and Voluntary Sector Responses to Violence Against Black Women in the Home*. London: Race and Housing Research Unit/Runnymede Trust.

Melia, J. (1989) Sex education in schools. Keeping to the norm. In

C. Jones and P. Mahony (eds) *Learning our Lines*. London: The Women's Press.

NUT Working Party on Lesbian and Gay Issues in Education (1991) *Lesbians and Gays in Schools. An Issue for Every Teacher*. London: NUT.

Oakley, A. (1981) Interviewing women: a contradiction in terms. In H. Roberts (ed.) *Doing Feminist Research*. London: Routledge.

Rich, A. (1979) *On Lies, Secrets and Silence*. New York: Norton.

Rich, A. (1980) Compulsory heterosexuality and lesbian existence, *Signs: Journal of Women in Culture and Society*, 5 (41), 631–60.

Spender, D. (1982) *Invisible Women. The Schooling Scandal*. London: Writers and Readers Publishing Co-op Ltd.

Spender, D. (1985) *Man-Made Language*. Routledge: London.

Spender, D. (1987) Education: the patriarchal paradigm and the response to feminism. In M. Arnot and G. Weiner (eds) *Gender and the Politics of Schooling*. London: Hutchinson in association with the Open University.

Stacey, J. (1991) Promoting normality: Section 28 and the regulation of sexuality. In S. Franklin, C. Lury and J. Stacey (eds) *Off-Centre: Feminism and Cultural Studies*. London: Harper Collins Academic.

Trenchard, L. (1984) *Talking About Young Lesbians*. London: London Gay Teenage Group.

Trenchard, L. and Warren, H. (1984) *Something To Tell You*. London: London Gay Teenage Group.

Weeks, J. (1991) *Against Nature. Essays on History, Sexuality and Identity*. London: Rivers Oram Press.

Walkerdine, V. (1981) Sex, power and pedagogy, *Screen Education*, 38, 14–24.

Wolpe, A. M. (1988) *Within School Walls. The Role of Discipline, Sexuality and the Curriculum*. London: Routledge.

CHAPTER 4

A Burden of Aloneness

KOLA: BIRMINGHAM BLACK
LESBIAN AND GAY GROUP

Introductory note (by Debbie Epstein)

This chapter is the result of my request to KOLA to contribute
to this book in the way they felt was most appropriate. The
group's decision was to provide me with a transcript of a meeting in which they discussed their experiences of schooling in
relation to both racism and sexuality. The meeting was organized in such a way as to ensure that all those present had a
chance to testify to their experiences of each stage of their
education, and is thus organized around these phases.

Primary schools: Racism and difference

Ranee: I started primary school on an RAF base. Our father
was in the forces, and we were the only black people on that
particular base. I haven't got very many memories of it, other
than that, if ever a kid had to do really grotty jobs or get
the nasty bits in the plays, I was the one that got them. If
they were going to use anything that belonged to you, if they
were going to throw some things away or stomp on them,
then it would be mine that they'd do it to. And I remember
the language that was used – people saying 'Paki' and using
the words 'wog' and 'nigger' and things like that – words
which were used mainly to describe me.

Robert: My beginnings are far more mundane. I went to a local
school and I think that's where I began to be aware of the

whole business of not fitting in: as if there were something wrong. There was a feeling that there was always something wrong. It was distinct from bad behaviour; it was as though there was something intrinsically wrong, with a teacher protecting white children from people like me, and parents feeling that I was a threat to their children and making themselves very clear about it. It was a church school and there was a lot about it that I enjoyed. But I think that there was the whole question of not being quite 'one of us', and of being focused upon in a very negative way.

Rajah: My school was predominantly Asian with a few white people. My parents were Sikh, so at that time I wore a turban. While I was in that school we were picked on all the time, by white kids and by Muslim kids, for being Sikh. I was always the one who was being victimized. I was the only one in that class that no one really got on with. After about two years, since I felt different, I had to prove myself in other ways. I took to studying a lot to do that, so that I could be recognized as someone who was a 'brain'. So, in the last few years of primary school my reputation picked up.

David: I went to a predominantly West Indian school with very few white children. There were a few Asians. All the teaching staff were white, and I suppose that became natural and it was always when you saw a black face, that it was something strange. It was a nice school with a nice atmosphere. I enjoyed primary school.

Ranee: I think the thing that Robert said – about it being verbalized that you were different – is something that I've always felt. I'm not sure how much of that was because of what people put on to me because I was black, but I was always aware that I was different and I was always fighting for my own identity. People would identify me, culturally, as something that I wasn't. I'd be called Chinese or Maltese and actually have to fight for my own origins and say, 'Well, I'm not that'. There's always been a feeling of being different and of not being able to identify why. It was because I was the only kid who wasn't white.

'I wasn't like other . . .'

Michael: It's all to do with race. It's all to do with your race and your religion, and not being able to identify the sexuality question until later on, until you go to the secondary school.

Robert: I think it's definitely that kind of burden of aloneness. I can remember growing up and at each stage there was my mother saying, 'You're different'. I've never known quite how to manage this. I wasn't the archetypal delinquent child that causes a lot of hassle or stays out late, or is particularly challenging to authority. I was largely a goody-goody child. Yet there was that message that I was difficult, different and there was an uncertainty about how I would cope – particularly if I were to go and work in a factory. I can remember my mother saying that! She was picking up on a softness – that I somehow wasn't like other boys, and that was certainly true of my own feelings from a very early age – finding other males somewhat fascinating – the same, but not quite the same.

Ranee: I think that I always knew that there was something I found attractive about other girls at that age. It wasn't anything to do with their clothes or their hair, because I hated all of that. I hated the little girlie dresses which we were supposed to wear because we were girls. But I always knew there was something about my feelings. I'm not sure that I could particularly identify it as lesbian feeling then. I can remember at about 10 or 11, being shit scared of my feelings. But I'd never even heard of what those feelings were.

Rajah: I think that when you're at primary school, especially if you're a boy, you can get away with a lot of playing and no one will take it as being something sexual, which you can't perhaps do when you're older. You can get away with things like having a bath with your friend. That was quite acceptable when you were kids, and maybe your perceptions of having a bath with your same-sex friends were different to their perceptions and maybe the experimental things that happened between kids were different for you. I remember having a bath with a friend. We used to take it in turns to be the man and the woman, and to do what we thought men would do, like get on top of each other! When I'd had my bit of being the man, I would be the woman. I'm not sure

whether my perceptions were very different from those the
other children had. For me it wasn't just about exploring;
it was about something that had this tremendous effect on
me.

Michael: When I was in junior school I thought I was supposed
to have sex with girls (whatever we thought sex was at that
time). I don't think we knew what sex was, but we knew that
we were meant to have sex with girls. I'm wondering how we
felt about ourselves. People talk about experiences of feeling
different because of colour and because of sexuality. If we
were being picked upon because of our colour, then, how did
we feel about people actually liking us [sexually]?

'A question of what was in the foreground'

Robert: For me it was a question of what was in the foreground. Initially, it was always colour. It was the race question. But, as people went beyond the skin to the individual,
then the whole issue of sexuality came to the foreground, so
a lot of the time the race issue took a back seat. Within that
there was a kind of powerlessness, because I wasn't setting
the agenda. I actually couldn't set the agenda in terms of
which issues were being dealt with or the degree of abuse and
how it would be pointed; but it was very much the difference
between the fire and the frying pan. But I think overall, it
was predominantly sexuality that was made overt. If people
wanted to abuse me it was around being sissy and not quite
fully masculine and only the 'daring' would be overtly racist
in their abuse.

But it was also about colour and about my internal
agendas. I think a straight, black child, would have triggered
a different agenda, because of what he or she may have done
or not done and his or her different responses to racism.

Rajah: I felt that being attracted to girls was wrong as well,
because I'd been brought up that way by my parents. I had
a period in India and we were always brought up to think
it was terribly wrong to have relationships, full stop. So I
knew it would be wrong if I was attracted to girls, from my
family's point of view. But I also knew it was wrong to be
attracted to boys.

Michael: So basically issues around actually knowing what *our* sexuality was, really came through in our secondary school years?

John: I know I didn't understand about homosexuality. I don't think I'd even heard the word until I was 17. At junior school, in the third year, we were taught sex education by a white teacher and we thought, 'We're never going to do this! We're never going to do that!' and *that* was just between a man and a woman.

When I was at secondary school I had to confront racism. I went to a predominantly white school, so I had to deal with that first. When I had any [sexual] feelings, they were geared towards black women. I started having feelings towards men in the third year of secondary school. I saw it as a phase. Boys are attracted to other boys in a pally-pally way, so I thought that was what it was. I don't think there is anything at all for black youngsters to teach them about feelings that they might have, or any form of support at present.

Robert: I didn't know there was a black gay community!

Secondary school: 'Just trying to exist'

Ranee: Especially if you go to a predominantly white school, there's a constant battle about your identity and about facing racism, not just from pupils, your colleagues – but from teachers as well. There were teachers who would stand at a window and watch you getting stoned down the playground, and hear all the abuse being given to you, and not do anything! I knew there were things about sexuality although I didn't know the terms at primary school. At the beginning of secondary school, the predominant thing was just trying to exist and carry on.

Michael: Did you actually remain in Norwich for secondary school, or had you moved by then?

Ranee: It was still in Norwich.

Michael: Were your problems mainly because of that part of the country?

Ranee: I don't know that it's just because of that area of the country. I'd see it more as going to a school that was all white. I don't think my experiences would have been different in a different geographical area, if it still had been all white.

Michael: So you're saying that in the change from primary to secondary school, the situation didn't change a great deal?

Ranee: No, it was just the same. There were just more kids who could stand in the playground and throw stones at you and kick you and throw you into things. Because I was little they used to hang me up on coat pegs and leave me there, and put me into dustbins and leave me there and things like that.

John: My primary school was predominantly black and then going to a white school was a shock to the system. I'd never encountered so many white people before. I could deal with that. But what I couldn't deal with was that it was the first time I'd ever encountered racism. I didn't know racism had existed until that moment. I became very frustrated and unhappy and I disguised it. I started to put more into my lessons and study to shut myself off from the unhappiness, at least until the blacks in my year could band together. You always had clusters of blacks. That's how I dealt with it. Also you achieved a place in the pecking order. I had quite a few scraps in my first year.

Robert: I found the transition quite difficult. In a sense racism began to speak its name, in loud, raucous terms. By the time I was ready to leave junior school, I was obviously senior. I had been in the environment for a number of years, and as I grew it had shrunk proportionately and felt like mine, and there was a degree of comfort about all that.

Moving from that to the secondary school was almost like moving to a different town. I can remember standing outside the gym and thinking to myself, 'God! this is almost as large as the school that I've just left'. Everybody lined up, and in that cold autumn morning, felt like refugees.

It was extremely difficult, and there were lots more white children. My junior/infant school was predominantly white, so in that respect things hadn't changed, but it was certainly on a much wider canvas and the unguarded racism of older children started to make itself felt. By the time I'd been at secondary school for a few days, I'd already had one boy, who was probably a couple of years older than myself, offering to have a fight with me with a drawn knife! And it was quite clear that it was about my colour. I had done nothing to him, hadn't been in an argument, hadn't messed with anything that belonged to him, and there had been no offence, accidental or otherwise. But somehow I threatened this boy. And when I went to the form master he said, 'We're going to reframe this. This didn't happen the way you're telling it.'

Rajah: For me secondary school was pretty much the same as primary, in that there was still that same racial mix and it was predominantly Muslim. There were more white people than there were at primary school but I was again in the minority, being Sikh. Most of the racism came from Muslims as opposed to white people, though white racism was there. I also thought the teachers were less compassionate than at primary school, and I was more afraid of them.

I'd built up quite a reputation in primary school, and I was quite respected by the end of it. And then, coming to a new school, I had to rebuild all that. At the beginning there was a lot of racism and being picked on. It wasn't until a few years into my secondary school that I began to work hard again. There were periods when I just completely gave up on my work. Then at the end I really picked it up. It was the same sort of pattern as at primary school.

David: My school was mostly black. There were a few whites and a few Asians. It was the same at primary school. So you know I had really no problem, no racism at my school. There was no one saying anything racist to me.

Michael: What about on sexuality?

David: I used to know from an early age that I felt sexual towards other guys, but I used to think to myself, 'I'm sure this is wrong'. I wouldn't go to see an elder, because they'd probably say to you 'Boy, like you're having this sort of feeling? What's wrong with you, boy?' The only person I asked at primary school was the teacher. I went and said 'What is it about two guys going to bed that's bad?' She said to me. 'Then you're classed as homosexual', and she asked why I'd asked and I said 'Oh nothing, it's just this book I was reading'.

When I was growing up I had an older brother who used to put questions to me, like 'What have you done?' I couldn't really say anything to my parents, or he would get into trouble for putting certain questions to me. So I dealt with my problems by myself.

School in Jamaica

Michael: Clinton, do you want to briefly go over your experiences for us?

Clinton: All right. In primary school it was a bit difficult. I didn't look on myself as being gay then, but I used to be called names, a lot of names. I've never been called 'poof', but 'sissy with electric tittie' and all those things! I used to hate it when they called me names. I used to hate it and it used to annoy me a lot. When I went to high school, it was basically the same. I used to be called 'sissy', and 'batty man' and all that shit, but in my recent training course I haven't been called any names at all. I haven't had any difficulty at all. I doubt if people know I'm gay there.

Michael: You went to school in Jamaica didn't you, so was there racism in Jamaica? Were you at school with black people or with white people?

Clinton: I was with black people. The majority were black, and Indians. Black [people] used to call black [people] names. Black [people] used to call light skinned black people 'dum does' and the light skinned black people used to call darker people 'pot bottom'. They used to call the Indians 'coolie' and they used to say stuff like 'coolie shit' and 'coloured boy'. In high school it wouldn't go that far. They'd say 'coolie' and that was it really. And then some would say 'anything that's too black's not good', but there was nothing really serious!

When I came to England, it was quite frightening. Racism doesn't frighten me. I just look on people and think they're daft or stupid, but I am experiencing much more racism now, in my twenties, than when I was in my teens.

Michael: Is that mainly in college, or is that outside of college?

Clinton: I think it's outside of college. I think it's trying to find a job where I find it most difficult – finding a job.

University was completely different

Michael: Is there anyone here who actually went through higher education, and what were the main differences?

Ranee: I went to sixth form college and my experiences were different in that I'd got really into education by then. What was being said to me, was that I was never going to go to university. I was bloody determined that I was going to go to university. So I worked and I worked and I worked. Issues about my sexuality sank into the background. During my last few years at senior school they'd been really prominent, because I'd been accepted by then, although there was still racism. So, during the last few years at senior school there was stuff about sexuality. I was really confused. I didn't understand all the things I heard in the playground about 'He's a poof. She's a lezzie. Yes, she's got short hair, oh my God!' University was completely different, because there were lesbian and gay groups. It was also getting away from my parents.

I moved to an area that was mixed. I lived in an area that was predominantly Sikh and Afro-Caribbean and there were very few white people. It was wonderful. It was brilliant. It felt like coming home! It was just like a huge relief.

So higher education was much better, because I had the space and the time to sort out my identity, and that's where I came out and where I verbalized the things I'd learned since I was a little kid.

Michael: You're saying that there were societies within the university specifically for you as a sexual person? What about societies for black people? And what about the tutors, the lecturers and the students themselves?

Ranee: There weren't very many black people, so again, within the institution, I was in a minority and I was in a situation where I again could have been vulnerable. But there was a difference in that you're not made to sit in this place from nine till four. You can leave it. You don't have to stay within the university. So my needs as a black woman weren't met, but the space was there for me to understand who I was and what I was and identify myself as a black woman as well as a mixed-race woman. There was that space, but it was still very anti-me as a black woman, and a lesbian. There happened

to be a group of lesbians and gay men, which was very small
but it existed. For three years I knew it existed and, in the
last term, I started to go to it. It took me that long to actually
walk through the door of one meeting and say, 'Hello, I'd like
to join'.

David: When I was attending college in the London area at
the age of 22 I felt a lot different than when I was attending
school because of meeting new people at college. Most of
them were really straight people. I hated myself, knowing
that I was gay. One year on the course I knew that lots of
straight guys that I was hanging around with were getting to
like me. Now, some of them had feelings [towards me], even
though they'd never experienced gay feelings. Even though I
didn't let them know about the way I felt, they started letting
me know that they had this feeling toward gays. But I
couldn't say nothing much to them about gay men's feelings.
What I had to say to them was, 'Go and talk to someone
who's more inclined, who knows more about it'. In the area
where I lived then, I used to see gay people whom I didn't
even know. They were friendly and used to say 'hello' and
I'd say 'hello', and from there it would lead into conversation
and you'd get to know someone. Suddenly I started going to
clubs and partying. I started enjoying myself, and I thought
'Well well!'

[My college was in a] mostly white area, but generally, I
have no problem with racism in London.

Robert: I find it very interesting hearing that so many people
have gone through the education process in a black majority
situation in terms of the institution, yet, in a sense, within
a white majority context. That certainly wasn't my experience. In terms of higher education, I went to college where
the courses are arty, and there were a lot of young gay men
on the course.

Michael: What was the course?

Robert: It was a course in theatre/dance in London. It was
very interesting being in 'the big city', living in Notting Hill,
having several gay pubs near to hand, knowing that they
were there, and knowing something about what they were
about. I didn't really use them very much. I didn't make contact with the gay scene until I came home. I spent the time
denying to other people that I was gay, but not denying it

to myself. I was still having a relationship with a woman and I was living in hostels which were directed towards young men who had difficulties at home, so all those issues arose in a very macho environment. In that very disturbed environment it was certainly necessary to deny being gay vehemently, though my gayness was obviously showing itself as well.

Rajah: I found at sixth form college that I couldn't not address sexuality any more. I'd managed in secondary school to detach myself from everyone, and just worked very hard so no one ever questioned me about sexuality. I found myself having to sort of pull away from everyone, so I didn't make any friends so that no one could confront me about this. When I went up to university I went to a completely white city. That was a terrible mistake, because this was my first experience of racism.

Up till then I'd been in majority Asian schools, and now I was in a completely white city, in a completely white middle-class university and department. To start with, I'd loads of problems trying to find my identity there, and trying to make people understand me. I tried to get on with them and then found that I couldn't. So I had to completely detach myself from them, so the race issue took over. But I came out as well and, at the beginning, was very active. I went to gay societies, but I didn't have anything in common with anyone because they were all white. So then in a way, I had to go back into [the closet] again, because there wasn't any support for black and Asian gays in that part of the country.

Ambivalent support

Ranee: What Raj says about going into the groups and realizing that you don't fit in, was an experience for me too. But going into the group actually made me say 'I am a lesbian', which was good after years of knowing I was a lesbian but denying it to everybody. If someone came into a room and mentioned the word lesbian, I'd hit the ceiling. I'd be so uptight, so nervous, I could feel my heart in my throat. Going into the groups, the clubs and the pubs helped me say 'Yes, I'm a lesbian'. But I also became very aware that they were predominantly white, and they didn't take anything into account about being accessible for black people because they weren't dealing with racism within the groups. So it was like getting into a group and having your identity, but also knowing that within that group they could oppress you.

Robert: Yes, I've just completed a second year of a university accredited course and I don't think the race issue is adequately addressed. I don't think they begin to do that on the course. They are a more mature group of people. It's a mixture of black and white Christians from black majority and white majority churches and there's a lot of very typical Christian 'Well, let's see how nice we can be to each other from our different denominations and our different traditions'. So things get, not pushed under the carpet, but the contradictions are smoothed over for fear of conflict. But having said all that, it's ironic that real community for me has been found in the church that I go to – real, real support. It's this invidious situation, as a black gay man, of having to deal with racism every bit as much as a heterosexual black person, but not having the confidence that you can turn to the black community for support because of all those issues around shame and fighting for our dignity anyway, and not wanting the extra burden of homosexuality or the stigma of that attached to us.

Michael: That's a really interesting point. For a lot of people, including myself, religion played a part in our lives initially. But most people I know have gone away from religion because of the pressures of their sexuality. It's interesting to hear you say that Christianity is giving you something that a lot of black people whom I know feel it's taken away from their lives.

Robert: I think it's because it had nurtured me before my sexuality had become an issue, so there was a kind of abiding need for it. There was conflict – and it was a very long drawn out process – moving away but not feeling comfortable with being outside of [Christianity], not feeling comfortable with being inside of it, and having to separate out institutional religion from my experience of God. Not everyone can do that successfully, but what has helped me enormously was to find Christian fellowship in a context where people were convinced that their sexuality was OK, and that they could integrate that to their faith system. It's about positive lesbian and gay person-of-faith experience, and if you can find inroads early enough into that kind of community setting, then that can help you. I think a lot of people don't find that. It's not just a question of sexuality. It's about how churches operate. So often one doesn't experience more than a set of institutional processes, and people don't get to sense the personal one-to-one [experience] of the divine. So when problems and conflicts arise, particularly around our sexuality, then there's just a letting go.

Failures of the education system

Michael: I must add another experience of mine here – something that I find quite disturbing. I went to sixth form college after I left school. My experience was that the primary school and the secondary school that I'd gone to were predominantly black. It was about 99 per cent in both cases. I went on to a sixth form college that was vastly white and I had the most awful experience of my life, which made me leave education. I knew at the time that I hadn't fulfilled my potential, but I left none the less. At about 28, I found myself going back to college and I know a lot of black people who're in the same boat as myself. Thank God the education system does cater for mature students. My experience took me away from education, which puts me at a real disadvantage. I know a lot of white people who don't have the same problems.

Ranee: I think that's very important. I think there's a failure in the educational establishment to come to terms with the impact of systematic oppression upon academic attainment and I don't think it's about not knowing. I think that there still needs to be a lot of work done around issues of sexuality, but certainly there has been a lot of academic study in terms of race. It's not an absence of research, but it's somehow not being addressed.

John: It's not addressing the way that white teachers have low academic expectations of black kids, which means that if you're in a mixed class, you can guarantee that the kids who will get the materials first and the help first will be the white kids, because the expectation is that because you're black you're not going to do very well. If you're not going to do very well, what's the point of spending any time with you? Therefore, you get very little time spent on you. You find that you become a self-fulfilling prophecy. You get fed up with your hand being in the air for 15 minutes while the teacher goes to see the white kids first.

So I think it's about actually addressing the needs of black children and challenging the low expectation there is of any black child. Even in predominantly black schools, there are mainly white teachers and there's been this huge discrepancy between the number of black teachers and pupils. It's just the same with regard to issues of sexuality! How do you deal with being black and gay if it's bad having low expectations because you're black?

Robert: I think teacher expectations are very important. When I worked with small children, I wasn't terribly lovey-dovey. As far as I was concerned, I was a teacher, not a nanny. Because I inflicted a very firm discipline upon the poor darlings and took the attitude that 'we're here to do this thing and we're going to do it: we're not going to mess about, and when we've done it, then we can play', the performance levels went up. The once-a-week child was doing things that people who had been teaching them for years did not expect and did not see. It was interesting to see how children keyed into that and performed according to expectation. They performed at one level when I was running the class, and then the principal of the school would come in and the performance would just plummet.

For me, a lot of the problem was that I was inappropriately placed in class. I was put in classes because I was black, and there was expectation of low attainment; and because certain skills hadn't been given to me earlier on, which seemed to confirm that [expectation], I was then put in a lower stream than I should have been, with people who didn't want to work anyway. So I had that sort of unhealthy environment pulling me down.

Rajah: Perhaps being gay helped in a way, because I achieved a lot more out of education, in terms of results, than I would have – perhaps, because I saw it as a way out. If I hadn't got the grades, I wouldn't have been able to go to university, and I wouldn't have been able to come out, so . . .

Michael: I just wonder what it's like now for kids in schools, when you've got Section 28. Before, things about lesbians and gays may have been mentioned – although it may have been very negative. I wonder if the words are even mentioned any more, because people are so frightened of Section 28.

Robert: I think they're mentioned in an informal setting, in the playgrounds and the toilets and the changing room – that kind of environment – within the peer group. What Section 28 has effectively achieved is that the rubbish [from the tabloid press] cannot be countered. You cannot feed in positive, accurate, truthful information. It's about where [young people] pick up their data, bearing in mind that most of what we learn about sex and sexuality tends to be in an informal rather than in a structured, formal manner. It is very important, I feel, to create a climate where those informal structures can be invaded.

Ranee: I just think the whole education system is really racist and homophobic – not just in terms of pupils but in terms of teachers and curriculum.

Robert: One improvement that I would want to see, if I were a little tot going to school again, would be to have racism awareness on the curriculum, and to have positive images, so that I could learn to understand my oppression from an early age.

Michael: Thinking about a point Ranee was making, I don't think it's all about racism, or about homophobia, but it's also about class. When I was at college I came from an area called Highfields, which was a mainly black area; and just to mention that I came from Highfields would make people draw in their breath in horror. All these people lived in these huge houses with tennis courts and swimming pools, and there was me from lowly little Highfields.

Robert: Yes, there's this whole issue of language in relation to class as well. I found one of the inhibiting factors for me was the pressure against using particular words, wanting to expand one's vocabulary, because that was perceived as not being appropriate to where I was coming from.

If we could change the system . . .

Michael: If we were given the opportunity to change the system, so, for instance, if I was seven again and going back to school, and I wanted to change the system so I felt comfortable in it, what changes would we suggest?

Rajah: I think, I think the education system reflects society, and that we'd only have a better education system if society was more positive towards black people and gay people. But things that could take us in that direction would be things like racism awareness and presenting positive images of gay people and of gay black people, so that we wouldn't have such a hard time coming to terms with it. That's what holds us back from higher education. I remember times when I had lots of relapses because I couldn't handle the racism and homophobia. It detracted from my work.

Robert: The other thing that I was thinking, was an extension of the whole system of college counsellors, where a person can go and discuss issues privately and know that it's not going to be referred back to the teacher. It's just us and them, and you can pick up a variety of information.

Ranee: I think they ought to implement equal opportunities. I think they should actually implement them in terms of curriculum content and behaviour. That includes positive images; it includes awareness; it includes stuff about not oppressing people; and I think it has to be done from day one.

David: As far as I'm concerned, there'll never be any change.

Michael: Why's that? If you *could* make a change, what would you do?

David: First thing I'd say is that there shouldn't be any racism at all, but it's going against what generally happens.

John: I'd say that somewhere during the junior school stage, there should be some input into sex education with angles about homosexuality, or being a lesbian; and also information on where they can find assistance any time it might be needed.

CHAPTER 5

Are You a Lesbian, Miss?

SUSAN A. L. SANDERS and HELENA BURKE

Introduction

The following is a piece written by Sue, a white lesbian who is a supply teacher in a London school, and Helena, a heterosexual teacher in a different school. They compare their experiences of dealing with lesbian and gay issues with the young people they come into contact with and the effect it has on them.

Sue's story[1]

The all girl school in which I am a supply teacher is in an Outer London suburb. It is a fairly large comprehensive and predominantly white. Equal opportunities is an issue which is being addressed and there is an equal opportunities policy (EOP) task force of which I am a member.

I am also a co-founder of an education workers group researching lesbian and gay issues which is supported by the local authority. We are starting with a questionnaire which is being sent to all schools in the borough. Once the information has been collated and analysed we will design and offer training and supply networks and resources. I volunteer my time to this group because of my experience of being 'out' over the last five years, in all the schools in which I teach.

I had heard the term 'shock horror', of course, but I had never witnessed it until the day, several years ago, when I said, 'yes' to a student who asked the question, 'Are you a lesbian?' The scene has been replayed many times since and my response is always the same – grave concern for both of us. It's painful to imagine what is going through the students' hearts and minds when I see this reaction. One morning I walked through the main doors of the school to be greeted with the call, 'Who are you going to rape today?' What have the young women I teach (aged between 11 and 16 years) heard about lesbians that produces such a response? What lies have they been told?

In a school for adolescents, there are many reasons for workers to be 'out'. The research figures from the London Lesbian and Gay Teenage Group are frightening. They show that in London, one in five lesbian and gay students attempt suicide. One could be forgiven for assuming that in London, large and cosmopolitan as it is, attitudes would be more accepting and flexible. However, their research shows a high level of intolerance for lesbians and gays in schools (Trenchard and Warren 1984).

Few of those taking part in the research had any support from school. In fact, the attitudes of both staff and peers in schools were far from helpful. There was little or no information about lesbianism or gay sexuality, coupled with the most negative of stereotyping behaviours.

To decide whether to come out or not is always a complex decision. There is a cost to pay either way. On balance, though I have lost jobs in the past, I prefer to be out. Having an EOP in the school which addresses lesbian and gay rights certainly facilitates this.

As a supply teacher, being out has its advantages and disadvantages. I work part-time and my main income is through my work as a freelance management consultant. My contract with schools is verbal and flexible. However, having no written contract, I am potentially less protected by the union or any EOP in the school or local authority.

My relationship with the staff and students takes longer to develop. Even in my main school, one of my difficulties is that I frequently don't know the names of the pupils, so it is very difficult to follow up problems. Were I a full-time teacher in a school like Helena's, my approach to dealing with offensive remarks would be similar to hers. As it is, I tend to deal with problems on my own.

As I have no control over the content of lessons, my policy is not to initiate any discussion about sexuality. I wear two badges most days: a pink or black triangle and a 'Teachers against Section 28' badge. They make subtle statements about a part of me, just as a wedding ring does for others.

I deliberately wear the triangles rather than an obvious gay or lesbian badge, as it enables the students to have a choice whether or not to notice or ask questions. The triangles also bring up the whole issue of oppression and prejudice. This, to me, is the heart of the matter.

The acceptability for lesbian and gay workers and students to be out in school is linked to our attitudes about discrimination and prejudice. The shock for some students in discovering that they are sitting in front of a self-defined lesbian is enormous. Many can't fully take it in and they need to ask several times. Others, hearing the rumours round the school sensibly need to check it out and hear it 'from the horse's mouth' as it were. (Like Helena, I find that the staff seldom check out the 'rumours' they've heard.)

It is not unusual for students to ask, 'Aren't you ashamed to admit it?' In many cases other students answer for me and say that there is no need for me to feel that. There often follows a few minutes of lively debate on the issue. When I explain that the triangles come from the concentration camps of Nazi rule where many minority groups were imprisoned, tortured and killed, I am aware that for some students this is new information.

Sometimes in the classroom I am less prepared to answer questions, especially when it is clear to me that students are trying to avoid the work set. While it is my job to make sure that they do their work, compromises can be made: 'Do that piece of work and then we'll talk.' How important the questions really are is easily measured by how quickly the work is tackled! Sometimes I will be talking to the whole class. More often it is a small group that has asked me over to talk to them.

The students' most frequent concern is that I will fancy them. Some even think it is illegal for lesbians to be teaching them. Girls are often concerned that I could be having fantasies about them. There is no instant way to allay their concerns, but given time, my behaviour demonstrates that I am not a threat. This means I need to be particularly aware of what constitutes disrespectful verbal and non-verbal language. Respect for students' boundaries is essential. It is difficult for me when students obviously, and insultingly, move away from me. I am still experimenting with ways to deal with this, as I have no desire to erode any young woman's right to choose who comes near her.

Sometimes it can be difficult when they ask questions like, 'How do you know when you are a lesbian?' I always answer with my own experience, emphasizing that it will be different for others, and that there is more information about that now than there was when I was an adolescent. Some students have asked me what I do in bed. I do not give them details about my sex life. I tell them that the answer is too personal, that there are books on Lesbian sex available and that some book shops stock them. I point out that there is no such person as a 'typical gay person' and that we are represented in all sections of the whole community: black and white, mothers and fathers, able-bodied and disabled, middle class and working class, young and old.

Most are more than aware of the prejudice against lesbians and gays. Indeed, it is clear that many pupils share this pre-judice and assume that their attitudes are based on factual evidence. It is easier for those attitudes to be maintained when lesbians and gays are silent and invisible in their institutions.

I have, over the last two years, taught most of the young women in the school. The fact that I am a lesbian is now common knowledge, the grapevine being what it is. The word lesbian can be said with many different intonations. When it is yelled at me in the corridor, it does sound vile, even to *my* ears, and there is a part of me that wants to deny it, as I am sure that their definition and mine are vastly different.

At all times I attempt to be calm and clear and do not 'put down' students while challenging negative attitudes. This is not always easy, especially when a student said that all lesbians and gays should be shot. However, to lose my temper or pull teacher power on them would be totally inappropriate. After all, I am attempting to set up a situation where the students can feel safe to speak their minds. It is important to me to model constructive feedback while exploring the students' realities. It is hardly the students' fault that they have only heard one side of our story.

Some students are very supportive of my being out. They will say so quite explicitly and volunteer information about other lesbians or gay men their family know. Some say that it is a good idea that there are teachers prepared to talk about such things and be open about themselves. Others will simply be very deliberate about saying 'Hello' to me in the corridor, especially when some students are giggling or pushing and pulling each other into or out of my path. That takes bravery on their part because they are challenging peer pressure.

Time is a very important ingredient in this work. We all grow and change. I have been teaching now in a variety of settings for over 20 years. During that time I have taught students of all ages and some of them have been initially very angry and oppositional to me or my views, but in time some have dramatically reappraised their attitudes and lifestyle. No one's views are set in stone.

The students are stating attitudes they have before they have had the personal experience to test them. It is essential, therefore, to keep my ground, not to take things they say personally and to continue to question their assumptions and ideas while giving them facts and information that they can think about.

Though there are some teachers who find my presence a challenge, most realize the dangers if we don't challenge the prejudice. The subject is there in the playground. 'Lezzie' is used as an insult and to pressure the 'other' to conform to stereotypical roles. For the moment, until we have our EOP in place, it is up to each individual to decide how to bring the issue into their classroom.

Schools can be oppressive places for children. In many ways, it seems to me, we have yet to take seriously the rights of young people. If, however, we do not enable students to have self-knowledge and self-confidence we are encouraging them to be oppressive to others and themselves. Discrimination and prejudice not only harm the receiver, they stunt the growth of the giver as well. All too often, people put someone else down to feel good about themselves. This is made easier if they are ignorant about that person or their way of life.

Heterosexism exists in our schools both by design and ignorance, as does racism, classism and disablism, for schools are a reflection of our community. That they can be a place to challenge such attitudes is vital. Young people have a passion for fairness. They have been told many lies about many people by the media. Various people have been made invisible in their textbooks.

Many of you reading this will remember with dread your schooldays. That we have made some inroads in schools is clear, otherwise there would have been no demand for Section 28. There is however a long way to go. It is clear that there is a section of the government and their friends that will only be happy when lesbians and gays are unable to work with or help raise children. The recent attempt to stop us fostering and adopting makes this clear. We can all work to dispel the web of lies that is fed to the younger generation, and encourage them to question their 'shock-horror' of meeting a real, live, out lesbian or gay man.

Helena's story

The aim of this piece is to look at reasons why I, as a teacher who chooses to be heterosexual, believe we all have a responsibility to raise issues of sexuality in our classrooms. As issues of equality have arisen in society it has always been the oppressed groups who have raised them first. Others then join the debate and some choose to support such struggles. In education, some teachers have been involved in supporting issues of equality, related to gender and race for years. Others have taken on a range of other issues, but few, and very few outside of the gay and lesbian communities, raise issues of sexuality and equality.

I am very aware that I am writing for a book which may be read predominantly by gay and lesbian teachers (simply because many heterosexual teachers will see this as 'nothing to do with them'). Because of this, I feel I need to make clear that I am writing from personal experience. My aim is to initiate ideas and to indicate ways in which this challenging but productive area can be tackled.

Looking back to when I first talked about homosexuality with pupils, it was in the most low-key way possible. If you were to look through my syllabus or worksheets, there would be no sign of such work. As a probationary teacher of sociology, it would come up because we were discussing sex or inequality, or because pupils were abusing each other. I cannot claim that this was thought out or structured in any real way. It was my response to a commitment to equal opportunities.

The process of putting into place equal opportunities policies has had a complex history, and we are still learning. In the past, there was a danger of segmenting and sectionalizing various groups, setting up a hierarchy of oppression and denying the reality of people belonging to more than one minority group. This could easily set up a pattern of 'race this year, gender next'. At such a rate, many schools would never get on to gay and lesbian issues.

Schools need to recognize that equal opportunities is about everybody and present the concept that oppression and power cannot be sectioned off into separate categories or issues. The danger of such sectioning is that some issues, particularly lesbian and gay issues, will be perceived as dangerous and controversial, while others will be seen as less important.

I teach in a school that has a holistic approach to equal opportunities and has worked with parents and governors throughout its development. To put this approach into practice requires all teachers to address gay and lesbian issues in their classrooms.

If we allow pupils to use the abusive language of heterosexism and allow stereotypes to continue, we are playing a part in the oppression of gays and lesbians. We are also doing a disservice to all young people in our classrooms. It is anti-educational to collude with the ignorance that surrounds gay and lesbian lifestyles. It is now broadly accepted that all pupils benefit from an education that challenges sexist or racist oppression. All pupils will benefit from the opportunity to discuss their sexuality and that of others, to understand the range of lifestyles that exists in our societies, and to understand the role they in turn have to play in challenging prejudice and discrimination.

Sue has referred to the horrific figures of teenage lesbian and gay suicide attempts and the fact that few of those young people felt school offered them any support. Can teachers really continue to consider it a matter of choice as to whether we can discuss these issues or not?

My own fears about tackling this work have, in the main,

been allayed. This is obviously due to the specific atmosphere in the school created by the EOP and the practical
support of out lesbian and gay teachers who have listened and
worked through my anxieties. What has been of great value
to me is the personal work I've had to do around my own
sexuality. In so doing, I was then faced with recognizing my
position in society not only as a victim of oppression as a
woman but also as a potential oppressor in that I am a white
heterosexual.

Pupils' positive responses to work around lesbian and gay
issues has far outweighed the negative in my experience. Yet I
am stunned to hear teachers who confidently deal with issues
of race and gender, and have the structures and support in
place to enable such work, blame predicted pupil response for
not dealing with lesbian and gay issues: 'I couldn't do that
with my kids, they would just sit and talk about poofs.' I
seriously doubt they would. I believe this is an underestimation
of pupils. However, if that is what the teacher really believes,
it seems the strongest reason in the world for starting such
work. Would it be acceptable to say, 'I'm not going to study
oppression and racism in my school, because the kids are too
racist'?

Sue has made it clear how vital it is to have out lesbian and
gay teachers in our schools. Heterosexual teachers, too, have
a role to play in this. It is our responsibility to work towards
the creation of a safe environment that challenges stereotypes
and assumptions and celebrates diversity. Ways in which we
can do this include:

- working towards policy and structure which celebrate gay
  and lesbian lifestyles and challenge heterosexism;
- being aware of how we speak in the classroom and staffroom,
  e.g. not saying 'don't be such a poofter' to a boy combing his
  hair;
- using examples of both heterosexual and same sex couples in
  teaching materials;
- making sure we openly work with students on these issues in
  the formal curriculum;
- always tackling prejudice ourselves rather than waiting for
  lesbians or gays to take it up, whether with adults or
  students;

- enabling and facilitating students to fight prejudice within the school and the wider community;
- not presuming the heterosexuality of students or staff;
- not assuming that because a gay or lesbian person is out to you, that it is OK to discuss this with others.

Many of the above, and more, have been excellently documented by the Lesbian and Gay Rights Working Party, City of Leicester Teachers' Association (1988). By playing a part in enabling such an atmosphere, thereby giving gays and lesbians a better choice to come out, heterosexual teachers gain an enormous amount. As heterosexual teachers it is *our* responsibility to initiate such work or join the conspiracy of silence which presumes heterosexuality and defines homosexuality as against the norm.

I have tried to build this work into the formal curriculum. This has a number of benefits:

- it gives work on lesbian and gay issues the status of other topics and encourages all pupils to engage in them;
- it contextualizes lesbian and gay issues alongside other issues of oppression, prejudice and liberation;
- it ensures that all members of the department deal with the issues.

If such work is included in GCSE and A level, pupils will have to involve themselves in it in order to complete course requirements. This takes away the element of 'waiting for it to come up in discussion'.

We've dealt with lesbian and gay issues in a number of other ways as well. Images around the school can support pupils who choose to raise issues with staff. It may well be that a pupil needs someone to talk to about their sexuality in their own time. By having posters of prominent gays and lesbians, campaigns by lesbian and gay groups and help lines, we are showing that staff are open to discussion and are indicating other paths young gays and lesbians can follow for advice. We also have assemblies which celebrate Lesbian and Gay Pride Day alongside other festivals which reflect the diverse society of our pupils.

The above work can only be done within the context of a school where an equal opportunities structure, and at least some of the staff, support you. I am in a secure position within my school. I hold a middle management position, I have developed relationships with like-minded staff and, most importantly, with pupils, having been in the school for three years. All of the above are extremely important, as dealing with lesbian and gay issues has personal consequences. It is frequently assumed that we must be lesbian or gay to raise the issues, and from the time I began such work, I was presumed by many staff and pupils to be lesbian.

This is no longer something that concerns me. This must be seen, in part, as a result of the hard work of out gay and lesbian staff in creating the specific atmosphere I have referred to. This is illustrated by the behaviour of one particular group of pupils who spent several days reassuring me that it was 'fine with them' if I was a lesbian, but they just wanted to know. This was clearly no more than a request for gossip on staff. It resulted in a number of hilarious encounters as they enlisted the help of an openly gay member of staff to glean this information from me.

However, I am also aware that to be presumed to be a lesbian is not a risk for me, for I could choose to 'deny' this at any point. Gay and lesbian teachers risk much more: if not out, they risk being outed; if out, they risk persecution and the potential loss of job or status.

Whilst I have the option to state my heterosexuality, after much discussion and guidance from out staff, we find the most useful strategy is to respond to pupils' questions by asking 'What difference does it make?' (Other teachers never ask, they just wonder!) We find that this can engage pupils in thoughtful and provocative discussion. If heterosexual teachers simply confirm their sexuality, it can immediately close down discussion. Pupils need to acknowledge that lesbians and gays are 'just like everybody else', that 'you can't tell by looking at them' and that lesbians and gays are potentially their teachers, friends, members of their families, and idols.

At the same time, it is important to challenge the concept that only lesbians and gays would tackle such work. Therefore, it is my policy that, at a carefully judged time, if the pupils have persisted and the question is no longer about how I should be defined and treated, but rather a light-hearted desire for 'info', I will acknowledge my heterosexuality. This information is, interestingly, often not passed on to other pupils. Rather it falls into the body of background information on teachers – who is married, who has a boyfriend, where so and so goes out, etc.

Like Sue, I am also asked about lesbian, gay and bisexual sex. I, too, have to acknowledge that this needs to be dealt with in particular contexts. However, when asked in a way which clearly indicates a serious question by a pupil, rather than an opportunity to giggle or merely distract from work, I will discuss it. This particularly occurs within the context of sex education, where we try to examine the range of sexual expression in our society, such as celibacy, heterosexuality, bisexuality, transsexuality and lesbianism and homosexuality. If it is within the context of a GCSE unit on 'attitudes to sexuality', I will be less willing to discuss it. I feel it is vital to get pupils away from the notion that to be lesbian or gay is simply about sex.

By bringing the issue out in our classrooms, we are attempting to prevent homophobia and heterosexism. But we cannot hope that this will eliminate the weight of 'evidence' given in the media, some homes, peer groups, etc. that to be gay or lesbian is unacceptable. When dealing with abusive language, I try to ensure that my first response is to make it clear to the offender, and to all other pupils, that such homophobia is not acceptable. This would usually be followed up with an 'educational' discussion with the pupil, asking: what does the word mean? why use it as an insult? how would it make the young lesbians and gay men in the class feel?

It is obviously the aim that a pupil should become aware of what they have done and why it is wrong. This does not always mean a complete change in behaviour but rather a clearer awareness of the issues involved. For instance, a young man who had done some excellent work in this area (see Patrick and Sanders, this volume) 'inadvertently' called another boy a 'poof'. Before I could do anything, the young man went very red, and apologized profusely and continuously for the rest of the lesson. His behaviour hadn't completely changed, yet, but the work had obviously had a real impact in raising his awareness that such name calling was offensive and unacceptable.

Unfortunately this awareness cannot always be achieved and,

as a last resort, a continuous offender would be subject to discipline. We have an EOP to protect oppressed groups and challenge prejudice. Whilst our aim is to educate, we also have a responsibility to protect young gays and lesbians and all oppressed groups.

My approach to homophobic attitudes expressed in discussion is different. I feel I have to allow pupils to explore their own views and only through open debate can they be challenged. We have rules about the sort of language that can be used, but I still feel concerned about the young gays and lesbians who have to listen to these views. I haven't resolved what I feel is best here.

Pupils' responses to being faced with issues of gay and lesbian sexuality vary enormously. I have had a group who took the issue to their school council. They didn't feel it was anything to do with them and that they therefore shouldn't have to study it. This instance alone shows why it is so important to ensure that you have support in your school before starting work on any scale with pupils. Their concern was obviously the result of fear and insecurity and a great deal of time was spent talking to them, by teachers who worked with the school council and eventually by the headteacher. Without this support I could not have continued with this work. However, it was eventually made clear to them that the bottom line was that this was a piece of work which was part of the school's EOP, and they would do it.

We also have very positive responses from pupils. One of the joys is the lightness they can bring to such work, showing a sense of humour and simplicity when teachers are regarding it in a 'serious, soul-searching' manner. They frequently surprise me. Last week, as pupils were writing a piece describing their feelings about two imaginary lesbian girls, and how they were mistreated at school, a young man wrote, 'I cannot understand how these people behave like this, it's abnormal'. The piece was a little unclear. However, I presumed I was dealing with a boy who was expressing his prejudice and I sat down to explain that there was nothing abnormal about lesbians. He then patiently explained to me that the abnormality he had been referring to was the prejudice of the pupils and not the young lesbian's sexuality!

One of the exciting things about this work is that it

continuously shows how open people are to changing their attitudes and opinions – not only young people in our classrooms, but also parents, staff and governors. It has been really rewarding to be part of such work.

Conclusion

Working on this article together has been a fascinating process. We set out to show the different ways in which lesbian and gay issues could be tackled by a lesbian teacher and a heterosexual teacher. Interestingly, what it has highlighted are the similarities in our approach and ideas, though the experiences that have led us to this are very different. We certainly found our practice is different at the moment, but that is more to do with the different situations in which we find ourselves. We discovered a political mutuality which was strengthening and heartening.

Note

1 I would like to acknowledge the Brisson Veor Trust for the special place where I did the bulk of the writing of this article. I would also like to thank my partner, Jeane L. Nadeau for her belief in this work, her support and editing skills.

References

Lesbian and Gay Rights Working Party, City of Leicester Teachers' Association (NUT) (1988, revised 1990) *Challenging Oppression: Lesbians and Gays in School. A Resource Pack*. Leicester: City of Leicester Teachers' Association.
Trenchard, L. and Warren, H. (1984) *Something to Tell You*. London: London Gay Teenage Group.

CHAPTER 6

Victim of a Victimless Crime: Ritual and Resistance

ROY BARTELL

This story is about a teacher who is arrested for indecency and the consequences which that arrest has for himself and his family. The narrative explores the policing of a *victimless crime*, the nature of a local education authority's response, and the *resistance* of the teacher to this persecution. The facility with which the authority marshals the use (or ab/use) of *procedure* and the *power to define* indicates *ritual* practice.

A victimless crime

For Freddie Parkes these late evenings were now regular week-end events. It was 'purple pansy' duty – that's what fellow white officers called it. Chatted up by vice-squad detectives, black constables posed in Shire City's underground toilets on Friday and Saturday nights. It was all tight clothes, hard or wayward glances, maintained eye contact, and a dick out at a urinal with rhythmic hand movements. Surprising how many arrests they could make. Your vice-squad superior was outside ready to close in once you had 'a chicken or two in the coop'. Not official Home Office stuff, but the Shire's new chief constable was keen on getting a reputation. Freddie could expect promotion soon if things continued to go as well as they had over the last four months. He had the body. And the nice thing about this assignment – the detective did most of the paper work.

He had been standing alone at a urinal for some time when he heard footsteps coming down the stairs from the street. It was December, a dank night, and he felt the cold through his heavy black cotton T-shirt. It wasn't long before he caught the glance and kept it of a client. He was white. Freddie judged him to be in his late 40s. Same height, bearded, and dressed warmly in a ski jacket and knitted cap. He stood three urinals further down the wall and despite his glasses, he seemed to be responding to Freddie's plaintive stare? It *was* late – usually they didn't have to wait too long when it was this close to midnight.

More footsteps! Colin wouldn't be coming down this soon. Another white man, rather short, went to the urinal beyond this bearded bloke. He was lighting up – a sure sign that he intended to stay a while. This could be it. Freddie hoped Colin wouldn't be too hasty about closing in. Colin had blown a chance already this evening when he hadn't let the chickens roost for long enough.

Freddie kept offering to meet their glances. Then he noticed some body contact. He moved his arm rhythmically and brought himself away from the urinal a bit. It looked like display *and* it gave him a better chance to see what was happening. The bearded man was beginning to wank the little man.

Footsteps! The wanking ceased. Another man came in. Maybe not white. Freddie couldn't quite see. It sounded as if he went into one of the cubicles at his back. Footsteps . . . then Colin lingered in the door frame. Like Freddie, he tried to get eye contact with the two men in the corner. The room was now filled with snatched glances. The wanking resumed. Freddie and Colin watched as if absorbed.

When Colin reached towards his coat pocket with his left hand, that was the cue. Freddie moved quickly and seized the bearded man by his left arm. 'We are members of the Shire vice squad and we are arresting you . . .' Freddie's spiel was interrupted by Colin's ferocious shout at the man in the cubicle. 'Get out of here!' His voice implied the violence he was prepared to use. Freddie didn't tighten his grip, however. In a moment he and Colin took two acquiescent middle-aged men to an unmarked car. They were on the way to two more arrests – arrests that would look good on their summary sheets.

For Freddie the rest of that evening was procedural. He and Colin interrogated the men in the car and, once at the central police station, on the way to the charge desk. Compliantly, Freddie found out as much as possible about the bearded man. He was, as Freddie had hoped, 'soft bait' – a teacher, one of the professionals that the local paper could give pictorial as well as verbal coverage to. Too bad he wasn't from the clergy. Freddie's game of trust blew, however, when he asked, 'And where do you teach?' No more information after that. He'd have not to seem so interested another time.

His client was a Dr Bartell. His accent told Freddie that he wasn't born in this country. Bartell knew something about his rights on arrest, picked up a leaflet that lay on the charge desk and asked to telephone home. Then he wanted to speak to a solicitor. Colin told Freddie to warn Bartell that he could be here all night – they didn't know where the duty solicitor was. But it hadn't worked. Sensing that this could be an awkward customer, Colin decided they'd interview his bloke first.

Colin did all the work when they got around to Bartell. It was about two o'clock, Saturday morning. Freddie was tired and wanted to go home. They might be easy arrests but things could get drawn out. Colin said the usual about people in the community being concerned. He kept trying to get Bartell to admit to being gay or homosexual. He made sure that the nature of the arrest was never discussed on tape. It wasn't too difficult – Bartell was evidently frightened. His voice was terribly dry.

Like almost all of them, Bartell was a married man with family responsibilities. He was intensely anxious about publicity. Freddie had taken him to be fingerprinted, photographed and to have the charge of Gross Indecency read out. As Freddie took him back to a cell, Bartell asked him, 'Will there be reporters outside when we leave the station?' They were unbelievably naïve. On cue, Freddie got changed into his uniform. He and Colin would drive these buggers home in a police car just in case any of the neighbours might be up late. Next week he would be back on his evening beat in the centre of Shire City.

Freddie liked watching out for what *The Messenger* made of these arrests. To his surprise there wasn't anything about

Bartell. When he and Colin were working the loos a few weeks later, Colin told him that some solicitors from London were chasing up details. He'd made a statement. Freddie needn't bother. These queers didn't stand a chance in magistrates' court.

In June Freddie had to do something he hadn't bargained on when Colin first approached him about doing the loos. He was asked to sign a statement about the arrests which didn't reflect what actually took place. He wasn't too happy about this. He got one small concession. He gave the time he entered the toilets as different from what Colin gave. It wasn't likely that a defence lawyer would take this matter up, especially when *The Messenger* would be giving front page publicity to the case if it was contested in court.

In July Freddie was at the Crown Court. Bartell was exercising his right to have the case heard by a circuit court judge. Bartell's barrister was even trying for a bind over – the Crown Prosecution agreed, Colin had said he and Freddie agreed, but Freddie didn't think their boss would agree. He and Colin had got some real soft bait in June – a headteacher in the county. The chief wasn't about to let Bartell off the hook – there was the prospect of a lot of publicity that made it look as if the police were doing a fine job.

In the end Bartell had to plead guilty. He was only fined £50. The Crown barrister even spoke up for the teacher. These barristers had little respect for the game the chief constable was playing. Freddie and Colin, in uniform, stood at the entrance to the court as Bartell left with his wife and a close friend – this time Freddie couldn't catch Bartell's eye.

In May 1989 Freddie found himself in uniform again over the case. There was to be a hearing at the school where Bartell had been teaching for just three months before his arrest. Freddie suspected it was Masonic links that got a lot of this going. He wasn't likely to be asked into Freemasonry, that was for sure! But he knew there was a big fight brewing in the vice squad over unfair Masonic promotions. Colin had told him. There were rumours of county hall Freemasons running things as well.

Bartell had claimed that Freddie had been masturbating in the toilets that evening. He would certainly deny that. Freddie wanted to put this vice squad detail behind him now, anyway. The chief constable was losing interest. What publicity was to

be gained had been gained. New toilets were being installed
– the one where Bartell was arrested had been bulldozed long
ago, and there was pressure being brought on the chief by one
of Shire City's MPs. A gay and lesbian campaign had gathered
too much information on the use of *agents provocateurs*. It was
getting harder and harder to get convictions in court, especially
against a person on his own. A vicar and a headteacher were
both taking their cases to the High Court.

Freddie shuddered to think of the cost to the taxpayer of the
chief constable's campaign. Bartell must be earning somewhere
in the region of £15,000 a year and was still pulling that in
– almost a year and a half after being suspended from work.
And how many people at county hall, in the Crown Prosecuting
Service and at the Constabulary had spent time dealing with
this one arrest? That added up to something like £50,000. With
the arrests they had made the cost of the chief constable's concern was probably in the region of a million pounds. The constabulary's proportion of that money could be much better
spent on domestic violence and attacks on the vulnerable in
public places. Freddie left work that day hoping he'd seen the
back of that single arrest one night in December 1987. He wasn't
sure what Colin's career hopes were – he was white after
all – but he, Freddie, was on a course at Shire University. He
hoped to improve his promotion chances that way rather than
as a 'purple pansy'.

Ritual Ab/use of procedure

Smythe Gollum, Shire's director of education, first knew of Dr
Bartell's arrest on Monday morning when Will Err, head of
Humbold Community College, telephoned him. Bartell had
rung one of Err's deputy heads Sunday evening. Err wanted to
know what to do; he'd never heard of anything like it before.
Gollum was very reassuring. 'Make certain he doesn't come in
to teach. If you can, get him in to clear out his room this
afternoon. I'll have a letter hand-delivered to Bartell by
tomorrow morning.' Err was relieved. He hadn't taken to
Bartell – far too inclined to rock the boat, to introduce new
ideas. As he put down the phone Gollum thought briefly to
himself, 'Here's a chance to get rid of another of these wets. I'll

have to find out a bit more about this Bartell character. I hope Err doesn't get too agitated.'

When Gollum had a message to contact Duncan Wanders, regional union officer, about an hour later, he knew what it would be about, and he wasn't worried. Wanders understood himself to be a friend, someone who could telephone, or be telephoned by, Gollum day or evening, at work or at home. There was plenty of room to come to understandings. Bartell's case wouldn't upset that.

When Gollum got around to telephoning Wanders that evening, he already had more information on Bartell. He had taught for many years at one of the county schools, Butler, and was held in very high esteem by colleagues there. That could create problems. Gollum's predecessors had appointed heads in the county who had minds of their own. In turn they had appointed independent minded staff. Butler had often pressured the authority into granting additional funding. There was a lot of political know-how. Gollum might have to watch that.

Err at Humbold was a different matter. He was near retirement and not very well, and his school was really at the mercy of the authority – it was a wholly council estate catchment area. Not much parental or influential political power there. When Err rang in the afternoon to let Gollum know that Bartell had come in to collect his belongings, Gollum was unequivocal. 'You won't see him back in your school – rest assured.'

The conversation with Wanders went well. Wanders agreed that Bartell should resign and accept a few weeks' payment. He could apply for retraining. Wanders understood how similar Bartell's case was to that of a local union official – someone a bit too radical for their liking – the authority got rid of him after a police raid on his house . . . party, drugs, pupils and all!

On Tuesday morning Gollum had a letter delivered by hand to Bartell: 'Suspended until the outcome of the proceedings is known.' Gollum could count on the editor of *The Messenger* to give the case publicity at the magistrates' court. Bartell didn't stand a chance.

Six months later Gollum had to put his mind to this matter of Bartell again. It was now June and still nothing had been resolved. Bartell was turning out to be less amenable than he had hoped. Wanders informed him that Bartell had obtained the services of an out-of-town solicitor. There had been no publicity in the local papers. Bartell was getting a lot of support from former colleagues at Butler. Gollum told Wanders that he had had a lot of letters concerning Bartell from Butler teachers. Yes, Wanders confirmed, a campaign had been organized.

Gollum did have something on Bartell, however. Will Err was anxious to take early retirement this year. He had seen to a report on Bartell during his three months at Humbold which was fairly damning. Gollum was sure this could be used. And now there was to be a new headteacher at Humbold. When staffing provision was discussed for Humbold this month, he would let it be known that Bartell's post might be permanently replaced.

September 1988 saw a flurry of activity concerning Bartell. Gollum had approved the permanent appointment. Lance Curry, the new head, was pleased with that and was preparing another report. Bartell had got a conviction but only a £50 fine *and there had been no publicity*! All the same a Freemason connection at the police had provided a somewhat lurid account of the arrest for county hall. They should have enough to hang Bartell. Wanders was anxious, however. Supporters were putting Bartell up to things. Wanders had mentioned to him something about a classroom incident. Bartell was demanding to see any reports that had been prepared on him.

Gollum moved decisively. He wanted Bartell to face a hearing at Humbold School. Curry wasn't too happy about risking publicity for his new school, however. Gollum decided it was time to distance himself from the case. Patty Mallis, one of his deputy directors, would take over. Her first act would be to set up the hearing at Humbold School. She wrote to Wanders giving 10 days notice of the hearing. She also mentioned the request for Humbold documents. 'I have said I am referring to you in this case and that it is inappropriate to discuss the matter in any other way.'

Ritual: Power to define 1

When Patty Mallis took over Bartell's file from Smythe Gollum, she did not relish the task. Gollum had proceeded towards dismissing Bartell before any satisfactory hearing had taken place.

There was only a £50 fine, and *no* publicity. And now the latest was that the DES was not taking action against Dr Bartell. All this left the authority vulnerable in its course of action. Furthermore, there was a file full of correspondence from colleagues trying to find out what the authority was going to do to help Roy Bartell.

Mallis had to be careful. There were some things she could count on to affect Gollum's design. He had succeeded in obtaining reports on Bartell at Humbold which could be used damagingly. The police account of the arrest was valuable. And most importantly, Mallis knew that she could count on Wanders, the union regional officer. He would not affect union policy over access to documents. Gollum had seen to that. Mallis turned her mind to preparing a case against Bartell knowing full well that the documents she was using would not be subject to detailed scrutiny.

At a hearing Bartell would be able to produce positive character witnesses on his behalf, and they could be impressive. Mallis needed to find a means of discrediting him as a teacher. It would not be enough to rely on his conviction for Gross Indecency. It had to be demonstrated that he was a menace in the classroom.

Thus it was she who hit upon an event which took place in Bartell's classroom on the day of his arrest. A male pupil had exposed himself to some girls. Bartell had sent for the year head, who had seen the male pupil and subsequently disciplined him. Bartell had later discussed the event with the year head. Mallis turned this incident over carefully in her mind.

She prepared the education authority's case against Dr Bartell. She alluded to Bartell's arrest and conviction. It was the 'nature' of the arrest that concerned the authority. It was also, however, an incident in the classroom that day, an incident which Dr Bartell claimed had 'set him off' – seeing a male pupil expose himself. Bartell was neither 'trustworthy' nor of good 'judgement'. He could not be allowed to return to the classroom.

At the end of September Mallis arranged for the hearing at Humbold to take place immediately. Suddenly, however, one of Mallis's securities slipped away. Wanders was dismissed by Bartell for failing to obtain education authority documents he made reference to. Bartell was going to be represented by a group of London solicitors. The hearing had to be postponed. Issues of natural justice were being raised. The local union representative was seeking meetings with her. She needed to buy time.

By December 1988, a year after Bartell's arrest, Mallis decided she now had enough in place to go ahead with a hearing at Humbold. She sent a copy of the authority's case to Bartell's solicitors and gave them 10 days to prepare for a hearing. She was unprepared for their reply. They insisted on having the document which was the basis of the accusation about the classroom incident. No hearing could take place until this document was produced. Mallis needed advice. She turned to the county solicitor.

Ritual: Power to define 2

I. M. A. Mason, Chief Administrator and County Solicitor, had already come across the Bartell file. When Gollum needed a summary of Bartell's arrest and conviction, Mason knew who to contact at Police Central. The detective inspector was a member of Firnwood Lodge, like himself. Mason was a man with connections.

He was not happy when he read Roy Bartell's file. He understood why Mallis wanted to use the classroom material. He also understood why Bartell's solicitors wanted a copy of the basis of the accusation. He was going to have to stall. In his reply to the London solicitors he enclosed a copy of the police report. That was going to be included in the education authority's case at the Humbold hearing. Concerning the classroom incident, this hearing was not the same as one in court. Evidence did not strictly have to be adhered to.

He sent that off and waited. In the meantime he adapted Err's report on Bartell. He visited Humbold School and spoke to two of the teachers mentioned in Err's report. He was ready for the London solicitors' next letter. He replied sending a copy of a document that he said didn't make very nice reading. The education authority didn't really want to produce it. But here it was, 'a copy report', submitted by Miss Herringdon. It would be Exhibit A. The education authority had also decided to call the two arresting police officers to give evidence at the hearing.

When the solicitors continued to press for a signed, dated and complete document, Mason replied that knowing how embarrassing the document was the authority would only use two paragraphs from it. Both Miss Herringdon and a deputy head had agreed to give evidence at the hearing. It would be the first week of May. Another solicitor would represent the authority. Submissions from Dr Bartell must be received a full working week before the hearing. Mason arranged for the Clerk to the School Governors to take over arrangements and for there to be a stenographer present to record the proceedings. With the police in uniform and the actual document still not handed over to Bartell's solicitors, the authority stood a good chance. The Clerk to the School Governors and the chairman were both fraternal order men.

At first, Mason thought the result of the hearing was what he wanted. The Governors, although not unanimously, had recommended Bartell's dismissal. There were one or two complications, however. The Governors also recommended that further consideration be given to Dr Bartell's case because of all the evident support and concern expressed by professional colleagues. When Mason saw the transcript of the hearing he was dismayed. Neither of the teachers supported the authority's version of the classroom incident. The authority could be in trouble over that.

Ritual: Ab/use of procedure and power to define

Mason was particularly concerned about Bartell's right of appeal to a county hall committee. There would be county councillors present and even though officers could generally count on members seeing things their way, anything too extraordinary could not go unnoticed. He arranged a meeting with the Clerk to the Governors. Had the Clerk prepared the summary of the hearing? It needed to be brief. Would he send it along for looking over? These London solicitors could be very clever.

The Clerk's summary required careful editing. Mason finally approved of a version of the two teachers' evidence: Miss Herringdon recalled telephone calls being made and the deputy 'did not record Dr Bartell using the words "set me off" but the sentence was factually correct'. It was sent to Dr Bartell as 'The Notes of the Hearing' with a 10 day notice for appeal. The reply from London was categoric. 'The Notes' must include all questions asked and all answers given. Mason replied, 'The process being followed is not that of a court of law. The note of proceedings for the purposes of the disciplinary process is whatever the .Clerk to the Governors produces as "the note of proceedings".'

The London solicitors would not accept this explanation. An accurate record of the hearing must be available for the committee as the only fair basis for appeal. Mason was now in considerable difficulty. It all stemmed from Mallis's going ahead with her clever case without first consulting the legal department. When would these education people stop expecting the legal officers to cover up for them! On 29 June 1989 Mason wrote to the London solicitors:

> The stenographer, Mrs Withers, was taken to the Governors' meeting by the Clerk to the Governors not for the purpose of taking a verbatim record of the meeting but to provide the Clerk with a backup point of reference should he need it. I am told that Mrs Withers did not take notes of the whole proceedings, since she understood her role to be to pick out the salient points. Subsequent to the Governors' meeting Mrs Withers . . . was told by the Clerk that he had produced his notes of proceedings . . . She had been impressed at various times with the view that the proceedings were sensitive and confidential . . . she destroyed the notes to preserve the confidentiality. The position is, therefore, that the notes no longer exist and cannot be transcribed.

Resistance

Roy and Harriet were in many ways young adults of the 1960s. Harriet had come from a family whose parents had been nourished by the political ferment of the 1930s, had been a part of the intellectual community in Shire City which had vigorously supported the Republican forces in Spain. For her part, the Aldermaston marches had been formative in defining political initiative. She had met Roy, seven years older than herself, in Nigeria just at the time and place Biafra was forming.

Roy had come late to the issues of the 1960s. From a west coast USA city still very much parochial in its outlook, Roy had rebelled against his parents' McCarthy era sentiments, as much through liberal Christianity as through politics, and had found himself in the Peace Corps in the full flush of JFK enthusiasm just before Kennedy's assassination. The years in Nigeria, culminating in the year when Harriet arrived, had been most radicalizing. Vietnam was to be campaigned about, not just avoided.

When Roy and Harriet found themselves in Metropolis in the late 1960s, fresh from West Africa, they particularly took up issues around racism – apartheid in South Africa, inequality in inner-city English schools. In his secondary school Roy's department offered the only black studies course outside London; Roy and Harriet were founder members of their city's branch of Teachers Against Racism.

It was during those years in Metropolis that Roy and Harriet built up alliances and furthered their awarenesses: the Free University, encounter groups and the quest for Gaia. When the education authority (under Labour control) attempted to close down his department, Roy found these associations and alliances crucial. In the end, however, the LEA succeeded – as Metropolis went comprehensive, Roy's school was closed in favour of a school with fewer radicalized staff. Roy, Harriet and their friends learned a hard lesson in the perfidy of political parties.

It was at this time that Roy and Harriet had their first son; he was disabled from birth. When Roy found work at Butler Upper School, in the Shire, on the outskirts of Shire City, he and Harriet were changing – slowing down to meet the needs of their first born. It was in Shire that the older generation of Harriet's family had grown up and lived.

The community college where Roy was now working was an exceptional school. Its principal was a patron of the arts, locally, and with his wife, who was not British, he collected around him teachers who had experience of worlds far beyond the confines of Shire England. The upper school reflected this ethos in its curriculum and in its social relationships. After their second son, born a little over a year later than their first, Roy and Harriet adopted a third child. He was black and joined a group of such children adopted by members of the college community. Eventually Roy and Harriet also fostered a South Asian student at Butler; she was facing compulsory ejection at 16 from a children's home.

With Harriet, Roy now focused on ecological and anti-nuclear issues as well as those around race and disability. Harriet found work in adult education, and through it financed post-graduate work in cultural studies. It was at this time as well that the two of them began exploring their sexual identities. The ferment of parenthood added to that of the growth movements. For Harriet the feminist movement gave important nourishment. Roy followed in time with an anti-sexist men's group. At his school Roy was active in supporting his trade union as well as an innovator in community events. Between them Roy and Harriet were part of a complex network of colleagues and friends.

Encouraged by some of these colleagues Roy took a year on secondment to study dance. This was in 1986. At the end of that academic year he was redeployed to Humbold. The family had just moved into Shire City itself, where their black son could have more non-white friends. It was a lovely house vacated by one of the older generation of Harriet's family. Butler was now far away from their home. Humbold was their side of Shire City. In September 1987 Roy's brief three months at Humbold began.

Roy's arrest brought intense distress to the Bartell household. Harriet spent the weekend telephoning everyone close to her. The arrest had been a terrifying shock, but she was determined that it was not going to silence her. Friends came to see them and to stay with them immediately. There were long angry and tearful sessions in the best of the co-counselling tradition. Both Harriet and Roy sat with their sons. She spoke directly: 'Your Dad has been arrested for playing with another man's willy, but you don't have to worry. He isn't going to jail and he hasn't lost his job yet. We have a lot of friends who love us and don't think anything less of your Dad.' The older two sons wanted to know about publicity. 'There won't be any for now, but when there might be we will talk with you about it. You can go away for a few days and stay with your aunts if you want.' 'The police were not doing what they should have been, and that's one reason our friends are giving us the support they are. They don't think what the police were doing was right.'

During the next week, Roy contacted the teachers at the boys' schools who were involved in their pastoral care. He told them what had happened. Because his middle son wanted it, Roy went with him to his school and talked with his form tutor, someone that Roy knew from his past membership of the Society of Friends.

Harriet's professional and social life provided an important network at this moment. The partner of the local secretary of the trade union was a colleague of hers. This woman affirmed Roy's importance at a time when the local secretary knew very little of Roy. (Roy's involvement at Butler was with another branch of the trade union.)

The local secretary and a colleague at Humbold, who was in charge of equal opportunities, put Roy in touch with the trade union's lesbian and gay rights group. A copy of *Outlaws in the Classroom* (City of Leicester Teachers' Association 1987) was immediately to hand. Counselling and concern from one or another member of this group continued throughout the years following the arrest. Again and again in the days (then months and years) that followed, Roy benefited from the full range of sexual politics.

Lesbian friends immediately suggested alternative solicitors to the man preferred by the local gayline network. These friends had a complex understanding of the event; practical suggestions were made as well as longer term issues discussed. The wisdom of their advice was borne out over the coming weeks, months. A solicitor in London was evidently less readily 'available' to accommodate Shire City machinations than a local solicitor. A barrister from London negotiated the first appearance at the magistrates court without publicity – a feat the local gayline solicitor had virtually ruled out.

With their Christmas/Solstice cards Roy and Harriet sent out a note about the arrest. The telephone hardly stopped ringing in the evening, and there were constant offers of help. Roy's colleagues and Harriet's friends joined together in setting up a support fund. This response fully comple-mented the determination of Harriet that Roy was not going to resign and that the injustice of the arrest was going to be challenged. She was particularly incensed by the lacklustre concern of the trade union regional officer. As word spread Roy began receiving letters and cards from former colleagues:

'Fight 'em!' 'Good Luck' 'Don't let them get you down!!'

In dealing with the LEA and the trade union regional officer it was colleagues from Butler who proved most helpful. They listened carefully to what Roy told them was taking place, and they gave advice as to what to expect, what questions to ask and what demands to make. In turn they found out through their own friendship networks what was happening, for instance, at Humbold School where Roy had only just begun to make friends. They also came up with names of colleagues who wanted to act as referees. It was possible to keep closely in touch with what action the LEA was taking in this way.

During the months ahead colleagues kept up correspondence with Gollum on Roy's behalf. At the forefront of letter writers was the former head of Butler, not long retired, a scholar in his own right, and not a person that the LEA relished tangling with when he was negotiating allowances for his school.

Colleagues, also close friends of the family, some going back to the days in Metropolis, were in constant touch. Through them Roy had the sound advice of a chair of education in another LEA. A reunion of pupils taking the black studies course was arranged to coincide with one of Roy's traumatic hearings, as a boost to his morale.

As this network of support fell into place, Roy, not British born, was interested to observe that Harriet was the only Shire person really involved in the action. There were other close English supporters, but enormous support came from two Scots, a New Zealander, a Bajan, and two close friends from Irish backgrounds. It was one of these friends who opened up a crucial avenue of information – teachers who had been arrested on indecency charges and had had very different treatment from that which Roy was receiving.

It was ironical that what might well have come from a supportive trade union framework at a national level had to come only through personal contacts. By the end of May 1988, Roy knew of teachers who had successfully kept their jobs with such arrangements as a letter in a file to be removed after two years' non-offending, simply being moved to another school, or as in one instance, being kept on the school complement of teachers until the governors changed their minds and decided to accept the appointment. Roy met one of these teachers and was in contact by telephone with another. He was able to share his experiences and to benefit from their advice.

About the same time another friend of Roy's told him about a primary school teacher who had kept his post in a school where the governors were so sympathetic with the industry of the teacher that they did not want to lose that level of commitment to the school. By the time Roy appeared in the Crown Court in July 1988 he knew there was every reason to expect that the LEA could keep him on as a teacher if they wanted to.

Through the lesbian/gay working party of his trade union, however, Roy began to find out about the tension that existed between the politics of homosexuality and the views of the director. The working party had received national publicity for one of their campaigns. Not long afterwards there seemed to have been a personal vendetta carried out against one of the women prominent in the group.

It did not come as a complete surprise then that in September 1988 Gollum began distancing himself from the case. Mallis was put in charge. The staff at Humbold were reported to be angry that the LEA was trying to shift a decision onto the school which the LEA could easily be settling in a low-key manner, given the paucity of publicity.

In November the trade union members at Humbold passed a resolution, virtually unanimously, requesting that there be no hearing for Roy at Humbold and expressing dismay that teachers at the school had been required to contribute to a report nine months after the brief time Roy had taught in the school. It was an action taken at local trade union level, underlining the difference between the support Roy could expect from members and the treatment meted out by officers at regional and national headquarters.

Gollum was reported to have been furious about this resolution, saying there were a lot of incompetent teachers in the authority and this was a good chance to get rid of one. The comment was made to Curry, new headteacher at Humbold. The director in correspondence with Roy's London solicitors was later at pains to deny he had ever said it.

By December, a year after his arrest, Roy was receiving references from his former colleagues and friends in preparation for the hearing at Humbold which Mallis was intent on pursuing. There were 31 references in all. They made very moving reading. Some were from teachers who far from being concerned about Roy teaching their own children (the issue of judgement and trust), actively wished that he could. One was from the deputy headteacher whom the LEA was going to call as one of its witnesses. He wrote: 'I strongly believe that Dr Bartell should not be dismissed by the Authority because of a minor offence he committed outside of school'. Many referees called attention to Roy's outstanding capabilities in working with disaffected students and in youth work.

One contribution to the references was to set a pattern resistance might take after the hearings. It was a letter to Mallis from Roy's head of faculty at Butler:

> The Crown Court considered that Roy's offence merited a fine of £50 (3 or 4 parking tickets, these days?); I find it extraordinary that the Authority should think the same offence deserves, as a secondary penalty, the severest sanction it can impose [*viz.* dismissal].

For her part Harriet felt especially angry that the outcome of the LEA's persecution of Roy would be the victimization of his family. For a victimless crime, she would have to find secure full-time work no matter at what distance from Shire City and their sons would live in fear of the local newspaper printing Roy's photograph as it had done with the headteacher in September 1988. Criminalization would be taking place.

But Harriet was right in insisting that he not resign. The resistance which took place between his arrest and the final dismissal from his post two years later enabled her to find a permanent full-time post and for Roy to explore avenues of work other than teaching in secondary education. As a result of the rigours of resistance to the closure of his department in Metropolis, combined with those of an active researcher, Roy maintained a comprehensive grasp of what was taking place. He had files of documents, a system of briefing notes and notebooks of daily events. He was able to supply, on a regular basis, summaries of what the issues were at a particular point in what came to be the confrontation with the LEA. He also knew how to convene meetings and effect strategies.

For Roy, the issues around criminalization were, however, most distressing. They took him back to moments such as that

late February morning in 1988 when he had been taking a bath
and had been overcome with remorse. He had telephoned one
of the friends who had said, 'Ring any time', and she had come
round and Roy had been in floods of tears. 'The one thing I have
wanted to be was a good father, because of how my Dad was
towards me. But I haven't changed things. I've just made them
the same.' On an afternoon in April when, in the midst of
writing a letter to his older brother in the States he was overcome by the distance he felt between his father and himself.
Again he telephoned friends, and they came and sat with him
as he read aloud the letter he had written and shared with them
his grief. Little did Roy know at these moments what his mother
would reveal when she came for something of a surprise visit
a few months later.

Resistance had depended on alliances across many groups:
colleagues, personal friends, family, friends from political and
growth movement allegiances. These alliances, where the
politics of gender and sexual orientation were concerned,
bridged conflict and self-interest. It was the power of these
friends to embrace an image of diversity set against hegemonic
forces, which overcame so much adversity for Roy and his
family. The support fund raised about £10,000, very material
support. An analysis of its contributors would undoubtedly
reveal a predominance of unmarried women and men who were
in one sense supporting the institution of the family, shoring it
up as Roy's livelihood was threatened. The cost of the prosecution of this victimless crime was unthinkable.

Homophobia

The story of Roy Bartell has been a reconstruction using facts
from the case but narrated by various personae. These people
all existed but connivance is projected. It is true that I. M. A.
Mason was powerfully placed as a Freemason in the county and
was shortly to be appointed to one of the most lucrative county
hall positions in Britain. There were scandals that broke over
Freemasonry both at county hall and in the police force. The
extent to which such brotherhood operated in effecting homophobic action has to be left conjectural.

It is around homophobia, however, that the action of the LEA coheres. Any of the police or county hall figures involved in this action would deny they were homophobic, of course. Lance Curry, headteacher at Humbold who had never even met Roy Bartell, was brought as a witness by the LEA at Humbold. This is what he said at the hearing: 'I would be reluctant to appoint someone like Dr Bartell. It has nothing to do with his being homosexual. I have met some wonderful homosexual teachers. It is the public nature of the act.'

So it is enough to have *met* some homosexual people (nothing too intimate), and, of course, they are all right . . . *until they step out of line*! Then we are entitled to ignore our humanity, our sense of justice, and proceed since we have the power to do so. And we can count on *homophobia* to do part of our work for us. Under cross-examination, Curry said he would not be so reluctant over the appointment of someone convicted of a drink-drive offence, even when such an offence meant people might be killed. 'No . . . it is not the same. Dr Bartell's offence is about relationships.'

The LEA, in conjunction with the county legal department, continued to use its considerable power to obtain Dr Bartell's dismissal. The county hall committee stage hearing was eventually held in November 1989, and once again the LEA prepared a damaging document which made much use of 'the nature of the offence'.

The issue of homophobia was taken up by many of the correspondents who supported Roy Bartell in his resistance to dismissal. Most of the letters were sent directly to Gollum himself. In the early stages before Bartell outmanoeuvred the union regional officer by replacing him with the London solicitors, Gollum brought pressure on Wanders to discourage Bartell's supporters from writing on his behalf. Once Wanders was out of the way, Gollum no longer had this leverage.

An excerpt from one of these letters might account for why Gollum was concerned about receiving them. In this case, four signatories review Roy's case and raise important questions about the LEA and homophobia.

> Dr Bartell was arrested while masturbating another man his age in public toilets late one December evening. He has never denied his doing so. The arrest was made using an *agent provocateur*,

a plainclothes policeman in an 'entrapment'. A spate of similar arrests were made by the Shire constabulary about this time. It has since been reported that the constabulary have agreed, after strong representations from a Lesbian/Gay Rights working party and a local MP, to discontinue these kinds of arrests/this kind of surveillance of public toilets. Some of these arrests have been discredited in the courts as you will be aware.

Dr Bartell's case was heard in the Crown Court where he was convicted and fined £50. Dr Bartell was later notified by the DES that it was taking no action in response to this conviction. It would seem that legally and educationally the assessment of the significance of such arrests/convictions is that they are not worthy of considerable opprobrium. As the judge said in the Crown Court at the time of Dr Bartell's conviction, 'Least said, soonest mended'.

The LEA, however, proceeded against Dr Bartell in a highly prejudicial manner in response to his arrest. For both of the hearings that Dr Bartell appeared before, the LEA prepared documents which focused on 'the nature of the offence'. We can only attribute the persistent use of this phrase to the LEA's intention to stir, in hearing members' minds, images of debauchery and lasciviousness intolerable in the behaviour of any classroom teacher.

Considering the 'nature of the arrest', we would have hoped that the LEA had honoured Dr Bartell as other LEAs we know of have respected their teachers facing similar convictions. At the Humbold hearing the LEA went so far as to bring in uniformed police, to put forward an unsubstantiated claim concerning a classroom incident, and to use a headteacher unknown to Dr Bartell to voice anxieties about his judgement as a teacher. This action by the LEA smacks much more of homophobia than it does of genuine concern for the lives of the pupils/students Dr Bartell taught/would teach.

Shire LEA had made quite a display of its equal opportunities policy when it first came out in the early 1980s, and with regard to race, it still did. Where it concerned sexual orientation, however, it was prepared to be as evasive as possible. Like Lance Curry, it was quick to point to a token acquaintance; like the plainclothes police interrogators, however, it was also quick to access latent homophobia, rather than to challenge it. Its equal opportunities policy in fact had no biting or *educational* edge.

After/maths: Sums that don't add up to a conclusion

In June 1989, a year and a half after his arrest, Roy Bartell was still suspended on full pay and continuing resistance to his dismissal. His London solicitors did not let the education authority get away with Mason's casual account of how the stenographer's notes to the Humbold hearing came to be destroyed. After consultation, the authority agreed to a summary being prepared by London. This 'note' included every question asked and every answer given (the solicitors and the local union representatives had made their own careful record at the Humbold hearing!). By late September an account of the proceedings was agreed.

In early November the education authority once again used ab/use of procedure: it prepared a document against Roy Bartell for a forthcoming hearing at county hall which brought in new evidence. It set a date for this hearing which again, as in December 1988, gave Dr Bartell virtually no time to prepare against it.

When the hearing at county hall took place the third week in November, the London solicitors and barrister, Dr Bartell and Harriet and two local union representatives all withdrew when the hearing committee refused a request for additional time to address the new accusations. Resistance was met with ab/use of procedure, this time involving elected members. In his absence the committee dismissed Dr Bartell from his teaching post with the education authority. Dr Bartell's solicitors began the process of taking the education authority to the High Court.

It is from the time of his dismissal, the loss of income and the intense domestic upheaval which that entailed, that the story of Dr Bartell begins to become dispersed. Up to that time the resistance was focused on the courts and the education authority. Now, other institutions/parallel institutions, are drawn in to effect the punishment of Roy Bartell and his family: Legal Aid poses severe constraints, unemployment benefit is denied and Dr Bartell finds himself contesting his dismissal from a part-time teaching post in adult education, an appointment made with full knowledge of his arrest and conviction.

The education authority continues to use ab/use of procedure; it does not reply to union letters demanding information about this latter dismissal. Dr Bartell and his supporters meet with his county councillor. He is a person who helped expose county hall's Freemasonry connections. He is furious, however, when asked to write a letter to Gollum requesting information about this latter dismissal.

And the power to define takes on new dimensions: a DSS tribunal adjudicator draws on a *para*legal decision to justify withholding benefit, a commissionaire's decision made shortly after the 1967 Sexual Offences Act and one which refers to 'certain professions'; and knowing 'they are expected to maintain a high standard of conduct'. It is a decision (paragraph 11 of Commissioners' decision R(U) 1/71) which begs questions of general practice and general knowledge in an increasingly mobile and international society.

Roy also finds out in conversation with his mother, who is visiting him, that his father had 'the tendency', knowledge which casts a particularly traumatic childhood event in a new light. And Roy's brother, living on the west coast of the USA, is worried about any financial help he gives Roy which might go towards promoting homosexuality.

Resistance continues to take the form of correspondence addressed to Gollum over Dr Bartell's dismissal: a petition signed by 150 of his colleagues and letters from his MP, MEP and friends – 'the Educational Authority has squeezed all the poison it could from a triviality, squandering time, trouble and expense' – and a document signed by 16 headteachers:

> It is our view, based on many years of experience as teachers and head teachers, that
>
> – there are many teachers continuing to teach after such a first offence;
> – there is no correlation between adult male homosexual behaviour and child sexual abuse/paedophilia;
> – there is however a campaign by some local police forces to set up such arrests as part of anti-homosexual campaigns (there is no equivalent heterosexual offence);
> – it would therefore be all the more fitting that an 'Equal Opportunities' Authority should view such a case compassionately and be seen to deal with it in a sophisticated manner;
> – such a course, together with the School Governors' recommendation that Dr Bartell's case be carefully considered, could

then be seen as part of the process in which the school engages in educating the community;
- finally, the main consideration involved in an arrest of this kind is an assessment of the person. Having known Dr Bartell over a long period and known him to be utterly professional and trustworthy, we would concur in offering an entirely favourable assessment.

For all of this resistance, there is no conclusion to this story of Roy Bartell that is satisfactory. Harriet has the unenviable burden of providing a livelihood for three sons advancing through their teenage years. The toll on all their lives is a story they may want to tell in far less heroic terms than that of resistance as given here. After almost two years of seeking justice through a High Court decision, Roy Bartell withdraws his action. The constraints of Legal Aid and the slow progress of the law overcome resolve. Roy has opportunities to follow an academic career, and a High Court decision is still a long way off. There are some outstanding legal debts. And Roy has to find ways of exploring his sexuality which are not encased with the bitterness which resistance too easily entails. The costs of an arrest, conviction and persecution for a victimless crime are very high: for the police, for the education authority, for the classroom, for the loving and loved ones and for the criminal. The price we pay to keep homophobia in place is enormous.

Reference

City of Leicester Teachers' Association (1987) *Outlaws in the Classroom: Lesbians and Gays in the School System.* Leicester: National Union of Teachers.

CHAPTER 7

Black in the Closet[1]

AKANKE

Our relationship is a closeted one, even to the children. Although we feel that we are sharing something beautiful and worthwhile, we are 'forced' to keep it 'secret' as we fear repercussions, not necessarily for ourselves but for the children.

However, to say that we are 'closeted' is a contradiction and belies the fact that, in practice, many of our friends, both straight and gay, are aware of our relationship. So within this context it simply means that our 'secret' applies only to people outside our immediate circle of friends and acquaintances. In my first year at university, when I was feeling particularly isolated and felt I was getting negative vibes from a few of the Black students on the course (for reasons I am still unsure of), I told one of my lecturers, who had been especially helpful to me in the past, about my sexuality and about the unhappiness I was experiencing. He immediately arranged for me to meet with a postgraduate student who was also a lesbian. From this experience I recognized that I needed to network with other lesbians, as well as confide in a few of the other Black students, with whom I had become friends, about my sexuality. In so doing, I have been able to keep in touch with these friends both in and out of the university. I no longer have to pretend to them that there is no one special in my life, and I have become less paranoid about them ringing me at home. Similarly Terri no longer has to pretend to be my baby-sitter.

Although Terri spends a lot of time at my house, we tend to hide our affection for each other when the children are around. This is a practice we've come to regard as 'normal'. However, quite recently, we were made to wonder just how discreet we've been, following an incident with a Mother's Day card. My youngest daughter told me that she had a present, which she had made at school, to give to me. She handed me an envelope and, beaming from ear to ear, she demanded that I open it and read what she had written inside. To my horror, it read 'Happy Mother's Day to mummy and Terri'. Fearing the worst, I said to her, 'Did your teacher see this card?' 'Yes', she said, 'my teacher said it was a lovely card'.

By this time I must have aged about 20 years. With much difficulty and as much calm as I could muster, I asked what her teacher said when she saw Terri's name. In a most conspiratorial manner my daughter replied, 'I added her name in the bus on the way home. That's why it's written in a different colour crayon'. The sense of relief that came over me was so obvious that we both started to laugh. This incident, though seemingly funny, lost its humour when, for those few minutes, my worst fears surfaced. It also points to the fact that my daughter is/was obviously aware that something was going on of which the school would not approve.

Being 'closeted' is not a choice I wish to make. Nevertheless, because of the pervasiveness of racism, it is one that I *choose* to make. Being Black, however, is not a choice. As a black woman my colour is my most obvious feature, not my sexual preferences. Within British society, black people's lives, sexuality and culture are regarded negatively. Our colour often dictates our level of income, housing and educational attainment. This is not to imply that there are no exceptions to this rule. The fact that a particular social group suffers from disadvantages or inequalities does not necessarily imply that all members are equally affected.

Terri and I are fully aware that, as Black lesbians, raising Black children in a white, racist, sexist and homophobic society, we are fighting against a system that threatens to devour us and 'our' children. The dominant white culture impresses upon our children, from an early age, values that are alien to their experiences at home. This can often cause conflict, anger and frustration, and when no other outlet can be found, we eventually fight amongst ourselves. I have found that Terri, who was born in this country, holds differing views to myself (who was born in the West Indies) on issues of race. Our differences sometimes threaten to alienate us from each other. It is at these times that we have to remind ourselves that we are not each other's enemies.

Being part of at least two 'minority' groups which are both stigmatized and marginalized, we find ourselves retreating into the background (particularly when government actions, such as Clause 28, legislates for further discrimination against lesbians and gays). For while we are able to empathize with white lesbians who are out, their fight is not our priority. Their oppression is not a result of both their race and their sexuality, but only of their sexuality. This brings me back to my earlier assertion, that our colour is our most obvious feature, not our sexual preference. Our concerns are, therefore, more focused on issues to do with, for example, the dismantling of the apartheid system; the inadequacies of the Race Relations Act; the state control of Black women's reproductive rights;[2] and even more immediate, our daily survival.

We have found that, while racism is not as overtly visible within the white gay community as within the white straight community, it is very much alive and kicking. This is not to deny the fact that we have, at times, had the personal support of white lesbians. However, the fact that racism remains a constant feature is probably indicative of the nature of the struggles with which each group is separately involved. It cannot be assumed, therefore, that by virtue of being part of a minority group, there will be a congruence, which will inevitably break down the negative stereotypes that many white people hold about other groups in society. Implicit within this assertion is the undeniable fact that white people, however anti-racist, cannot escape the material benefits of being white in an unequal, racist society. In that sense, white people are implicated in racism regardless of their commitment to anti-racist struggles.

Within our own Black communities, our sexual preference is seen as a 'white man's disease', inherited from white society/ people, which will eventually lead to the demise of the Black race. Others have pointed to the notion of the disintegration of the 'Black family structure' to which we are contributing. Even more absurd is the notion that our problem is to do with the fact that we have yet to find the right *man*.

Over the last six years, I have lost a few Black friends whose friendship and support I had come to rely on. One person in particular, whom I had regarded as a close friend, told me that she found my sexuality difficult to cope with, as she wondered whether or not (throughout the years of our friendship), I had (through friendly gestures) touched her in a sexual way. She also told me that the very idea that this might have happened made her sick. Although not a religious person herself, she went on to impress on me that God made woman to be man's mate and vice versa. She also said that He did not make man for man or woman for woman. She then asked me whether or not I was contemplating a sex change and if my sudden interest in trousers was a part of that process!

This experience made me more aware of the prejudices that are held by many Black people with whom I identify, and of the pain that it causes when you are made to feel alienated. It has also reinforced for me the importance of maintaining 'secrecy' about my sexuality: I feel that being Black is essentially more important to me than being a lesbian – a label which I choose to wear only when it is convenient, whereas being Black is not a choice. This is in no way meant to undermine the strength or the importance of the relationship I share with Terri, but merely points to the fact that I/we would prefer to have the support of other Black people while denying our sexuality, rather than the support of some white people and feel alienated from Black people.

So being 'out' holds no attraction for us. We do not see it as a source of empowerment for us or our children but as a possible weapon to be used against us. Mind you, it is arguable as to whether or not 'coming out' as lesbians could provide further ammunition for discrimination. As far as we are concerned, every effort has been made, every tactic has already been used, and every facet of Black people's lives has already been affected by the legacy of racism, a legacy which will be inherited by our children and their children.

I feel that in many ways I have had much richer childhood experiences, growing up in Jamaica, than my children will or could ever have in terms of cultural input. I came to England in my teens and, now that I am in my early thirties, I have come to realize the importance of those early childhood years and how they have influenced the way I am now bringing up my children. Those early years gave me a sense of belonging that is lacking in most young Black people born in this country. I can see it even in my own children, who have expressed a desire for us to go and live in Jamaica. Quite frankly, I am tempted. If I was able to change one important aspect of my life in Britain, it would have to be my children's education. I would like for them to have experienced an education devoid of the kind of racism they now encounter.

Until I came to Britain in the 1970s, the word 'racism' was not a part of my vocabulary. This is not to deny the legacy of our imperial and colonial past, but compared to what we experience here in Britain, the extent of our oppression was not so glaringly obvious. I did not wake up every morning to a white, racist society. I did not attend a school where I was a 'minority' with minority feelings, minority intellect, minority pathology and minority achievement, who shared minority housing, minority employment and received minority rewards. Whatever prejudices I encountered came from people who were not white. I was not made to feel alienated, worthless or ashamed of who I was and at the mercy of an ambivalent white society. I did not feel that I was being ignored by my teachers and they did not parade my shortcomings in front of society. Basically I was not ignored for being a girl, or even a Black girl. I did not experience antagonism and distrust between my teachers and my parents.

In contrast, within the British school system my children have had many labels attached to their colour. When my son, Robert, was still in nursery school, one of his teachers told me that he was immature for his age. When I asked by what criteria he was being judged, she told me that he preferred to play alone rather than join in with organized play activities. She even told me that she had included these comments in the report she was about to send to the adjoining primary school. At that time I was unsure of what to do about this, but, after discussing it with other mothers, I decided to speak to the head. I asked him to justify the comments on the form written by one of his staff, and he agreed with me that they were extremely negative things to say about a four year old. He then suggested, to my great relief, that under the circumstances he was quite willing to destroy the form, which he did in my presence. Even after all this time, I can still remember clearly the blue form on which the comments were written.

However, when we moved away from the area, I had to find a new school for my children to attend. From the outset, the relationship between myself and their new headteacher was one of coolness. At the time, I did not perceive this to be a problem, since I was more concerned about the standard of teaching than with my personal relationship with the head. Things began to deteriorate when Robert began to come home often very upset because of things which were said to him either by the 'dinner ladies' or teachers, who had all 'branded' him a bully.

Things came to a head one particular parents' evening, when I was offered a lift to the school by a friend because I was feeling unwell but felt it was important to attend. Rather than have her wait in the car park, I asked my friend to accompany me to see Robert's teacher. Maybe her presence was a source of discomfort to the teacher, but regardless of the reason(s), his teacher started off by telling me that my son was guilty of disrupting the whole school and that she was unable to control him. She became extremely agitated when I asked her for specific examples of Robert's disruptive behaviour. She told me to go and speak to the head, as he would be better able to fill me in on the details.

It transpired that over a period of time my nine year old son (who was taller than the other children of his age group) was constantly sent to the head to be disciplined for incidents in the playground. Robert's version of this was that, whenever he happened to be around younger or smaller children, the 'dinner ladies' always wanted to know what he was doing. If for any reason a child was upset or crying, Robert was automatically blamed and marched off to the head's office for his due punishment. He and other Black boys from his class were made to stand outside the head's office for at least three hours each day. When I asked why it was necessary for Robert to have missed so much class time, I was told that he not only picked on the younger, smaller children in the playground, but that the teacher was afraid to discipline him. Hence it became the head's responsibility to do so.

I asked the head why I had not been informed of this 'change' in Robert's behaviour, since they were finding it so difficult to exercise control over him. The head then asked me if there were any problems at home to which Robert's behaviour could be attributed. I told him 'No!', and that, in fact, Robert was quiet and extremely well behaved at home. I was surprised to hear that, as soon as he entered the school gates, my son was transformed into some kind of monster, wreaking havoc throughout the school. I remarked to the head that they were failing miserably in their efforts by using such punitive methods of discipline. I made it clear that they were teaching the child to fail by their predominantly negative attitudes towards him and other Black children in the school. From then on the relationship plummeted to an all-time low and, eventually, I was told by the head to remove my children from the school because 'they would be better off if they were placed elsewhere'.

I was, to say the least, very surprised at this but refused to move them for various reasons. I told the head that I hoped that he and his teaching staff, as well as the dinner ladies, were above taking retaliative actions against young defenceless children. Given the open hostility which has existed since then between myself and the teaching staff, my children have frequently remarked on the 'dirty' looks they have received from their teachers; and on occasions, especially whenever they were feeling particularly vulnerable and stated their desire not to attend school, I have allowed them to remain at home.

Whilst I have had a lot to say about Robert, I have said very little about my older daughter's experiences. This is not to imply that they are not relevant; it means that what Karen experienced was far more subtle. When she was eight I noticed she found reading and other related subjects extremely difficult to master. Eventually I started to pay a teacher to give her private lessons. This helped to improve her confidence and her reading ability a little. However after a period of time I did not feel that the improvements were substantial and, moreover, I found it impossible to continue to afford these private lessons.

At the time I did not feel it necessary to inform the school about the lessons, as I felt that they were already exercising enough negativity towards my son and would probably use her extra lessons as a reason to spend less time helping her. I was convinced that she was dyslexic but had no way of confirming this without the help of the school. I felt that the teachers had come to expect very little in the way of intelligence from the children and they would therefore find it impossible to associate something as 'civilized' as dyslexia with a 'dumb' Black child.

Despite this uneasiness, I decided to mention to the teacher the difficulties 'I' was experiencing in trying to help my child with her reading, without necessarily allowing them to see just how deeply concerned I was.

For a short time they provided extra reading lessons for her. However, after one term I was told they could no longer provide this service due to lack of resources; a lack of trained staff; and the fact that there were younger children whose needs were far more urgent. However I was encouraged not to worry as she was doing extremely well in physical education!

I was extremely shocked to hear that they were continuing to use this age old rhetoric, told to many West Indian parents in the past when they had, on occasions, voiced their concern about their children's performances in school. I have heard young Black people who have passed through the education system complain that those remarks only gave their parents a false sense of security (by believing that, although their children were educationally backward, at least they were good at something, that is sports). So I discouraged Karen (rightly or wrongly) from competing in sporting activities.

This was an extremely worrying time for me. Each time I tried to help Karen with her reading, it became progressively more and more frustrating for both of us, as I felt that I was getting nowhere and she was desperately trying to please me. Eventually I decided to find out more about dyslexia and contacted several private practitioners. Their prices were extremely high. Consequently Terri offered to pay for the tests to be carried out. The tests showed that my child was, in fact, severely dyslexic. I was very relieved to know that at last my suspicions about her were confirmed (no thanks to the school).

I do not wish to romanticize my own childhood experiences in comparison to those of my children. However, I am proud that the people and community in which I grew up helped me to believe in myself because of my colour. I had a sense of self and of belonging, which I am positive have enabled me to lead a more enriched existence.

Terri was educated in this country. From her recollections, her school days appeared to have been quite a positive experience. She went to a Catholic convent school (there is a view held by many West Indians that Black children have better educational opportunities in Catholic schools) where her 'colour' was not an issue, although she acknowledges that this was not always the same for other Black children. She was the exception rather than the rule: all Black girls who happened to be in the top streams in their year were exceptions. However, she grew up with constant reminders from her mother that, if she wanted to achieve, she had to work 'ten times' harder than the average white child. This added pressure produced the 'right' results for the wrong reasons.

For many Black children the fear of failure provides the impetus for greater achievement. This fear, however, stems from the knowledge that the colour of their skin is an indicator of the kind of results they are destined to achieve. Although I did not experience the British education from an early age (but only as a mature student), I am now experiencing it through the predominantly negative experiences of my children. Whilst I realize the importance of a good education, I fail to understand why it has to be such a painful experience for most Black children, who then have to experience further discrimination on most levels when they eventually enter the job market.

By investing more of our time and energies in their education, both at home and at school, I hope my children will be better prepared to face the challenges they will undoubtedly encounter. They are more than aware of the inequalities that exist between themselves and their white peers and, given the negative attitudes that are held about Black people and about lesbians and gays, it is not my wish to further 'disadvantage' them by advertising my sexual preferences.

Some may argue that being up front with the children about my sexuality would be far better for them as I would no longer have to hide a very important aspect of my life from them and all our lives would be made far richer by my revelation. Personally I am not convinced. I am more than happy to explore with them general questions about lesbians and gays but not on a personal level. However, due to a particular incident that occurred recently, I have been reminded that it is not always possible to control the circumstances in which such revelations are made. A few months ago their father found it necessary to retaliate against me by verbally abusing me to the children. He told them a catalogue of lies, saying that he regarded me to be a bad mother. He also said that I was a lesbian.

Robert was so disturbed by this that I was left no other choice than to confirm what was, in effect, a suspicion of his father's based entirely upon my refusal to return to him. At the time I/we were unsure of how detailed our explanations to Robert should be. However one day, while they were out together, Terri decided to talk to him about it. She asked him to explain to her the way he felt about what his dad had said to him and my confirmation of that. Robert revealed that he was unsure of how he felt, because his father was always 'bad-mouthing' me, and he thought this was another of his lies. Now that he had found out that, in fact, his father was right (at least about my lesbianism), he was not happy about it. She explained to him that the negative things his father had told him were similar to what white people often say about Black people. She asked him whether or not he believed these negative things to be true of Black people, to which he said, 'No'. She then explained to him that, in a similar way, people often say negative things about lesbians which are not true. He seemed to have accepted this along with the assurance that, if at any time he wished to know more, then he was quite welcome to talk to either of us.

Despite this incident, I am still of the opinion that if I could turn the clock back I would certainly do so. I felt that I was 'forced' into a situation for which I was ill-prepared, and one which caused me a lot of personal grief. Surely there is nothing wrong in wanting to protect children from painful situations, either inside or outside the home environment. However I am conscious that is not always possible.

I am especially sensitive to the fact that, from an early age, we give up our children to a system that is hostile and damaging; a system that despoils, disempowers and teaches them to fail, where every weekday between the hours of 9 a.m.–3.30 p.m. we deposit our children into the hands of people, many of whom we deeply distrust, and give them permission to abuse our children both psychologically and physically. Under other circumstances we would be facing criminal charges for not providing a safe environment wherein our children would have the right to develop their full potential. And far too often they leave the system with less than they entered it, especially if they happen to be boys.

Society on a whole does not work favourably for Black boys and our 'disempowered' teenagers become an endangered species. Almost always African-Caribbean boys are assumed to be a problem. Their 'failings' are then blamed on lack of parental care and discipline, on Black pathology or on the matriarchal family structure. In this situation the 'victims' are blamed.

Most educators still have low expectations of Black children's ability to succeed and are blind to the fact that, if it is said often enough and loud enough that Black children and their parents are society's failure, then that self-fulfilling prophecy will come to pass. If the past few years are anything to go by, then Black children's chances of a successful outcome would appear to be very marginalized. Many of their experiences within the education system have been traumatic and painful. I am a very angry person, weighed down, not by the 'chip on my shoulder syndrome', but by the massive log of racism. I am angry that my children at such tender ages have had to (and continue to) channel their energies into being aware of and dealing with the daily ration of racism from their headteacher, teachers, peers and society as a whole. However in the last two years my children have changed schools, are a lot happier and are achieving at a rate that I did not think was possible, even though I was of the opinion that they could do better.

Unfortunately this does not detract from the fact that it is high time white teachers within the system begin to realize that they too are part of the institution of racism, which perpetuates racist views, myths and stereotypes, and are more than active participants of a system that thrives on disempowering and deskilling our Black children in preparation for a depraved/deprived adulthood. It is also time for them to stop apportioning the blame entirely on Black parents, especially when teachers find it too painful to accept their own racist attitudes.

From what I have experienced with my children, I now have little regard for the teaching profession and many of the professionals within the institutions of 'learning'. My analogy for this system is of a large white fish which, having made a meal of our children by swallowing them whole, regurgitates their dismembered and disembowelled bodies back to their anxious parents. The parents then blame their 'dead' children for allowing themselves to be eaten alive and the disempowered parents are accused of not protecting their offspring. (The biblical version of Jonah and the fish is a less sinister version.) Intrinsic within this concept is the fact that Black parents are invariably blamed, as are their children, and even the large imaginary white fish called institutional racism, which is blamed for the disproportionate number of 'underachievers', allows the teachers within the system who actually perpetuate a racist 'culture' to continue blameless and unheeded.

Terri and I are united on: 1) the children's education and 2) the need to remain 'secretive' about our relationship. She is very involved in the educational aspect of their lives and will try, whenever possible, to help them with their homework, trips to the library, purchasing of essential books, and providing a secure and happy home environment. However the part that she plays at home does not extend to activities which take place at school, such as parents' evening, school plays or being able to go on school outings without attracting undue attention.

Like all other constraints within which we have to work, this is just another one that we have both come to accept. While I may choose to refer to myself as a single mother, in effect I am not. This situation is far from ideal and one that I am uneasy about, as I often feel that I am actively denying my partner's existence and the part she plays in our lives. Invariably I am the one who receives the praise on parents' evenings for the high standard of homework that my children produce, regardless of her input. It saddens me that she is unable to accompany me to hear first-hand the praise awarded to the help she gives to the children.

Being a Black woman, who also happens to be a lesbian mother, I am conscious of the extent of the inequalities that exist, affecting not only Black lesbians and other Black people but other social groups as well. For me this holds particular significance as I have to weigh up carefully the options and benefits, if any, of being more open about my sexuality or remaining in my semi-closeted position. At this point I am unable to justify being 'out', particularly when taking into account what I said previously about the children.

It would be foolhardy of me to turn my back on the opportunity of receiving and giving my support to the Black community as I cannot deny that being amongst, and spending time with, people with whom I identify on so many levels and with whom shared commonalities offer temporary escape from racism, far outweighs any desire to 'openly' assert my sexuality.

Notes

1 I would like to thank my partner, Terri, for her support in the writing of this chapter.
2 Historically, the main fight for white (heterosexual) women in Britain and the USA in relation to reproductive rights has been for the right to choose abortion. For Black women, the struggle has been more complicated than this and has included the fight not to be experimented on by medical manufacturers of contraception and not to have enforced sterilization.

PART II

Issues of Policy, Curriculum and Pedagogy

CHAPTER 8

Lesbian and Gay Equality within a Whole School Policy

DEBBIE EPSTEIN

As noted in the introduction, this chapter was commissioned and written but, at the last minute, the headteacher of the school on which it was based withdrew permission for publication, although the school was not, in fact, named in the piece. This head is concerned that her school will suffer in the 'market' if it has a strong visible equal opportunities policy. Bearing in mind the school's long record of such a policy – and one which has included lesbian and gay equality for many years – this is indicative of a major loss in the ground gained by education for social justice.

I have decided to include this short statement in the book to indicate to readers the threat of current government policies. I do so in memory and emulation of members of the Jewish *Kulturbund*, an organization of Jewish writers, artists and performers working in Nazi Germany. As more and more of their work was banned and censored, they continued to perform, using silence to indicate that they were forbidden to say or do something. In the end, their performances consisted entirely of silence, with the performer standing in front of the audience for the length of time it would have taken to perform the piece in question.

CHAPTER 9

Lesbian and Gay Issues in the Curriculum

PAUL PATRICK and SUSAN A. L. SANDERS

Equal opportunities should affect all areas of school life. It is vitally important that it is not just seen as a set of rules – a list of dos and don'ts – it must celebrate the diversity of lifestyles, languages and cultures in a school as well as empowering young people to develop an understanding of both the origins and practice of oppression and to enable them to act upon those understandings. Unless all issues of equal opportunity inform the curriculum such an aim cannot in my view be realized.

(Bob Hodgson, deputy headteacher, south London mixed comprehensive)

The view that equal opportunities should inform all areas of school life is one more frequently stated than acted upon. This is because it is often difficult for teachers, who labour under the many pressures of organizing and running a curriculum that is under constant review, to envisage what such curriculum development may mean without a degree of INSET that is now more and more difficult to achieve.

Bob Hodgson, quoted above, works in a south London comprehensive that has consistently attempted to address equal opportunities through the curriculum and has given the time for that INSET to take place. From this school we have taken some examples of how it is possible to include lesbian and gay issues within a curriculum that also matches the other demands placed upon it. We present these examples of work as an indication of what it is possible to achieve in a school where commitment to equal opportunities is seen as central to the delivery of high quality education for all.

Within the hidden curriculum it is important that the school's commitment to equal opportunities is clearly delineated in any displays around the school. In this south London comprehensive this means not only the display of the school's equal opportunities policy in the foyer, around the corridors and in each classroom, but involves the display of a wide range of materials, including pupils' work which highlight equal opportunity issues. Such materials include, along with anti-racist, anti-sexist, anti-disablist, class, language and religious issues, materials that address equal opportunities in the area of lesbian and gay sexuality.

In this school such posters include the 'Real Families' and 'We demand the right to learn and to educate without fear' (Figure 9.1) posters produced by the 'Stop the Clause Education Group', posters from Pop against Homophobia, Greenwich Lesbian and Gay Centre, helplines posters and a range of materials produced by the school's pupils.

The pastoral curriculum is an area which presents many opportunities for the development of equal opportunities work. In this school the emphasis is placed upon an understanding and challenging of the issues of oppression and discrimination and a celebration of diversity. This has included a range of full school assemblies led by the headteacher with the involvement of pupils, parents, governors, teaching and support staff and outside speakers. These assemblies have marked International Women's Day, Martin Luther King Jr's birthday, World AIDS Week, May Day, Nelson Mandela's release from prison and Lesbian and Gay Pride Week. It is also the practice of the school that such issues be highlighted regularly through year and upper and lower school assemblies. During the first of the assemblies for Lesbian and Gay Pride Week a senior teacher who had taught in the school since it was formed took the opportunity to come out to the entire school.

The school's pastoral programme deals with all the equal opportunities commitments at an appropriate level for each year group, beginning with the Year 7 induction programme to the school and continuing to the senior school's work on

**WE ARE WOMEN,MEN,BLACK,WHITE,
JEWISH,GENTILE,DAUGHTERS,SONS,
LEARNERS,TEACHERS,MOTHERS,
SISTERS,BROTHERS,PUPILS,STUDENTS,
COLLEAGUES,DIFFERENTLY ABLED,
ABLE BODIED,WAGED,NON-WAGED,
FATHERS,WORKERS,FRIENDS,
OLD,YOUNG AND PROUD**

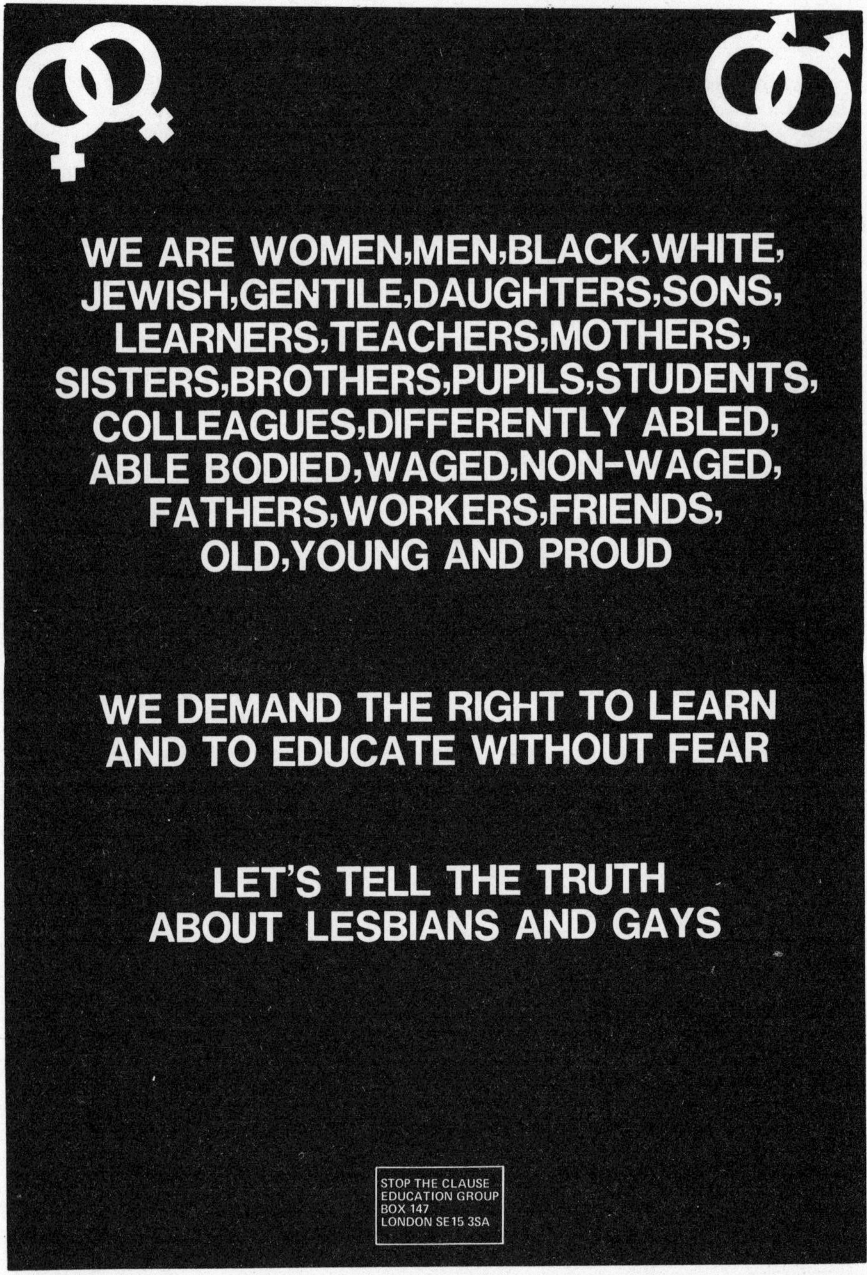

**WE DEMAND THE RIGHT TO LEARN
AND TO EDUCATE WITHOUT FEAR**

**LET'S TELL THE TRUTH
ABOUT LESBIANS AND GAYS**

STOP THE CLAUSE
EDUCATION GROUP
BOX 147
LONDON SE15 3SA

Figure 9.1

relationships and sexuality which includes an equal treatment of lesbian, gay and heterosexual relationships and a research project on helplines which includes Lesbian and Gay Switchboard and Lesbianline along with such organizations as the Samaritans, Childline, Rape Crisis and AIDS helplines. Such work is part of the curriculum for all pupils and it is frequently supplemented by discussion with individuals, small groups or whole classes or years, in reaction to incidents that may occur within school, the local community or the wider world.

All sexuality education, which begins in Year 7, provides parallel information on lesbian/gay sexuality with heterosexuality, raising issues of choice, taking control for oneself, respecting self and others, Some of the materials used are illustrated in this chapter. Some sexuality education with Years 7, 8 and 11 takes place within the Science Department. When this occurs the subject is presented in an emotional and social context as well as dealing with the biology and is informed by the same ideological base as within the pastoral curriculum.

At the end of Year 7 or beginning of Year 8, to coincide with the students having received a bulk of knowledge on these matters, they are given several lessons in single sex groups (with teachers of the same gender). These sessions are intended to enable the students to raise the issues they are particularly concerned about or interested in and is designed to be student-led. This enables students to look at various issues in a supportive environment. These sessions are a valuable chance to form close relationships with staff working with them, which offers them an opportunity for individual discussion should the need arise, a chance to talk about their feelings with peers, and gain further specific information.

In Year 9 there is a single sex programme for the whole year taught by PHSE specialists where they cover assertiveness, bullying, sexuality, and anti-racism; the boys study child care and the girls self-defence. The specific work on lesbian and gay lifestyles includes an analysis of societal and personal attitudes and uses material from 'Taught not Caught', teachers' materials (Figure 9.2), role play, and written work.

The following work was produced by a group of girls taught by a parent working with them on this course after watching the video *A Different Story* (ILEA 1988). They were asked to create a problem page:

3.   SEXUAL PREFERENCE

This is your sexual response to other people, which may
include both sexes.

Many people have their first sexual feelings about a friend
or person of the same sex. Since your friends are people
that you like and want to like you, it's not surprising
that you feel close to them.

We can't choose what sex we are born into or how we are
brought up, though we may not accept either.

Sexual preference is not fixed and we may find ourselves
attracted to all sorts of people all through our lives.

We are not all attracted to the same things and same
people.

Some people choose not to express their sexual
feelings.....

and some people don't know how they feel
yet....

However you feel, be ASSERTIVE : do only
what is right for you and anyone else involved.

Figure 9.2

PLEASE PLEASE HELP. I'm at the stage of killing myself. I'm 19 and a *lesbian*. No one knows that I am a lesbian but I want to talk to someone. I would like to tell my father but he won't understand. No one will understand. Please please help me I want to kill myself.

Well if I were you I would tell your parents because it would be a lot better for you, as you are a lesbian and that a lot of people don't approve of lesbians and gays, but it doesn't matter.

If your parents are sympathetic then tell them because you need to take some weight off your shoulders, so tell them and write back to me to tell me how it went and I will give you some more advice.

In Year 10 all students work in a mixed group for an hour a week with PHSE specialists and spend some time in a unit on relationships which includes lesbian, gay and heterosexual relationships.

Within the English course pupils study a range of texts and other materials, some relating to lesbian/gay lifestyles and produced by lesbian/gay authors. For instance in Year 8 the novella *Messer Rondo* (Aurey 1983), which tells the story of two 12 year old boys who are frequently bullied at school and, through a newspaper article, find common cause with the position of gay people. This leads them into many adventures which are eventually resolved with the help of a gay man. Having read the story, pupils use it as the basis for discussion, role play and creative writing.

As part of the GCSE course several texts with lesbian/gay themes are available for study including; the novel *Who Lies Inside* by Timothy Ireland (1984), the short story *Kestrels* by Kim Martindale (1984) and the play *Bent* by Martin Sherman (1979). Some of the work around these texts has been done in collaboration with the Sociology Department (see below). For the work on *Bent*, studied in Year 11 the pupils saw the National Theatre production of the play and interviewed Michael Cashman, who played one of the leading roles. The work then produced was published in pamphlet form under the title 'A Kind of Defiance' by two of the Year 11 group:

As Michael Cashman himself says, 'There are people who censor themselves. I don't, I am very proud of the fact that I am different, and I would be proud of this country if it celebrated the fact that you can be different and a valuable citizen.'

Cashman wants the country to accept the fact that there are people in the world who love the same sex, and instead of trying to fight it, just accept it and treat them equally . . .

He wants to be left alone without the fear of persecution for what he believes. As in the play where he is playing Horst he is telling Max all through the play that he should stand up for what he is. Max had a yellow star for a Jew when he was actually a homosexual so he should have had a pink triangle. However at the end of the play both characters take a stand for what they believe.

(Steven, Year 11)

The meeting with Michael Cashman was again reported by pupils for the school newsletter that goes termly to parents.

Kestrels is a short story which tells of the relationship between two 15 year old girls and was studied for both English and the GCSE Sociology unit, 'Attitudes to Lesbian and Gay Sexuality'. The pupils were asked to imagine they were friends of the two girls and write a letter to another friend explaining how they feel about the situation.

Dear Paula,
Thank you for your last letter and all the juicy gossip about everybody. Anyway I have just found out about my best friend, she is a Lesbian. Her father found her in bed with my other friend, that's Claire. I didn't even suspect Jakey and Claire to be lesbians and now Jakey's father has sent Jakey away. It's awful that Jakey isn't here. It was quite a shock when I first found out but it is not really my place to say anything anyway because it is up to Jakey and Claire and if they both love each other it is up to them.

At school Claire is being treated badly, so I am for sticking up for her. Because I am sticking up for her I am getting the same treatment. After school they wait for me to steal my money and beat me up. I hate it but I am going to stick by Claire until Jakey comes home. Because that's what friends are for and plus I did promise her.
     Love,
      Nicholas,
      Yr 10.

Dear Abi,
It's so weird not having you around to talk things over with, I'll just have to write instead.

Anyway, you know Jakey and Claire, and you know how they've always got on really well! Well they're now more than just friends, in fact they're sleeping together. Jakey's Dad got in one day to find them in bed together. He sent Jakey away so that she and Claire can't see each other. They're both really depressed though and Claire has been bunking school! I'm a bit stuck as everyone seems to think that being a gay couple is awful, but I think that if they are sixteen they are old enough to know what they feel and they love each other, so why shouldn't they be together? When I first found out, of course it was a shock because I wasn't expecting it. But I don't have anything against it and I just hope that not everyone is as prejudiced as Jakey's Dad and some of the kids at school. I may be heterosexual but it could just as easily be me that's as gay as them! It must have been a shock for Jakey's Dad, I mean it would have been a shock to find a boy in her bed. But I think it should have been their decision and Mr Smith shouldn't have split them up. I don't think he's been fair. He's only looking at the relationship from his own point of view and doing what's best for him, and not Jakey and Claire. Anyway that's what I think about it, what about you?

> Bye for now – write back soon,
> Beth,
> Yr 10.

In Year 11 the pupils study a range of poetry which looks at personal relationships. The poems are taken from a range of periods and cultures and included two poems, one by a woman, the other by a man without the pupils' knowing which was written by whom. The poems were in fact written by Aphra Behn and Sir Philip Sydney. From the poems the pupils constructed a whole theory about male and female attitudes to sexuality, totally unaware that the highly sexual description of making love to a woman was in fact written by a woman and the tender romantic poem to a man was written by another man.

One boy in the group summed up the lesson thus:

In English today we read two poems about romantic and sexual experiences. One was about a dream and the other about reality. The dream told the story of an imagined sexual encounter with a beautiful woman, but when the person awoke they were angry as it was only a dream. The second poem was about reality. Someone was expressing their love for a man. In fact they were so in love that their hearts were one. I thought, like many other people that the dream poem was written by a man and the true love poem by a woman. I was a little confused and shocked when I first discovered this was not the case as I thought that homosexual people did not write about their feelings like this and certainly not in the 18th century [*sic*]. But when I thought about it I got quite used to the idea and found it interesting.

(Danny, Year 11)

Throughout the course pupils look at the range of EO issues outlined within the school policy and use them as a basis for discussion, role play and creative writing. This has included work around World AIDS Week, International Woman's Day, Rosa Parkes' refusal to give up her seat on an Alabama bus, Martin Luther King Jr's birthday and Lesbian and Gay Pride Week. The following pieces were done by a group of Year 9 pupils as part of this work.

Joe

I came home from a party last Friday night.
Boy oh boy what a fright.
My parents found my letter from Joe.
I guess I really love him so.
They asked me one million questions.
What was it like? Don't you feel sick?
I can't take it any more, let me out quick.
'So you're a bender?' No I'm not
The word is Gay you know!
You love me and I love you,
And also I love Joe.

(Wayne, Year 9)

Just good friends

I was at Sara's birthday party. I was having such a good time. There was loads of food, drink and most of all people. It wasn't until they started playing slow music that I realized what was happening.

At first John asked me to dance. I said 'No.' I don't know why I just didn't feel like dancing at that moment. Then my friend Julie came up to me and asked me what the matter was.

'Nothing' I replied.
'So why do you look so down?'
'I don't know.'
'I know, nobody has asked you to dance yet have they?'

I tried to butt in and tell her the truth, but she carried on, 'Don't worry you can dance with me, then everybody will know how well you can dance, then you will have all the boys crawling at your feet. So come on then.'

I got up from my seat and went to the dance floor with Julie. She put her hands round my waist and I put my hands round her neck. I had a funny feeling inside me. I was scared she would tell me to get my hands off her and everyone would turn around and laugh. I wasn't thinking about anything, everybody was blocked out of my mind. It felt as if it was only me, her and the sound of slow music in the room. I pushed myself closer to her body and then I lay my head on her shoulder. I wanted to fall asleep, the feeling was so good and I hoped it was mutual too.

I was suddenly woken by loud laughter and screaming from the other people in the party. Everyone's heads were turned towards us, calling us weird names. Julie pushed me away from her and ran out of the room. I burst out crying and ran after her, but didn't catch her. I don't know what came over me, I just couldn't control myself, but the feeling was so good. It was much better than being with a boy. It felt as if we were made for each other.

(Jessie, Year 9)

The GCSE course in Sociology has a unit of work that looks specifically at attitudes to lesbian and gay sexuality using as its starting point either the novel *Who Lies Inside* by Timothy Ireland or the short story *Kestrels* by Kim Martindale. Both encourage pupils to look at their own attitudes and then their project, which forms a part of GCSE coursework, allows them to develop a mechanism to collect and review other people's attitudes to lesbian and gay sexuality and to test an hypothesis created from their own experience. It was a both useful and exciting addition to this unit within the course that in 1992 the school had as its guest Justin Fashanu, the openly gay black footballer, who split his time between answering budding sociologists' questions and running lower school football practice.

'I am comfortable with who I am.' Justin is a born again Christian and he feels that his religion helped him to realise he was gay and 'come out of the closet'. Justin said, 'The Bible is a wonderful book to live your life by.' Justin is very open and caring. He said he'd come out because 'I don't want to go to

| | **Attitudes to lesbian and gay sexuality.** 'Who Lies Inside" by T. Ireland. | |

1. Look carefully at the novel and the range of attitudes to homosexuality that the characters exhibit and make sure you understand them. (Use the worksheet provided to chart the characters' differing attitudes.)
What issues have been raised?

2. Choose a HYPOTHESIS.

For example : People believe that homosexual relationships are not as acceptable as heterosexual relationships.

3. Decide upon a method of research and explain why you have chosen it.
Example : I have chosen to use a questionnaire to conduct my research because .

4. Write up your questions. (Make sure you allow for all possible issues that arose in section 1.)

5. Collect your information.

6. Record your results. Remember to use graphs and charts where you can.

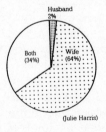

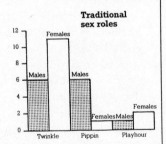

Pie chart to show answers to the question: 'Which member or members of the family should be chiefly responsible for the housework?'

Figure 9.3

my deathbed and not have lived.' Justin has helped me to understand more about homosexuality and to accept it.

(Sarah, Year 11)

The Sociology course (Figure 9.3) also provides pupils with
access to *Something to Tell You* (Trenchard and Warren 1984),
Leicester NUT Lesbian/gay pack (1988), the video, *A Different
Story* whilst allowing individual pupil research which included
speaking with members of lesbian/gay Christian movement,
Parents' Enquiry and Lesbian and Gay Switchboard.

Other Sociology units also raise lesbian and gay issues where
appropriate, for example, the unit on the family includes lesbian
and gay families and the unit on disability contains materials
on the situation of lesbian and gay people with disabilities.

The same commitment to the issues occurs in other depart-
ments. The Drama Department uses role play to analyse family
and other relationships. These frequently include attitudes to
lesbian and gay parents, young people and friends. Several of
the pieces presented for GCSE examination have looked at the
situation of lesbians and gay men and the reactions of their
friends and families. In History the lesbian and gay lifestyles of
people studied within the work are affirmed and issues relating
to the history of lesbian and gay liberation and oppression
raised. As part of the GCSE PE programme the unit on equal
opportunities in sport includes a section on sexuality in sport,
which is a part of the compulsory programme.

Finally there is a myth to scotch. It is the one that says if you
are dealing with these issues you are robbing children of their
'proper' education. This is clearly not so. You can teach poetry
appreciation as well through a poem that celebrates lesbian
and gay love; you can teach sociological skills through a look
at lesbian and gay lifestyles and attitudes towards them. You
must, when you teach about sexuality remember that a substantial percentage of the world chooses to express themselves
sexually and emotionally with a member of their own sex and
some of those will be in your classrooms and some of them
will be pupils' brothers, sisters, aunts, uncles, cousins, mothers,
fathers, friends and, potentially, children.

In this chapter we have looked at some of the ways in which
a particular school has included lesbian and gay issues in the
curriculum whilst falling in line with all the other demands

made upon it. While we have concentrated here on lesbian and gay issues we wish to make it clear that the curriculum is similarly attempting to fulfil all the commitments made in the school's equal opportunities policy statement. Without this it would be difficult to sustain the success that such work has been able to achieve within the school.

The work is based on the continuing study of the effects and causes of oppression for *all* people. Education must open the world up to understanding and empower people to make positive choices for themselves and respect the choices that others make. Without a curriculum based on equal opportunities this is not possible.

References

Aurey, S. (ed.) (1983) *Messer Rondo and Other Stories by Gay Men*. London: Gay Men's Press.

ILEA (1988) *A Different Story* (video). London: Albany.

Ireland, T. (1984) *Who Lies Inside*. London: Gay Men's Press.

Lesbian and Gay Rights Working Party, City of Leicester Teachers' Association (NUT) (1988, revised 1990) *Challenging Oppression: Lesbians and Gays in School. A Resource Pack*. Leicester: City of Leicester Teachers' Association.

Martindale, K. (1984) Kestrels. In L. Mohin and S. Shulman (eds) *The Reach and Other Stories*. London: Onlywomen Press.

Sherman, M. (1979) *Bent*. London: Amber Lane Press.

Trenchard, L. and Warren, H. (1984) *Something to Tell You*. London: London Gay Teenage Group.

CHAPTER 10

Shifting Ground: Rethinking Sexuality Education

PETER REDMAN

Introduction

Recently, a colleague and I visited a headteacher to discuss the possibility of conducting some research in the head's school.[1] During the meeting the head was polite, sympathetic but also extremely concerned. In our initial telephone conversation, she said, we had indicated an interest in the ways the school handled sex education, as well as relationships and HIV education. In our follow-up letter, however, we talked about 'sexuality education'. Why had the focus of our research changed?

Perhaps not surprisingly we were somewhat confused by the head's question. As far as we were concerned, 'sexuality education' meant education in precisely those areas we had raised in our telephone conversation: relationships, cultural beliefs, stereotypes and power relations, sexual identities and so on, as well as sexual activity itself – in short, the wider social and moral context in which sexual activity takes place as opposed to a narrow focus on sex and reproduction. The source of the confusion became rapidly apparent. 'Sexuality' as far as the head was concerned meant 'sexual orientation' , or, more precisely, lesbian and gay sexual orientation, and research on 'sexuality education' presumably meant talking to pupils about being gay or lesbian. For the head, it was this that set the alarm bells ringing.

The head's automatic equation of 'sexuality' with lesbian and gay sexual orientation and her anxiety about raising these issues in school are signs of the times. Her fears almost certainly have their origin in the intense period of moral Right campaigning over sex and sexuality in schools that took place in the mid to late 1980s, and which continues to reverberate today. This campaign, carried out by a loose alliance of moral traditionalists in the Conservative Party, sections of the press, and pressure groups like the Parents' Rights Group (PRG), focused on anxieties about 'the promotion of lesbian and gay rights' in schools and demanded the teaching of 'normal family values' in sex education (see Sanders and Spraggs 1989). These demands took concrete form in Section 28 of the Local Government Act (1988) and DES Circular 11/87. As is well known, the former attempted to restrict the 'promotion of homosexuality' by local authorities while the latter urged schools to help pupils 'appreciate the benefits of stable married and family life' (see below).

In effect, this campaign, and its continuing legacy in more recent legislation (see, for example, DfE 1993), represent a sustained attempt to actively promote what we might term conventional heterosexual familialism. This, as Veronica Beechey argues, refers to a system of beliefs and social practices which

(i) describe a particular kinship system and set of living arrangements (the coresident nuclear family) and assert that this form of family is universal and normatively desirable, and

(ii) assert that the form of sexual division of labour in which the woman is housewife and mother and primarily located within the private world of the family, and the man is wage-earner and bread-winner and primarily located in the 'public' world of paid work, is normatively desirable.
(Beechey 1985: 99; see also, Barrett and McIntosh 1982)

It is arguable that, at the very least, moral traditionalist campaigning has succeeded in establishing the agenda of sexuality teaching inside the boundaries set by heterosexual familialism. Of course, more liberal approaches have not disappeared. They have even found official sanction within the National Curriculum and *The Health of the Nation* (NCC 1990; DoH 1993). For example, Curriculum Guidance 5 (Key Stage 3) for Health

Education, states that pupils should 'discuss moral values and explore those held by different . . . groups . . . [and] . . . be aware of the range of sexual attitudes and behaviours in present day society (NCC 1990). *The Health of the Nation: Key Area Handbook on HIV/AIDS and Sexual Health* (quoting the Sex Education Forum) comments that sex education should 'encourage exploration of values and moral issues, consideration of sexuality and personal relationships and the development of communication and decision-making skills' (DoH 1993: 114).

However, although these liberal views reflect a genuine concern to give young people a broad and objective education in the area of sex and sexuality, they do not go much further than addressing same sex relationships as a 'special issue', limiting discussion to the arena of morality. This is inevitably very different to an approach which would genuinely seek to integrate the reality of gay and lesbian sexuality into the taken for granted life of the school as just one more aspect of social diversity.

Thus while falling far short of the extremes of moral Right positions, existing liberal approaches have given plenty of ground to the traditionalist agenda. Significantly, they have failed to mobilize a strong, coherent alternative to the new moral traditionalism. In the absence of such an alternative, moral traditionalist thinking has succeeded in creating a climate in which schools tread with extreme caution round issues of sexuality. This caution, I would argue, means that heterosexual familialism is actively and passively presented by schools as an unproblematic social and moral norm, both in those aspects of the formal curriculum addressing sex and sexuality as well as in the practices and meanings that make up the 'hidden curriculum'.

The consequences of this are far reaching. First and foremost, the real day to day needs of pupils beginning to identify as lesbian or gay are almost wholly erased from school life. In this context, Simon Watney has argued

> Gay teenagers predictably face loneliness, ostracism, and guilt about their most intense emotions; and at an extreme they face homelessness and clinical depression, sometimes tragically leading to suicide. To neglect their ordinary human needs amounts to nothing less than State-sanctioned child abuse, understood as systematic neglect, accompanied by the complete denial of the

forms of education and support to which they should automatically be entitled.

(Watney 1993: 93)

As he goes on to argue, in a situation where one in 20 young
gay men testing for HIV find themselves to be antibody positive, education's failure to address the needs of pupils beginning
to identify as gay is actively life threatening.

As well as marginalizing lesbian and gay experience, this
narrow focus on heterosexual familialism within schools tends
to ignore the reality of many other areas of young people's
lives. For example, it erases the reality of sexual violence and
women's relative subordination within conventional heterosexual relations. Equally it ignores the real diversity of *heterosexual* sexual relationships many of which do not take place
within 'the family'. Similarly it marginalizes the many family
structures that exist alongside the nuclear family. Perhaps most
fundamentally, however, it fails to take account of the meanings, values, feeling and activities through which different
groups of young people themselves experience and live out their
own sexualities. Teaching young people about the supposed
benefits of 'stable married and family life' may bear little relation to childhood or adolescent realities, whether heterosexual,
lesbian or gay.

In these circumstances there is a clear need for a new agenda
in the field of sexuality education, one that addresses gay and
lesbian sexuality as something more than a 'moral issue', and
one that gets to grips with relations of power, pupils' different
'sexual cultures', and the lived experience of their lives. However, establishing such a new agenda is easier said than done.
The major reason for this is that, unlike issues related to gender,
race and class, there is no readily available educational vocabulary through which to construct it.

In this chapter, I aim to explore some of these issues more
closely. The chapter begins by tracing the absence of sexuality
from critical educational thinking and moves on to argue that
this laid the foundation for the relative success of the moral
traditionalist agenda in the mid to late l980s. In the final section,
the chapter takes up some of the arguments from more recent
work (see in particular Wolpe 1988; Holly 1989; Jones and
Mahony 1989; Holland *et al*. 1990a, 1990b; Mac an Ghaill 1991;

Sears 1992; Sex Education Forum 1992) to suggest a possible framework through which to begin the process of developing an alternative consensus around sexuality education.

Sexuality education and the liberal educational consensus

Throughout the 1970s and 1980s, questions of class, race, gender and schooling increasingly occupied the centre stage of critical educational debate (see, for example, Bowles and Gintis 1976; Willis 1977; Spender and Sarah 1980; Arnot and Weiner 1987; Donald and Rattansi 1992; Troyna and Hatcher 1992). Questions around sexuality, however, were not taken up in the same way.

The relative neglect of sexuality as an educational issue is reflected most immediately in the state of sexuality education as a curriculum area. Despite the success of individual initiatives it is arguable that the overall position of sexuality education in secondary schools remains at best underdeveloped. For example, recent research by Mártín Mac an Ghaill concluded

> students reported a . . . picture of ill-prepared, under-resourced [sex education] lessons, that both lacked any sense of progression and were overly teacher-centred, with irrelevant information that was repeated frequently throughout their schooling. Ironically, at a time of much pedagogical rhetoric about student-centred teaching approaches and cross-curricular initiatives, there appears to be little movement among policy-makers or within schools to design whole school programmes of effective sex education that start with the students' experiences and needs.
> (Mac an Ghaill 1991: 295; see also Allen 1987; Measor 1989)

This underdevelopment of sexuality education in the classroom has been fostered by a distinct lack of critical thinking and research in the area. For example, in the editors' introduction to their watershed anthology of work on pupil cultures, *Life in School* (Hammersley and Woods 1984), Hammersley and Woods discussed the importance of studies on social class and schooling and went on to identify the then developing interest in questions of gender and ethnicity. They wrote

> Equally important, though, is the growing attention now being
> given to the effects of gender-related messages built into school-
> ing and to gender-based differences in responses to them. . . .
> The influence of ethnicity on pupils' perspectives and adapta-
> tions has received much less attention . . . [and] . . . much still
> remains to be done in this area.
>
> (Hammersley and Woods 1984: 3)

Sexuality was entirely absent.

While the *Life in School* collection can be seen as reflecting
the general lack of awareness around sexuality and schooling
in the early and mid-1980s, the period did see the first interventions in this field. These interventions came from two quarters.
Feminist work on girls in school began to identify the importance of sexuality to forms of girls' subordination within education, particularly in the form of sexual harassment and girls'
sexual 'reputations' (see, for example, Spender and Sarah 1980;
Walkerdine 1981; Mahony 1985; Lees 1986). At the same time,
Trenchard and Warren's groundbreaking work on lesbian and
gay teenagers began to uncover their experiences of schooling
and bring to centre stage the fact that not all school pupils identify as heterosexual (Trenchard and Warren 1984).

Growing awareness of these issues was reflected in the
development of new resources. For example, the Inner London
Education Authority (ILEA) developed the 'Relationships and
Sexuality Project', a resource for secondary level teachers that
addressed gay and lesbian issues (see Sanders and Spraggs 1989:
82, 98). As the 1980s progressed growing awareness of 'equal
opportunities' and the new imperatives occasioned by the HIV
epidemic fed into a burgeoning array of teaching resources
looking at such issues as gender roles, stereotyping, and relationships (for a comprehensive list of resources in this area, see
HEA 1991).

All of this has marked a discernible shift away from a sex
education narrowly focused on biological reproduction. However, developments such as these have remained on the fringes
of the educational mainstream and have not constituted a
wholesale change in either school or research agendas. As a
result, when the voices of the new moral traditionalism began
to be heard around 1986, no institutionalized educational consensus on sexuality and schooling existed to refute them.

The new moral traditionalism

The development of a conservative moral agenda in sex education has been documented with relative thoroughness elsewhere
(see, in particular, Wolpe 1988; Aggleton *et al*. 1989; Cooper
1989; Melia 1989; Sanders and Spraggs 1989, all of which provide the bases for the following argument). However, the
influence of this moral agenda continues to be so strong that
the headlines of the moral traditionalist campaign are worth
revisiting. The campaign reached its height in the run up to and
aftermath of the 1987 general election when elements in the
Conservative Party and the press, and moral Right pressure
groups organized against what they perceived to be 'loony left'
ideas on questions of sexuality and schooling.

For example, in 1986 Haringey Council introduced prelimin-
ary plans designed to improve support for lesbian and gay
pupils and staff, and to enhance good practice on lesbian and
gay issues in the curriculum. These plans resulted in a media
furore, government investigation, and even a hunger-strike by
a local clergyman. Tottenham Conservative Party was quoted
as saying that Haringey's lesbian and gay unit were 'a greater
threat to family life than Adolf Hitler' (Cooper 1989: 57). In the
same year, ILEA came under attack for stocking the Gay Men's
Press book *Jenny Lives with Eric and Martin* (Bosche 1983) with
its now well known sympathetic portrayal of gay parenting (for
details of both incidents, see Cooper 1980; for feminist concerns
about *Jenny Lives with Eric and Martin*, see Jones and Mahony
1989: xi).

In tandem with these developments the moral Right within
the Conservative Party began agitating for legal reforms in relation to schooling and sexuality. In the autumn of 1986, the Earl
of Harlsbury instigated a Private Member's Bill entitled 'An Act
to restrain local authorities from promoting homosexuality',
one of the key aims of which was to prevent the perceived 'promotion of lesbian and gay rights' in schools (see Sanders and
Spraggs 1989: 85). Although the Bill fell shortly before the
general election of 1987, its theme was not lost in the election
campaign. As part of its election propaganda the Conservative
Party ran a national billboard advertisement with the slogan
'Is This Labour's Idea of a Comprehensive Education?' under-
neath which it pictured three books, *Police: Out of School*,

Young Gay and Proud and *The Playbook for Kids about Sex*. In her Party Conference speech later that year, Margaret Thatcher reworked the same argument, claiming 'Children who need to be taught to respect traditional moral values are being taught that they have an inalienable right to be gay' (Maggie Champions the Moral Crusade', *Daily Mail*, 10 October 1987).

These interventions were followed by the introduction of Clause 28 of the Local Government Bill (later Section 28 of the Local Government Act 1988). Headed 'Prohibition on promoting homosexuality by teaching or publishing material', subsection (1)(b) of the section states that a local authority shall not 'promote the teaching in any maintained school of the acceptability of homosexuality as a pretended family relationship' (Sanders and Spraggs 1989: 109). It should be noted that the subsequent Department of the Environment, Circular 12/88, DOE 1988, states that, since Section 28 applies to local authorities, it does not impose any direct responsibilities on individual schools.[2]

The moral traditionalist tone was echoed (though not unequivocally) in the language of the Education (No. 2) Act 1986 and, more particularly, in DES Circular 11/87, *Sex Education at School*. The Education (No. 2) Act states that governors should

> Take such steps as are reasonably practicable to secure that where sex education is given to any registered pupils in the school it is given in such manner as to encourage those pupils to have due regard to moral considerations and the value of family life.
>
> (Education (No. 2) Act 1986)

Sex Education at School, DES guidelines on sex education, ironed out some of the vagueness of this statement, stating that

> Teaching about the physical aspects of sexual behaviour should be set within a clear moral framework in which pupils are . . . helped to recognize the physical, emotional and moral risks of casual and promiscuous sexual behaviour . . . Pupils should be helped to appreciate the benefits of stable married and family life and the responsibility of parenthood.

To underline the point still further, the guidelines go on to say

There is no place in any school in any circumstance for teaching which advocates homosexual behaviour, which presents it as the 'norm' or which encourages homosexual experimentation by pupils.

(DES 1987)

While the late 1980s marked the high point of moral traditionalist activity, moral traditionalist thinking continues to enjoy considerable favour in government circles. In the summer of 1993, for example, the DfE formulated a draft replacement for Circular 11/87 which not only reaffirmed 11/87's proscriptive attitude to sex education but also restated the provisions of Section 28 of the Local Government Act (1988), even though it acknowledged that the Act 'does not impose any direct responsibilities' on schools (DfE 1993). Equally, the Education Act (1993) saw the reversal of earlier liberal gains within legislation on sex education. In 1991, the Science Order of the National Curriculum had made basic sex education (including some non-biological issues) and HIV education a mandatory part of teaching for 11 to 14 year olds (National Curriculum Science Order 1991). The Education Act (1993) reversed this, removing both HIV education and all but the most rudimentary education about sexual reproduction from the National Curriculum (Education Act 1993). In effect the 1993 Act marks an uneasy compromise between moral traditionalist and more liberal positions. Although withdrawing HIV and most sex education from the National Curriculum, the Act acknowledges young people's need for education in these areas by making them a compulsory part of non-National Curriculum teaching at the secondary level. However, the Act also gives parents the right to withdraw their children from these classes, thereby denying children access to such education and making it extremely difficult for schools to teach HIV and sex education across different areas of the curriculum.

The new moral traditionalism has thus successfully mobilized a clear agenda on sexuality and education which, although it has not swept all before it, has succeeded in dominating official policy, and thus set effective limits on what is possible or attempted in schools. Within these limits, schools are expected to address questions of sex and sexuality within a framework that views heterosexuality as an unquestioned norm to the exclusion of other forms of consenting desire and that places sexual activity firmly within the context of 'stable married life'.

Coming to terms with sexuality and schooling

Like much of the Thatcherite project of the 1980s the new moral traditionalism in sex education succeeded, at least in part, because it had more ideas and was more vocal than alternative positions. Above all, the moral Right took the question of sexuality and schooling very seriously in ways that the majority of educational theorists, schools and opposition political parties did not. However, the last six years have seen a growing recognition of these issues. Building on the gay, lesbian and feminist work of the early 1980s, there has been a small but growing number of policy interventions and research initiatives that address sexuality and education (see, in particular, Wolpe 1988; Holly 1989; Jones and Mahony 1989; Holland *et al.* 1990a, 1990b; Mac an Ghaill 1991; Sears 1992; Sex Education Forum 1992). It is to this body of work that we need to look if we are to begin to establish a sexuality education that seeks to address the lives of all pupils.

Although this work is far from homogeneous, four issues stand out as being of particular relevance to the development of a liberal-left consensus on sexuality and education: the reality of sexual diversity, the centrality of power relations within heterosexual relationships, the construction of sexualities within the schooling process, and the need to address pupils' sexual cultures.

Sexual diversity and power relations

One of the starting places of much of this recent work on sexuality and education has been a focus on power relations, in particular young women's subordination and resistance in their sexual relations with young men (Wolpe 1988; Holly 1989; Holland *et al.* 1990a, 1990b). Equally both Máirtín Mac an Ghaill and the contributors to *Learning Our Lines* have focused on pupils beginning to identify as lesbian or gay and have sought to demonstrate the ways in which heterosexuality is institutionalized and sanctioned in schools (Jones and Mahony 1989; Mac an Ghaill 1991).

Taken as a whole, such studies make available a distinctly new set of priorities. Their focus on the subordination of lesbian and gay sexualities and girls' relative lack of power within the sexual economy foreground the absence of these issues from much current sex education. In the process, they draw attention to the need for educational strategies which recognize and can tackle the realities of power inequalities and sexual diversity.

Schooling and the construction of sexualities

Perhaps the most challenging argument in recent work on sexuality and schooling has been the assertion that schools operate as significant cultural sites in which understandings and practices concerned with sexuality are actively constructed, reproduced and lived out, both in the formal curriculum and the hidden curriculum. As Mac an Ghaill argues, even where sexuality is never overtly mentioned within the formal curriculum, it continues as a pervasive presence within relations between students and staff and students and students. Name-calling, staff preconceptions about pupil behaviour, the differential treatment of boys and girls, sexualized pupil resistance to teacher authority, the marginalization of gay and lesbian identities within both the playground and the classroom, all serve to carry important messages about sexual identities and sexual practices (Mac an Ghaill 1991: 295).

In this vein, Lesley Holly has written

> Of course pupils unofficially learn about sexuality and its inter-
> connections with power relations between the sexes. Although
> many aspects of sexuality may be unacknowledged it remains a
> resource on which pupils can draw to reinforce their sexual iden-
> tity. Boys can use sexual language to keep girls in their place . . .
> Girls can respond to sexual stereotypes by rejecting them or
> quietly living with passive femininity for an easy life. Teachers
> can also draw on sexuality in their relations with pupils . . . The
> effect of the sexualized encounters is to reproduce the idea of
> male superiority.
>
> (Holly 1989: 5)

Although Holly applies these arguments to gendered relations between boys and girls, the same point could be made about sexual identities. In effect, schools operate as important public spaces in which young people learn about and construct their sexualities and come face to face with the different value society places on heterosexual as opposed to gay and lesbian identities.

This argument marks an important shift in thinking about sexuality and education. The point being made is that schools are necessarily a significant place in which pupils learn about sexuality whether schools intend this or not. In some versions of this argument schools are said to reflect or reproduce versions of sexuality that are primarily located elsewhere. Thus Jacqui Halson has written

> Schools, as the Headmaster said, are 'reflections of society'. They help to reproduce rather than change the imbalance of power between men and women . . . not least by failing to recognize the extent to which young women are subjected to sexual harassment.
>
> (Halson 1989: 191)

However, in some other versions of the argument schooling processes and school cultures are assigned a more *primary* role in the process of constructing gender and sexuality. Thus, in this volume (p. 156) Mac an Ghaill writes

> Modern schooling systems are significant cultural sites that actively produce and reproduce a range of differentiated, hierarchically ordered masculinities and femininities. It is within this school gender regime that we may locate the development of black and white lesbian and gay sexualities.

This second version of the analysis is arguably the more productive of the two. If schools are said simply to reproduce homophobia, sexism and heterosexism, there is a danger that they are let off the hook. The problem becomes not the school but what the children bring with them through the school gates, for example, from their television watching, or from their family and community backgrounds. However, if the formal and hidden curricula are recognized as important sites in which young people learn about sexuality, then schools have an obligation to ensure that this learning is positive and useful.

This emphasis on the ways in which sexuality is *constructed* within schooling (and other cultural) processes tends to disrupt the educational 'common sense' that existing relations of sexuality are 'natural', 'normal', or, at least, unchangeable. In the process, it opens up the possibility of a radically new sexuality education. A perspective that focuses on the ways in which sexualities are constructed and lived out within schooling processes forces us to confront the ways in which heterosexualities are put in place, and maintained through complex social relationships which serve to marginalize and subordinate specific social groups (lesbians and gays, girls and women, black and minority ethnic groups, disabled people). If we look at playground name-calling, the implicit assumptions of the formal curriculum, staff typifications, pupils' interactions and pupil cultures, what we find is not an unproblematic and monolithic heterosexuality, as the moral Right would have us believe, but a vast diversity of sexual identifications (conscious and unconscious), beliefs, values, and practices, all of which are riven with relations of subordination, consent and resistance.

An understanding of the ways in which schooling operates to construct and reproduce sexualities thus offers the potential to shift fundamentally the agenda of sexuality education. Most obviously it brings to the foreground issues such as sexual harassment and homophobia as these are deployed and reproduced in schools, as well as the fact that different groups of pupils have divergent needs (for example, according to provisional sexual orientations, gender, ethnicity, class, age and disability). At the same time, it forces us to look at what is going on inside schools, in particular in the hidden curriculum, rather than assuming that sexuality education should address solely what happens 'out there'.

Such an approach is very different to the conventional 'equal opportunities' agenda. Existing 'equal opportunities' approaches tend to assume that the needs of pupils beginning to identify as lesbian or gay can be addressed by simply 'adding on' lesbian and gay issues to the existing curriculum as if they are somehow discrete entities or issues wholly divorced from other areas of sexuality education. Thus 'tackling lesbian and gay issues' becomes a matter of 'positive images' in textbooks, and classroom discussions on the value of extra strong condoms or the options for self-insemination. Valuable though such innovations would be, they do not go far enough. The problem lies in the fact that they work within a liberal framework that claims that gay and lesbian sexualities are 'different but equal'. While it would be nice if this were true, its assertion before the fact runs the risk of ignoring the very real ways in which lesbian and gay sexualities are subordinated, marginalized and constructed as 'other' both within the social formation at large and within schools themselves. Once it is accepted that schools operate as significant cultural sites in which the meanings of sexuality are constructed then it becomes necessary to address the precise ways in which schooling and school cultures operate to construct heterosexualities and homosexualities in relations of opposition and subordination. It is this, I would argue, that sexuality education should seek to address, as well as the more obvious issues that form the 'equal opportunities' agenda.

Addressing pupils' sexual cultures

The final major focus within recent writing on sexuality and education has been a concern to understand pupils' and young people's sexual cultures (Measor 1989; Holland *et al.* 1990a, 1990b). The importance of pupils' cultures to the educational process has long been recognized. In *Life in School*, Hammersley and Woods argue

> There can be little doubt that pupils' own interpretations of school processes represent a crucial link in the educational chain. Unless we understand how pupils respond to different forms of pedagogy and school organization and why they respond in the ways that they do, our efforts to increase the effectiveness, or to change the impact, of schooling will stand little chance of success.
>
> (Hammersley and Woods 1984: 3; although see Hammersley's more recent concerns about ethnographic research, Hammersley 1992)

As Hammersley and Woods suggest, educational interventions necessarily interact with and are refracted by pupils' cultures. Sexuality education will, therefore, necessarily interact with and be refracted by pupils' sexual cultures.

In spite of this longstanding recognition of the importance of pupils' cultures to the educational process, relatively little work exists on either sexual cultures themselves or their impact on the effectiveness of sexuality education. However, the work that does exist gives a clear sense of need for sexuality education to take pupils' sexual cultures as its starting place and to recognize the relations of power that are built into these. For instance, in her study of sex education and girls, Lynda Measor concludes

> By its 'open air heartiness', sex education in this school conflicted with the realities of adolescent sexual culture. I want to suggest that as a result it was difficult for the sex educators to reach or meet the needs of adolescents. The sex education remained a distant, unhelpful, adult thing.
>
> (Measor 1989: 51)

In this light, sexual cultures can be seen to be vitally important to the schooling process. They act as crucial sites of learning about sex and sexuality and they have the ability to both interrupt and resist the 'lessons' of formal sexuality education. Thus the Women, Risk and AIDS Project details the role played by the contraceptive pill in a particular version of adolescent heterosexual girls' culture, and the ways in which the social meanings ascribed to the 'pill' have the potential to interrupt safer sex education. They write

> [A] transition from condoms with new partners to the pill with steady partners is laden with symbolic meaning and can be used to signify the seriousness of a relationship, a way of showing someone that they are special. As one of our respondents put it, 'I went on the pill for him' . . . For the current generation of young women the pill . . . is closely associated with grown up status and grown up sex. This makes the prospect of long term condom use highly problematic.
>
> (Holland *et al.* 1990b: 18)

In a similar vein Rob Pattman has detailed the ways in which PSE lessons on relationships can completely fail to engage boys whose 'common-sense' understandings of sex construct girls as sexual prey. This fact is highlighted in the following exchange between Pattman and a group of boy interviewees. Pattman has asked the group the question. 'How do you talk about girls with your mates?'

Tony: I suppose one-sided really. When you're with your mates you don't really see them as other people, you see them as machines . . .

Me: Do you express these views in sex education classes?

Tony: No, not really.

Me: How are you supposed to talk about sex and girls in sex education classes?

John: You have to keep your mouth shut, don't you. You have to watch what you say.

Tony: You can't be that open. In certain matters you can. But when it comes to what you feel and your mates feel you don't say anything.

(Pattman 1991)

This exchange usefully identifies the fact that, for these boys at least, formal classroom discussions about sex and relationships bear little relation to their own understandings or the ways in which they handle sex and sexuality in the rest of the schoolday. Far from interrupting or opening up alternatives to peer group definitions, classroom discussions are experienced by the boys as a form of policing, a site in which you simply 'keep quiet' (or more likely, opt out and mess around) only to readopt your original position once the lesson is safely over.

Máirtín Mac an Ghaill's research, on the other hand, highlights the ways in which pupils who are beginning to identify as gay or lesbian tend to be wholly ignored within the formal curriculum. This, he argues, is in strong contrast to the informal curriculum in which gay and lesbian identities are endlessly and overtly policed. One of his respondents, Stephen, comments

Playgrounds are really cruel places if you're seen as different or weak. In our school the macho gangs treated girls very bad. And they persecuted me and a few friends, calling us poofs and queer and all that because we weren't like them, didn't act hard like them. We survived because we were big and did not show that we were afraid of them.

(this volume: 164)

A similar point is made by Marigold Rogers' respondent, Diane

My form tutor (who was a woman) once took me out of the classroom after registration and asked me if I could stop talking about my sexuality in front of the other girls because apparently it was upsetting some of them! I feel that this was a bit of a one-sided request because I had to put up with *them* going on about their boyfriends all day and no one asked *me* if I found that offensive.

(this volume: 35)

For pupils beginning to identify as gay or lesbian, official marginalization and playground policing are liable to make school a site in which very negative lessons about sexuality are learned (see also Trenchard and Warren 1984).

In all of these examples, forms of sexuality education are rendered relatively ineffective for particular groups of young people. Pupils are either ignored, their oppression is tacitly condoned, or the messages of sex education fail to take account of the meanings and practices which make up the pupils' own experience and understanding. Such findings have important implications for the content of sexuality education. They suggest that, to be effective, sexuality education needs to have an understanding of the particular sexual cultures of particular groups of young people and a grasp of the ways in which these sexual cultures are likely to come into conflict with educational interventions. This understanding will have to encompass a recognition of the ways in which young people are differently positioned within sexual cultures. White, working-class girls may well inhabit different forms of sexual culture to some white middle-class girls. Both will inhabit different positions to white boys. Similarly, growing up lesbian or gay may involve radically different experiences depending on the class, ethnic or even regional background against which this occurs. Sexual orientation, class, ethnicity, gender and disability as well as age will all throw up different sets of relations to available sexual cultures. All of these factors will need to be addressed in educational provision.

Towards a new agenda for sexuality education

Put together these four factors – the need to address sexual diversity, relations of power, the construction of sexuality in schooling processes, and pupil sexual cultures – offer the basis for a fundamental re-evaluation of sexuality education. As is surely obvious they do not in themselves provide any easy answers or a blueprint for 'how to do it'. However, what they do suggest is a new sense of direction; markers on the way to developing alternatives to the current submoral Right hegemony that holds sway over sex education in schools.

I would want to argue that a thoroughgoing integration of lesbian and gay issues into sexuality education needs to begin with just such a fundamental reorientation of the subject. If sexuality education really is to take on board lesbian and gay issues then it will need to address the ways in which heterosexuality is systematically built into and spoken by the everyday routines and structures of school life. By extension, it will also have to consider the ways in which gayness and lesbianism are systematically denied, marginalized and constructed as 'other'. Similarly, pupil sexual cultures will need to be taken into account. To combat homophobia, it will not be enough to tell pupils that 'poof' is an unacceptable word. Disciplinarian approaches will need to be underpinned by far more creative strategies which seek to understand the role of homophobias within boy cultures in particular, and which seek to enable pupils to find new ways of 'seeing' that make sense within their own lives and cultural formations.

Of course, legal realities and the burden of the National Curriculum will place major obstacles in the path of any potential reorientation of sexuality education. The demands of the National Curriculum mean that there is less and less space for 'time consuming' student-centred learning or subjects which fall outside curriculum orders. The Education Act (1993) has done little to offer schools encouragement in relation to sex education, and continues a rather sorry tradition of muddled official thinking and proscriptive policy-making when what is needed is clear sighted innovation and a willingness to address real needs.

While acknowledging these difficulties, the recent educational research that I have outlined does provide a real opportunity to rethink sexuality education. The Sex Education Forum's (1992) *A Framework for School Sex Education* has already integrated important elements from this debate into its recommendations and has secured extensive backing from key professional and voluntary bodies. Even the Department of Health quotes the *Framework* with approval (DoH 1993: 114). While the *Framework* is still a long way from an approach that really gets to grips with lesbian and gay issues, and while it is fairly vague on the hidden curriculum and relations of power, it does indicate the potential for building a liberal/left consensus within the mainstream of educational thinking. Such a consensus will only be built on the back of educational debate and classroom innovation. In this context there is real need for published research on the whole range of issues raised by sexuality and schooling and on the whole diversity of pupil sexual cultures. Equally, there is a real need for teacher innovation in good practice. In the meantime, many pupils, particularly those beginning to identify as lesbian or gay, will have their existence erased, their needs denied, and will continue to face day to day persecution in British schools.

Notes

1 The research referred to is the Sexuality Education Project, currently based in East Birmingham Health Authority. The project is conducted in association with Dr Debbie Epstein from the Sexuality Research Project.

2 The legal implications of Section 28 remain notoriously vague. Sanders and Spraggs suggest that 'In general, for an authority to cite Section 28 as grounds for disciplining a teacher or other employee it would have to show that they were 'promoting homosexuality', for example by urging pupils to adopt a gay or lesbian lifestyle or to experiment sexually with members of their own sex. It is generally agreed that there is nothing in Section 28 to stop teachers from discussing homosexuality with pupils in the classroom objectively and honestly, or counselling individual pupils in a pastoral context' (Sanders and Spraggs 1989: 115).

References

Aggleton, P. *et al.* (1989) Health education, sexuality and AIDS. In S. Walker and L. Barton (eds) *Politics and the Processes of Schooling*. Milton Keynes: Open University Press.

Allen, I. (1987) *Education in Sex and Personal Relations*. London: Policy Studies Institute.

Arnot, M. and Weiner, G. (eds) (1987) *Gender and the Politics of Schooling*. London: Hutchinson Education/Open University.

Barrett, M. and McIntosh, M. (1982) *The Anti-Social Family*. London: Verso.

Beechey, V. (1985) Familial ideology. In V. Beechey and J. Donald (eds) *Subjectivity and Social Relations*. Milton Keynes: Open University Press.

Bosche, S. (with photographs by Andreas) (1983) *Jenny Lives with Eric and Martin*. London: Gay Men's Press.

Bowles, S. and Gintis, H. (1976) *Schooling in Capitalist America*. London: Routledge and Kegan Paul.

Cooper, D. (1989) Positive images in Haringey: a struggle for identity. In C. Jones and P. Mahony (eds) *Learning Our Lines: Sexualtiy and Social Control in Education*. London: Women's Press.

DES (1987) *Sex Education at School*, Circular No. 11/87. London: HMSO.

DfE (1993) *Sex Education in Schools: Proposed Revision of Circular 11/87*. London: Department for Education.

DOE (1988) Circular 12/88. London: Department of the Environment.

DoH (1993) *The Health of the Nation, Key Area Handbook: HIV/AIDS and Sexual Health*. London: Department of Health.

Donald, J. and Rattansi, A. (eds) (1992) *'Race', Culture and Difference*. London: Sage/Open University.

The Education (No 2) Act (1986) London: HMSO.

The Education Act (1993) London: HMSO.

Halson, J. (1989) The sexual harassment of young women. In L. Holly (ed.) *Girls and Sexuality: Teaching and Learning*. Milton Keynes: Open University Press.

Hammersley, M. (1992) On feminist methodology, *Sociology*, 26 (2), 187–206.

Hammersley, M. and Woods, P. (1984) (eds) *Life In School: The Sociology of Pupil Culture*. Milton Keynes. Open University Press.

HEA (1991) *HIV/AIDS and Sexual Health Resource List*. London: Health Education Authority.

Holland, J. *et al.* (1990a) *Sex, Risk. Danger: AIDS Education Policy and Young Women's Sexuality*. WRAP Paper 1. London: Tufnell Press.

Holland, J. *et al.* (1990b) *'Don't Die of Ignorance – I Nearly Died of Embarrassment': Condoms in Context*. WRAP Paper 2, London: Tufnell Press.

Holly, L. (ed.) (1989) *Girls and Sexuality: Teaching and Learning*. Milton Keynes: Open University Press.

Jones, C. and Mahony, P. (eds) (1989) *Learning Our Lines: Sexuality and Social Control in Education*. London: Women's Press.

Lees, S. (1986) *Losing Out: Sexuality and Adolescent Girls.* London: Hutchinson.

Local Government Act (1988) London: HMSO.

Mac an Ghaill, M. (1991) Schooling, sexuality and male power: towards an emancipatory curriculum, *Gender and Education,* 3 (3), 291–309.

Melia, J. (1989) Sex education in schools: keeping to the 'norm'. In C. Jones and P. Mahony (eds) *Learning Our Lines: Sexuality and Social Control in Education.* London: Women's Press.

Mahony, P. (1985) *Schools for the Boys? Coeducation Reassessed.* London: Hutchinson/Explorations in Feminism Collective.

Measor, L. (1989) Are you coming to see any dirty films today?: Sex education and adolescent sexuality. In L. Holly (ed) *Girls and Sexuality: Teaching and Learning.* Milton Keynes: Open University Press.

National Curriculum Science Order (1991) *The Education (National Curriculum) (Attainment Targets and Programmes of Study in Science Order).* London: HMSO.

NCC (1990) Curriculum Guidance 5: Health Education. York: National Curriculum Council.

Pattman, R. (1991) 'Sex education and the liberal paradigm', unpublished PhD research. Department of Cultural Studies, University of Birmingham.

Sanders, S. and Spraggs, G. (1989) Section 28 and education. In C. Jones and P. Mahony (eds) *Learning Our Lines: Sexuality and Social Control in Education.* London: Women's Press.

Sears, J. T. (ed.) (1992) *Sexuality and the Curriculum: The Politics and Practices of Sexuality Education.* New York: Teachers College Press.

Sex Education Forum (1992) *A Framework for School Sex Education.* London: National Children's Bureau.

Spender, D. and Sarah, E. (eds) (1980) *Learning to Lose: Sexism and Education.* London: Women's Press.

Trenchard, L. and Warren, H. (1984) *Something to Tell You.* London: Gay Teenagers' Group.

Troyna, B. and Hatcher, R. (1992) *Racism In Children's Lives.* London: Routledge.

Walkerdine, V. (1981) Sex, power and pedagogy, *Screen Education,* 38, 14–21.

Watney, S. (1993) Simon Watney column: sex education, *Gay Times,* February.

Willis, P. (1977) *Learning to Labour.* Farnborough: Saxon House.

Wolpe, A. M. (1988) *Within School Walls: The Role of Discipline, Sexuality, and the Curriculum.* London: Routledge.

CHAPTER 11

(In)visibility: Sexuality, Race and Masculinity in the School Context

MÁIRTÍN MAC AN GHAILL

Introduction

> The society makes its will toward you very, very clear . . .
> the macho men – truck drivers, cops, football players – these
> people are far more complex than they want to realize. That's
> why I call them infantile. They have needs that for them are
> literally inexplicable. They don't dare look in the mirror. And
> that is why they need faggots. They've created faggots in order
> to act out a sexual fantasy on the body of another man and not
> take any responsibility for it. Do you see what I mean? I think
> it's very important for the male homosexual to recognize that he
> is a sexual target for other men, and that is why he is despised,
> and why he is called a faggot. He is called a faggot because other
> men need him.
>
> (Baldwin, quoted in Troupe 1989: 178–9)

History in school is really a long story that English people
need to tell themselves about how great white men civilized
the world. They need blacks to feed their imaginations with
their superiority. But as a black gay person you don't exist in
this society, publicly you don't exist because they need to tell
themselves there is only one way to live your life, in their
happy heterosexual families. But privately white straight men

fantasize about us, they envy us . . . So, when you bring together black and sexual oppressions it's very confusing and full of contradictions.

(Gilroy – student)[1]

Raymond Williams's (1961, p. 172) claim that: 'An educational curriculum . . . expresses a compromise between an inherited selection of interests', remains one of the most adequate and fruitful conceptions of schooling. More recently, in examining curriculum modernization, the focus has been on the internal philosophical divisions and compromises within the New Right project, which includes the neo-conservative emphasis on direct management and the neo-liberal emphasis on market forces. In response, much critical sociology of education, having moved beyond functionalist models of social reproduction in the early 1980s, has returned to an economic reductionist reading of what is presently going on in schools and what is to be done. Such a reading is marked by a major absence involving degendered, deracialized and desexualized accounts of the 'new curriculum' (Arnot 1992). We have witnessed the ascendancy of the New Right agenda occupying the moral high ground with its pro-jected atavistic representations of a consumer-based acquisi-tive individualism, the patriarchal family, the strong state and a patriarchic British nation. As Gordon and Klug (1985: 11) point out, the emergence of the social authoritarians' discourses converge around issues of 'race' and sexuality. They argue:

> For there is clearly an overlap in ideology which opposes black immigration on the grounds that white Britain could be swamped and one that advocates measures to strengthen the British family, both physically and ideologically, on the grounds that the moral integrity of the nation is at risk.

The response of the mainstream white male Left's response has been minimal, involving a defensive reaction in terms of vague conceptions of a social-democratic, welfarist, and multi-ethnic citizenship. The main political and theoretical challenge to this Tory 'high moral' discourse, that has been under-reported, has come from radical women's, black, lesbian and gay movements. For example, Liz Kelly (1992: 22) offers a radical critique of the legacy of the 1980s nationalist enterprise culture that involves, she argues, a hierarchy of oppressions approach that conceives of working-class black gays as triply oppressed, has limited explanatory power. Unintendedly, it serves to reinforce the pedagogical 'common-sense' view that recent policies, developed in response to the demands of the new identity politics of 'race', gender, sexuality and disability, have displaced policies on class, and are primarily concerned with minority interests and needs (Mama 1992: 80). Schools find themselves with disparate policy documents that fail to address the complex and contradictory articulation of different forms of oppression. Equally important they have failed to acknowledge the complex multifaceted nature and historical contextual contingency of the mediation of these oppressions in state institutions, such as schools, that are themselves sites of contradictions, ambiguities and tensions, located within a severe long-term economic and industrial recession. Weeks (1990: 92) has cogently summarized the issues involved. He writes:

> Nevertheless there are difficulties for the Left in an all-embracing humanism. As a philosophical position it may be a good starting point, but it really does not tell us how to deal with difference . . . If ever-growing social complexity, cultural diversity and proliferation of identities are indeed a mark of the postmodern world, then all the appeals to our common interest as humans will be as naught unless we can at the same time learn to live with difference. This should be the crux of modern debates about values.

The case study

The Asian and Afro-Caribbean young gay men involved in this qualitative study were aged between 16 and 19 years. They were all attending local post-16 education institutions situated in the Midlands. I taught a number of them, who were following A level courses. Within their schools and colleges they were not 'out' as gay. My own students informed me that they were open to me about their sexuality because of my anti-homophobic stance. In the staffroom, classroom and more informal school arenas I presented a pro-gay perspective. They introduced me to their friends, who in turn introduced me to their friends. We operated as an informal support group.

Mercer and Julien (1988: 97) contextualize for themselves as black gay men the positive political significance of the inner-city civil disobediences in opposition to the 1980s Tory hegemony.

> For us, 1981 was a profoundly empowering moment, mobilising energies and abilities to challenge our conditions of existence. The feeling of empowerment came from the collective identity we constructed for ourselves as black gay men, enabling us to overcome the marginality we experienced as black people and the individual isolation we felt as gay people. Politics is about making connections practically, with the forming of alliances between different social groups, and at a cognitive level with the recognition of diverse categories of race, class, gender, ethnicity and sexuality in articulation of power relations. The gay black group enabled us to start a conversation amongst ourselves, making connections between patterns of our common experiences to recognise the structures responsible for the specificity of the oppression in the first place.

There is a certain resonance here for me and for the young gay black men who took part in this study. Reading through this paper, we are surprised, at a time of the emergence of the New Right Moralism, that we continue to be optimistic (Weeks, 1989). Our being together provided the conditions for us to start a conversation about the politics of oppression with particular reference to contemporary state schooling. This produced an unexpected and unintended effect. By the early 1990s in post-primary schools there tends to be less evidence among minorities of the 'black unity' of the mid-1980s, with its emphasis on the shared experience of anti-black racism. The black gay students here, in exploring the politics of complex difference involving the articulation of homophobia, heterosexism and racism, are a sector of the younger generation among whom 'syncretic black identities are being formed' (Mama 1992: 80), focusing on racial, gender and sexual communalities as well as on the specificities of personal histories, memories, desires and expectations.

Methodology

Space does not allow for a detailed discussion of the study's methodology, particularly with reference to questions concerning the politics and ethics of researching oppressed groups (see

Mac an Ghaill 1989a). Much of the material reported here was collected from observation, informal discussions and recorded semi-structured interviews with the students and their teachers at their schools and colleges. The material is taken from life and school histories that involved discussion of family/kinship networks, peer groupings, work experience, political views/ activities and school/college experiences. This methodological approach helped to locate schooling within the larger socio-political processes (see Connell 1989 and Morgan 1992). Sharing our life histories helped to challenge the power asymmetries between the students and myself. My main influences include feminist methodology and praxis-based pedagogy (see Bryan *et al.* 1985; Freire 1985; and hooks 1991). In adopting a student-centred methodological approach that prioritizes their epistemological accounts of schooling, I have attempted to operate within a framework that served to empower the students who were actively involved in the construction of the research stance (Griffin 1987: 21 and Bhavnani 1991).

We are only beginning to understand the complex articulation between schooling, masculine cultural formations and sexual/racial identities. Feminist theory has enabled us to move beyond the ahistorical gender/sexual essentialism and determinism of sex-role theory, acknowledging that young people are not such '*tabulae rasae,* to be injected or even constructed with the ideology of the day' (Rowbotham 1989: 18). As Carrigan *et al.* (1985: 88–89) argue:

> The history of homosexuality obliges us to think of masculinity not as a single object with its own history but as being constantly constructed within the history of an evolving social structure, a structure of power relations. It obliges us to see the construction as a social struggle going on in a complex ideological and polit-ical field in which there is a continuing process of mobilization, marginalization, contestation, resistance and subordination.

Modern schooling systems are significant cultural sites that actively produce and reproduce a range of differentiated, hier-archically ordered masculinities and femininities that are made available for students to inhabit. It is within historically specific school gender regimes that we may locate the development of black and white lesbian and gay sexualities (Mac an Ghaill 1994).

A main argument here is that the major problem in the schooling of black gay students is not their sexuality but the phenomena of homophobia, heterosexism and racism which pervasively circumscribe their social world. Furthermore, these phenomena are mediated and reproduced both through existing formal and hidden curricula, pedagogical and evaluative systems that set out to regulate subordinated young people and through gender/sexual specific mechanisms, such as the processes of gender/sexual representations, which in turn are 'race', class and age specific. An idealist analysis of the curriculum that reduces the heterosexist structuring of schooling to aberrant teacher prejudice is insufficient to explain the complex social interaction of white male and female teachers with black male students in racialized, male dominated institutions. For example, the students' teachers claimed that they found it difficult to discuss lesbian and gay issues within the school context. However, at a deeper level specific age relations operate in English schools that serve to marginalize and alienate many young people. White teachers' difficulty in communicating with black gay students is not simply an issue about sexuality and racism. It is also premised on the low epistemological status ascribed to all students.

Administrative systems of teacher racial and gender/sexual typifications

As Westwood (1990: 56–57) points out within the context of the need to de-essentialize black masculinity:

> The essentialism of the constructions that surround the black man and black masculinity have given plenty of scope for racist accounts through stereotyping and the construction of black men as 'the other'. For black men of African descent the stereotypes have been fixed on the body, on physicality, physical strength, and as a site for European fantasies about black male sexuality. Orientalism has generated a different picture for men of Asian descent. The colonial designation of the 'martial races' of northern India produced an account of men of vigour who were at some distance from the wily Oriental, who by being tied to conceptions of manipulation and wiliness, became feminised in the eyes of the white men of the colonial era. The fixity

of these stereotypes places 'races', genders motivations and behaviours in such a way that they become naturalized and a substitute for the complex realities that they seek to describe.

For the young men in this study these processes of naturalization and objectification were most immediately experienced through the highly contradictory dominant systems of teacher racial and gender/sexual discourses which are 'embedded in social relationships of structured domination and subordination' (Bhavnani 1991: 181). These administrative systems operate as processes of teacher signification that form the basis for the creation of ethnically structured student hierarchies. In turn, they serve to establish regulatory criteria by which to develop allocative and exclusionary processes within specific institutional sites in relation to the Afro-Caribbean and Asian groups (Miles 1989).

In earlier work (1989a and b) I set out to reconceptualize black students' experience of schooling within a framework that moved beyond mono-causal explanations and examined the multifaceted dimensions of racially structured English schooling. The Afro-Caribbean and Asian young men in this study, all of whom are academically successful, recall schooling biographies that have significant convergences and differences. What emerges is how racialized social and discursive configurations with their own local histories are grounded in specific material cultures at classroom and playground levels. For the students, the white teachers' racial and gender/sexual typifications did not take a unitary form but rather were differentially structured and experienced, mediated by the specificity of different school cultures and individual and collective student responses. In particular, the racial and gender composition of each school was a significant variable in the construction of teacher typifications. So, for example, in working-class schools where there was a majority Asian student population with a mainly white minority, the dominant representations of Asian youths tended to be negative, with caricatures of them as 'sly' and 'not real men'. However, in working-class schools which included significant numbers of Afro-Caribbeans, the students felt that the Asians were caricatured in a more positive way in relation to the Afro-Caribbeans, who were perceived as of 'low ability', 'aggressive' and 'anti-authority'. In contrast, in middle-

class grammar schools with predominantly white student populations, such attributes as 'hard-working' and 'ambitious' were
assigned to Asian students (Rattansi 1992).

A major limitation of much 'race-relations' theoretical and
empirical work in education has been the failure to incorporate
psychodynamic explanations (Henriques 1984; Cohen 1987;
Nava 1992). As students point out, their schooling cannot be
reductively conceptualized in terms of a simple binary social
system, composed of a juxtaposed white straight superiority
and a black gay inferiority. The relations between white
teachers and black students also involve a psychic structure,
including such elements as: desire, attraction, repression, trans-
ference and projection in relation to a racialized 'sexual other'
(Pajaczkowska and Young 1992). This echoes one of the main
themes of Isaac Julien's film *Young Soul Rebels* (1991). In its
exploration of the construction of black masculinity, he focuses
upon such issues as white men's ambivalences, transgressions
and envy toward black men. There is much work to be done
in this area in order to understand the ambivalent structure of
feeling and desire embedded within social institutions (Fanon
1970; Williams 1977). In the following accounts the young men
discuss the range of split responses from white males to themselves that were manifested in terms of the interplay between
racial and sexual fear and desire and the accompanying contradictory elements of repulsion, fascination and misrecognition
(Klein 1960; Rutherford 1990).

> *Andrew*: It's like with the straights, all the bits they don't like
> about themselves or they're afraid of, they push onto us.
> *Rajinder*: Thinking about it, it's very complex. Straight men
> don't really have a problem with gays, they have a problem
> with themselves. Straight men seem to fear and love women
> but fear and hate gay men. Then whites, especially white men,
> have that fear and hatred for Asians and Afro-Caribbeans. So
> black gay men are a real threat to white straight men. Like
> James Baldwin says, they act out their fears on us, on our
> bodies . . . But then there's other complications. Like at our
> school, you could see some of the white teachers, the men,
> they really admired the Caribbeans and not just in sport and
> music, where it was really homoerotic, though of course they
> could never admit it to themselves. I think for a lot of teachers
> there, who felt trapped in their jobs, the macho black kids

represented freedom from the system. There were anti-school macho whites and Asians but the teachers with their stereotypes fantasized about the Caribbean kids, who they saw as anti-authority, more physical and athletic, everything they couldn't be but greatly admired.

Stephen: Like you say black kids know that most white teachers would never live in our areas even though they make their living here. English middle-class people have always lived off immigrants; the blacks and the Irish around here. The teachers' kids go to their white grammar and private schools on the backs of the miseducation that their parents impose on us every day . . . But at night the teachers creep out of their white ghettoes to live it up among the 'black folk'. Emotionally they're really screwed up. And somehow although they don't want us as neighbours, they are obsessed with our food, music, dance, with our sex. You see they fantasize about these poor black folk. They're not repressed like the whiteys and in a different way their kids are doing the same . . . another generation of patronization from the white boys and girls!

Subordinated black masculinities: Subcultural responses and self-representations

There is a danger in examining black gay students' schooling experiences of unintendedly adopting a passive concept of subject positioning, with the student portrayed as unproblematically accepting an over-determined racial and gender/sexual role allocation (Walkerdine 1990). In fact, as the students here make clear, they are active curriculum and masculine makers. Male ethnographic research on white and black working-class males has finely illustrated how subordinated youth, drawing on resources from their own communities and wider youth cultural forms, have actively constructed a range of masculinities. This has taken place within the interrelated nexus of teacher authoritarianism, their own survivalist peer-group cultures, the negotiation of their sexual coming-of-age and the anticipation of their future location in low skilled local labour markets. In the 1990s, for many black and white working-class young people, their post-school anticipation is for the status of a condition of dependency as surplus labour in late-industrial capitalism (Cohen 1987).

Cockburn (1987: 44) has pointed out that:

> The social construction of gender is riddled with resistance and
> the resistance is complex. While some boys refuse the macho
> mode of masculinity and pay the price of being scorned a 'wimp'
> or a 'poofter', others resist the class domination by means of
> masculine codes.

For black male students this resistance is also developed in
relation to racially administered schooling systems. Here, the
students reflected on the specific dynamics and interplay
between state schooling and the construction of black ethnic
masculinities. They were aware of how class-based differentiated curricula helped to shape differentiated masculinities,
with sectors of black and white working-class students developing compensatory hyper-masculine forms in response to their
experience of academic failure. They were also aware of how
black students defensively responded to racialized and gendered
discourses that constructed juxtaposed images of 'weak' Asian
and 'tough' Afro-Caribbean males. They acknowledged the
colonial legacy and present day validity of Mercer and Julien's
(1988: 112) argument that:

> Whereas prevailing definitions of masculinity imply power, con-
> trol and authority, these attributes have been historically denied
> to black men since slavery. The centrally dominant role of the
> white male slave-master in 18th and 19th century plantation
> society debarred black males from the patriarchal privileges
> ascribed to the male masculine role . . . Shaped by this history,
> black masculinity is a highly contradictory formation as it is a
> subordinated masculinity.

What emerges are the specific dynamics for young black
men of their psycho-sexual development within state school
systems and a wider culture that systematically devalues and
marginalizes black masculinities, while elevating and celebrating dominant forms of white straight masculinity. In the following extracts the students make clear the contextual contingency
in which racial and sexual representations and typifications
operate within specific sites.

> *Amerjit*: Teachers can't see the way that schools make kids act
> bad. For a lot of blacks, it's the low classes, the non-academic
> subjects and being pushed into sport that makes them act

macho. It's the way that black and white boys having been failed on the school's terms, try to get some status, some self respect . . . At school you only hear of all the great whites. Most teachers don't respect black men, so the kids think they have no choice but to act it out.

Assim: At our school when we started the whites and the Caribbeans were seen as the toughest. But by the fifth year, the Asian gangs were the worst. They were like the Warrior gang in *Young, Gifted and Black*. They formed gangs, smoked, wore the right gear, trainers and tracksuits, watched violent videos and hung around with older kids with fast cars and the music. Things that a lot of white working-class pupils do, acting hard all the time. But for the Asians, there is also racism. Outside of school, outside our own area, we are always under suspicion and likely to be attacked from the NF and respectable whites. We know that we get attacked because whites see us as easy targets, as weak. They also knew that the teachers were afraid of the Caribbeans because they saw them as tough. Like at school the teachers would avoid walking through groups of black kids but not Asians.

Stephen: In the last place [secondary school] the blacks were seen as the hardest and most against the teachers. There were only a few of them involved in the main anti-school gang but they were the leaders of the posse, as they called themselves. I think a lot of the teachers stereotyped all blacks as aggressive. And I think some of the kids came to believe this about themselves or thought the teachers believed it, so they may as well act it out as they were going to be picked on anyway.

Feminist scholarship in critiquing male ethnographic work on schooling and masculinity has argued that anti-school male student behaviour cannot be reductively read as simply a product of resistance but also acts as a 'legitimation and articulation of power and subordination' (Skeggs 1991; see also Walkerdine 1990 and McRobbie 1991). This research has established the widespread forms of sexual harassment experienced by female students and teachers. Sue Lees graphically describes the significance of the concept of 'reputation' in structuring women's sexuality as part of the wider construction of gender positioning. She argues that:

While everyone apparently knows a slag and stereotypically depicts her as someone who sleeps around, this stereotype bears no relation to girls to whom the term is applied . . . What is important is the existence of the category rather than the identification of certain girls . . . All unattached girls have to be constantly aware that the category slag may be applied to them. There is no hard and fast distinction between the categories since the status is always disputable, the gossip often unreliable, the criteria obscure.

(Lees 1986: 36)

The black gay students examined the links between the institutional and male peer-group surveillance, regulation and control of female and male gender and sexual reputations. They were surprised at the way in which male teachers and students conflated assumed gay behaviour with femininity in order to traduce the former. The assimilation of masculine non-macho behaviour to feminine behaviour was most evident in relation to the 'ubiquity of the term 'poof', which in 'denoting lack of guts, suggests femininity–weakness, softness and inferiority' (Lees 1987: 180; see Cockburn 1987: 41, on the development of the term 'lezzie'). Furthermore, they linked this form of 'gay-bashing' to that of the use of the term 'Paki' as a form of 'Paki-bashing'. Both these labels, 'poof' and 'Paki' have several meanings; sometimes they are used with a specific sexual or racial connotation, while at other times they are used as general terms of abuse. The notoriety and frequency of these labels acted as major mechanisms of policing gender and sexual boundaries with specific implications for Afro-Caribbean and Asian straight and gay youth.

> *Rajinder*: Nearly all the tough kids, the really hard lads, were in the bottom two bands, especially the bottom one. They got their status by fighting the system that they saw abusing them. Some of the toughest ones were the white kids from the estate, always in trouble with the police and teachers. They were obsessed with proving they were real men, like those kids you talked about with their fighting, football and fucking – that was really them . . . They hated 'poofs' and 'Pakis' and used to argue with the teachers when they tried to stop fights, say things like, 'sir, he's only a "Paki" or a "poof" '. They felt that the teachers agreed with them and in some ways they were right. A lot of the men teachers were really into violence but it was official, so that was OK to them. Anything seen as soft in their terms was despised. Like there was all this sexist

talk by teachers. They thought that the best way to control a boy was to say to him, 'stop acting like a girl'. And they always said it loud so all their friends could hear. You see then outside the class the lads could carry on the sexual bullying that the teachers had set up.

Stephen: Playgrounds are really cruel places if you're seen as different or weak. In our school the macho gangs treated girls very bad. And they persecuted me and a few friends, calling us poofs and queer and all that because we weren't like them, didn't act hard like them. We survived because we were big and did not show that we were afraid of them.

Vijay: The tough kids were the best at football, could threaten anyone, had the best reputation with a lot of girls, wore the best gear. They bullied younger kids and girls, and any boys who they thought were soft. White kids joined the gang and together the black and white kids abused Asian kids. They were always talking about 'Pakis' and 'batty men' [a derisory homophobic comment].

Assim: Looking back there wasn't probably that many fights but the physical pressure was there all the time. It was all to do with the way you looked. The clothes, hair and most important the way you stood, walked about, how you talked, just little things that signalled whether you were hard or not.

In contrast to the working-class forms of physical violence, former grammar school students recalled the centrality of verbal violence in serving to police gender and sexual boundaries. The highest peer-group esteem was assigned to those who combined a display of linguistic competence and 'put down' humour. One of the students, Denton Purcell, confided in his best friend that he was confused about his sexuality.

Denton: The next day when some of our mates were around, my friend said, 'your mom must be proud of you, that means she has two washing powders, Persil [Purcell] and Omo [homosexual]'. They all started laughing. They all got the message, as they already thought I was effeminate. It was one of the worst things that ever happened to me. I felt so violated. Thinking about it since we started talking, I can see it was my friend's way of distancing himself from me, not just for the crowd but also for himself. We were very close, not in a sexual way, more emotionally. Like most straight men, he just couldn't cope.

Visibility of 'race' – Invisibility of homosexuality or the normalization of white heterosexuality

Avtar Brah (1992: 134) has written very persuasively of the need to problematize the racialization of white subjectivity (see Hall 1991). I wish to apply her argument to the category of sexuality. In English schools there is a tendency to see questions of sexuality as something primarily to do with gays and lesbians. However, it is politically and pedagogically important to stress that both gay and straight people experience their class, gender and 'race'/ethnicity through sexuality. The sexualization of straight subjectivity is frequently not acknowledged by straights because 'heterosexuality' signifies 'normality' and dominance. Furthermore, there has been little understanding of sexuality as a relational concept in which different non-essentialist sexual identities are defined in relation to each other, with homosexuality always present in heterosexuality. A major task for educators is to deconstruct the complex social and discursive practices that serve to position teachers and students as 'black and white, male and female straights', 'black and white gays and lesbians'. Brah suggests: 'We need to examine how and why the meaning of these words (in relation to 'race' and sexuality) changes from plain descriptions to hierarchically organized categories under given economic, political and social circumstances' (1992: 34).

One of the major issues that emerged in the research was the question of the visibility of 'race' and the invisibility of 'homosexuality' within the context of the school. In order to understand more fully the absence of lesbians and gays from the curriculum, we need to examine the more general question of the official response to the place of sexuality within schools. Beverley Skeggs (1991: 1) has critiqued the way in which 'the discourse on sexuality is either ignored or subsumed within a more general discourse on gender'. Similarly, Wolpe (1988: 100) argues that:

> The ideology on sex and sex education, and its relation to the moral order, structure the official way in which sex and sexuality are handled within a school. In spite of these discourses and the tendency for teachers to accept these seemingly unquestionably, sexual issues are ever present but not necessarily recognised as such by teachers.

The visibility of the students' secondary schools' racial structuring included: predominantly white staff with majority black student populations, racially stratified curriculum and testing systems, the overrepresentation of specific ethnic groups in low status subject areas and racial divisions in classrooms and among student peer groups. More positively at their different schools multi-cultural/anti-racist policies were in operation. Athough these official local state interventions, often unwittingly, tended to reproduce reified conceptions of black ethnic cultures, and the accompanying reinforcement of images of 'them' and 'us', they also provided space to contest dominant racial representations. The students pointed out that 'skin colour' is often read as a key signifier of social exclusion. However, as for their parents, it also has positive, productive elements for young blacks positioned within specific racist discourses, thus enabling them collectively to develop positive social identities. As is argued in *Race Today* (1975: 56):

> This is not to say that there is no distinction between black and white immigrant labour. There is one important distinction, the second generation of white immigrants is not branded by skin colour. Those who are branded are able to maintain a continuity from the new arrivals to new natives.

The students recalled the invisibility of femininities and subordinated masculinities that the acting out of the dominant forms of white teacher and student masculinities served constantly to devalue, marginalize and threaten. Homophobia, compulsory heterosexuality, racism and misogyny circumscribed the prescribed boundaries of what constituted 'normal' male and female behaviour. The invisibility of homosexuality at their secondary schools was structured by a 'policy of omission' – it was as if lesbians and gays did not exist. Much important work on the racial and gender structuring of the curriculum has emphasized how discriminatory practices operate against subordinated groups. Here, the students point out that of equal significance is what is excluded in shaping differential curriculum experiences and outcomes.

> *Raj*: It's like you are black, right, and you can accept the white view of blacks or you can reject it and challenge it. But to say I am a black gay, what does it mean? At school they never suggested that there was a history of gay people or any books

on gays. They never presented any evidence of black gay
people. So, you could think, I must be the only one. At school
you are totally on your own. It's really bad, you know what
I mean? . . . The only times teachers talked about gays was
when they talked about AIDS a few times.

(see also Rogers, this volume)

As part of the research, I interviewed the students' former and
present teachers. Here, I am focusing on white male teachers.
Within the context of a broader concern with the question of
how schools produce a range of masculinities and femininities,
I asked the teachers how they would respond to gay students
'coming out' to them (Mac an Ghaill 1994). The following interview with a teacher in a senior pastoral care post was illustrative of their responses to the question of black students' sexual
identities. Holding on to notions of a unitary self, the teachers
were highly defensive in being unable to rationalize the contradictions of their own positions (Henriques 1984).

Teacher: I don't think a teacher is going to think an Asian or
  black kid is a homosexual, they just wouldn't. They've got
  enough problems dealing with being black. Like you wouldn't
  think of a handicapped person as a homosexual, would you?
  No, you just wouldn't, would you?
M. M.: You said earlier that you would advise a student, if he
  told you he was gay, that he was going through a phase.
Teacher: Yes, definitely. It's part of growing up. Often, these
  kids would be loners, one parent families without a father
  figure, you know?
M. M.: Is this phase true for all boys?
Teacher: I know, you are going to ask, did I go through it? It
  depends on what you mean. But no. I was close to friends,
  male friends as you are at that age. But I was brought up in
  a normal family and all that and I've always known where I
  stood with the ladies.
M. M.: But what about most boys?
Teacher: Well, the experts reckon so, don't they?
M. M.: But wouldn't that include Asian and black boys?
Teacher: You've tricked me. I must say I've never thought of the
  black kids here like that. Well like a lot of theories they over-
  generalize. If you saw the big black kids here, you'd see what
  I mean. We have to pull them away from the girls. The black
  kids are obsessed with them but to be fair to the lads, the girls
  do lead them on, hanging around all the time. I could say with
  certainty, there's no way they've got any homosexual ideas.

The intersection of these homophobic and racist discourses produced contradictions and confusions. On the one hand, in interviews with me, in relation to issues of gay sexuality, the teachers appealed to black parents' religious beliefs as a major legitimate justification for not taking a positive pedagogical stance towards gay students. On the one hand, as the students stressed, white teachers tended to caricature Asian and Afro-Caribbean male students and their parents as intrinsically more sexist than whites. In class discussions the teachers were preoccupied with explaining the difficulty of implementing an anti-sexist curriculum which they claimed conflicted with traditional ethnic cultures. Rajinder informed a teacher that he was gay and was most surprised that the teacher responded primarily in racial terms, projecting his own difficulties with the issue of sexuality on to the Asian community.

> *Rajinder*: At school there's no such thing as sexuality, so it seems. Then one day you come out and say you're gay and then you find out that it's the most important thing in the world. The teachers try everything to change you. 'It's a phase, you need psychiatric help, it's unnatural, it's against your religion, your parents won't accept you, your friends will reject you, you won't get a job'. I've heard it all. I think that teachers feel more threatened by gays than any other group.

What is heterosexuality? Or are straights 'born' or 'made'?

Lesley Hall (1991: 2) in her study of the hidden history of straight men's sexual fears and failures provides much evidence to reveal the 'considerable tensions between the ideals set up and the lived experience of men as they perceived it, and that the "normal" male and male sexuality were more problematic than they are usually assumed to be'. The gay students felt that these tensions took on specific cultural forms for young straight men within the context of secondary schooling that involved the performance of publicly exaggerated modes of masculinity.

> *Amerjit*: If you tell your friends you're gay, they ask you, what's it like? It's as if they think that it's totally different from their own sexuality. But you know that although they are straight,

at least publicly, they have a lot of doubts and difficulties about how they feel, about relationships, girls, sex . . . Girls are a lot more honest. If you're a man you can't show these doubts – not in public. But if you listen, you hear it all; that straights are scared of women, unsure about themselves and tired of acting things out. It's incredible you as the gay person are supposed to be the one with all the difficulties and they just turn it round. It's probably what women have to listen to all the time. And these straights are too arrogant to see that they may be afraid of us but they are a major cause of gay's and women's problems.

In an earlier paper (Mac an Ghaill 1991: 297) in which some of these students were involved, I wrote of how the gay students described the construction of ambiguous and transitional identities in their sexual coming-of-age. They spoke of:

the formation of their sexual identity as part of a wider process of adolescent development, with all its fluidity, experiments, displacements and confusions. For them sexuality could not be reduced to the conventional perception of a heterosexual–homosexual continuum, on which each group's erotic and emotional attachments are demarcated clearly and unambiguously. They spoke of the contradictions of the public–private worlds that gave them an insight into the complexity and confusion of young males' sexual coming-of-age. They have become experts at decoding the ambivalent social and sexual meanings of heterosexual behaviour involved in male bonding and rites of passage.

The black gay students developed their arguments concerning the contextual contingency and ambiguity of learning to become a man within an overall rampant school culture of compulsory heterosexuality (Cockburn 1987: 44). One of the main issues that emerged during the research was the question of the political and cultural meanings of modern forms of heterosexuality. For the students, most of whom held a social constructivist perspective, ambivalent misogyny, contingent homophobia and racism were contradictory constitutive elements of white male forms of heterosexuality. They recalled white boys, in learning to be straight men, obsessively distancing themselves from ascriptions of femininity and homosexuality within themselves and towards others. Hence gender/sexual identities were perceived as highly unstable categories that their schools, alongside other institutions, attempted to administer, regulate and reify. Most particularly, this administration, regulation and reification of gender/sexual boundaries was institutionalized through the interrelated social and discursive practices of staffroom, classroom and playground cultures. Much work remains to be done on the intersection of the specific social and psycho-dynamics of these processes at the local school level.

Plusses of being black gays

There is much evidence from lesbian and gay literature of the physical, psychological and verbal abuse that lesbian and gay people systematically experience in homophobic and heterosexist societies (Burbage and Walters 1981). The young men in this chapter report similar personal and institutional experiences of such abuse. However, it is important for educationalists in trying to understand the social positioning of these young people, not to adopt a reductionist pedagogical approach that sees gays and lesbians as mere problems or victims. In a recent *Guardian* article on the experience of young gays in England, two young lesbians suggest a guarded optimism about the future (Simpson 1992: 19). They claim that:

> 'Things are changing', Emily says. 'But in a confusing way,' Rebecca says. 'Attitudes are becoming more tolerant, but prejudice is responding by becoming more hidden and violent. But if we fight for our rights I believe that we can beat prejudice for good'.

The students provided much evidence in the study to support Peter Aggleton's (1987: 108) claim that being gay is in many circumstances a positive and creative experience.

> *Rajinder*: Teachers, especially male teachers assume your being gay is a problem but there are a lot of plusses. In fact I think one of the main reasons that male straights hate us is because they really know that emotionally we are more worked out than them. We can talk about and express our feelings, our emotions in a positive way. They can only express negative feelings like hatred, anger and dominance. Who would like to be like them?

Raj: It's like when you gave that talk at the university about having several identities. I don't think that most people could understand because really everything about them is taken for granted. Their Englishness, their whiteness, their culture, their gender and sexuality – it's just the norm for them. And that's what's really good about being a black gay, you have no choice, you have to question these things. I think what I've learned most in us being together for the last two years is that the questions can be on our terms, not theirs.

Denton: I agree. That's why people like James Baldwin and Langston Hughes are so important for us. Yes, the world is going to hate us but people like them got through and in a lot of ways it was worse, much worse for them. And you feel very proud that they are part of our history . . . They've made me more aware of other outsiders who are oppressed in this society. I used to feel really bad about being gay and I still get really down at times. But through being black and gay even if I don't stay gay, I know myself more than white men, than straights do.

Without reducing black gay masculinity to a unitary category the students' analysis finds a resonance in Isaac Julien's comment (in Bourne 1991: 27) that:

Where I see myself different from a number of white activists is that I think that they are more interested in sex and sexuality as an emphasis. When I was involved very early on in the Black Lesbian and Gay Group, we were interested in issues of policing and gender. These kinds of debates were related to debates around black masculinity and I think that generally this is a debate that takes a far more fundamentally important position in black politics than it takes in gay politics. I don't know how a gay political discourse takes on these questions of black masculinity. I think that black communities are written off as homophobic.

Stephen: I think that gays and lesbians have been really good at working through the differences between sex and gender to produce progressive politics. And the whole HIV experience and the response of the media has put gays, white and black, on the frontline. Now there's lots of differences among black gays but maybe we have taken a broader agenda, such as issues around gender and the treatment of the black community.

Andrew: Reading through this study it shows, yes we are pushed to the margins of society as black gays. But that doesn't mean we have to accept that position. We can educate ourselves to understand the different oppressions. And you can see here that our position can be positive in helping us to work out ways forward not just for gays and blacks but for others as well because we are questioning whiteness and heterosexuality that is usually very hidden.

Conclusion

Against a rather pessimistic English socio-political background, outlined in the introduction, Ozga (1990: 361) offers a way forward, arguing the case for the continuing validity in analysis of education policy of combining a state-centred perspective with detailed investigations of policy implementation. She writes:

> Explanations of education policy which take as their starting point the role of the state are inherently concerned with the contradictory nature of the demands made upon the state, and by the tensions caused by the requirement upon it to deal simultaneously with these requirements . . . Those investigations must of course be informed by individuals' perceptions and experiences, and the informing framework must be interrogated by such material and tested against it.

At present, young people, collectively and individually are constructing their identities, at a time of rapid socio-economic and political change, that has led to a major disruption in the process of coming-of-age in the 'enterprise culture'. For example, Willis (1985: 6) speaks of how the unemployed now find themselves in a 'new social condition of suspended animation between school and work. Many of the old transitions into work, into the cultures and organisations of work, into being consumers, into independent accommodation – have been frozen or broken.' As the students demonstrate above, their preparation for these transitions are further structured by an articulation of complex forms of social differences. Within this new social condition the young gay students here can be seen as an example of the new generation of black intellectuals, of whom Mercer (1992: 110) writes:

In the hands of this new generation of black diaspora intellectuals rethinking sex . . . [they] simultaneously critique the exclusions and absences which previously rendered black lesbian and gay identities invisible, and reconstruct new pluralistic forms of collective belonging and imagined community that broaden the public sphere of multicultural society.

Acknowledgements

A special thanks to the students, who collaborated in the production of the study, and especially to Rajinder. My thanks to the parents and teachers who have taken part. This chapter has benefited from the comments of Debbie Epstein and Richard Johnson.

Note

1 In order to maintain the anonymity of those involved, all the names of the students and teachers are pseudonyms.

References

Aggleton, P. (1987) *Deviance*. London: Tavistock.

Arnot, M. (1992) Feminism, education and the New Right. In M. Arnot and L. Barton (eds) *Voicing Concerns: Perspectives on Contemporary Educational Reforms*. London: Triangle Books.

Bhavnani, K.-K. (1991) *Talking Politics: A Psychological Framing for Views from Youth in Britain*. Cambridge: Cambridge University Press.

Bourne, S. (1991) Putting the record straight, *Gay Times*, 155, August.

Brah, A. (1992) Difference, diversity and differentiation. In J. Donald and A. Rattansi (eds) *'Race', Culture and Difference*. London: Open University/Sage, pp. 126–45.

Bryan, B., Dadzie, S. and Scafe, S. (1985) *The Heart of the Race: Black Women's Lives in Britain*. London: Virago.

Burbage, M. and Walters, J. (eds) (1981) *Breaking the Silence: Gay Teenagers Speak for Themselves*. London: Joint Council for Gay Teenagers.

Carrigan, T., Connell, R. W. and Lee, J. (1985) Hard and heavy phenomena: the sociology of masculinity, *Theory*, 14, 551–604.

Cockburn, C. (1987) *Two-Track Training: Sex Inequality and the YTS*. London: Macmillan.

Cohen, P. (1987) *Racism and Popular Culture: A Cultural Studies Approach*, Working paper No. 9. London: Institute of Education.

Connell, R. W. (1989) Cool guys, swots and wimps: the inter-play of masculinity and education, *Oxford Review of Education*, 15(3), 291–303.

Fanon, F. (1970) *Black Skin, White Masks*. London: Paladin.

Freire, P. (1985) *The Politics of Education*. London: Macmillan.

Gordon, P. and Klug, F. (1986) *New Right, New Racism*. London: Searchlight Publications.

Griffin, C. (1987) The eternal adolescent: psychology and the creation of adolescence. Paper presented at the Symposium of the Ideological Impact of Social Psychology, British Psychological Association Conference, Oxford University.

Hall, C. (1991) Missing stories: gender and ethnicity in England in the 1830s and 1840s. In L. Grossberg, C. Nelson and P. Treichler (eds) *Cultural Studies*. London: Routledge.

Hall, L. (1991) *Hidden Anxieties: Male Sexuality, 1990–1950*. London: Polity Press.

Henriques, J. (1984) Social psychology and the politics of racism. In J. Henriques, W. Hollway, C. Urwin, C. Venn and V. Walkerdine *Changing the Subject: Psychology, Social Regulation and Subjectivity*. London: Methuen.

hooks, b. (1991) *Yearning: Race, Gender and Cultural Politics*. Boston MA: Turnaround.

Kelly, L. (1992) Not in front of the children: responding to right-wing agendas on sexuality and education. In M. Arnot and L. Barton (eds) *Voicing Concerns: Perspectives on Contemporary Educational Reforms*. London: Triangle Books.

Klein, M. (1960) *Our Adult World and its Roots in Infancy*. London: Tavistock.

Lees, S. (1986) *Losing Out: Sexuality and Adolescent Girls*. London: Hutchinson.

Lees, S. (1987) The structure of sexual relations in school. In M. Arnot and G. Weiner (eds) *Gender and Politics of Schooling*. London: Hutchinson/Open University.

Mac an Ghaill, M. (1989a) Beyond the white Norm: the use of qualitative research in the study of black students' schooling in England, *Qualitative Studies in Education*, 2(3), 175–89.

Mac an Ghaill, M. (1989b) Coming-of-age in 1980s England: reconceptualising black students' schooling experience, *British Journal of Sociology of Education*, 10(3), 273–86.

Mac an Ghaill, M. (1991) Schooling, sexuality and male power; towards an emancipatory curriculum, *Gender and Education*, 3(3), 291–309.

Mac an Ghaill, M. (1994) *The Making of Men: Masculinities, Sexualities and Schooling*. Buckingham: Open University Press.

McRobbie, A. (1991) *Feminism and Youth Culture*. London: Macmillan.

Mama, A. (1992) Black women and the British state: race, class and gender analysis for the 1990s. In P. Braham, A. Rattansi and R. Skellington (eds) *Racism and Antiracism: Inequalities, Opportunities and Policies*. London: Sage/Open University.

Mercer, K. (1992) Just looking for trouble: Robert Mapplethorpe and fantasies. In L. Segal and M. McIntosh (eds) *Sex Exposed: Sexuality and the Pornography Debate*. London: Virago.

Mercer, K. and Julien, I. (1988) Race, sexual politics and black masculinity: a dossier. In R. Chapman and J. Rutherford (eds) *Male Order: Unwrapping Masculinities*. London: Lawrence and Wishart.

Miles, R. (1989) *Racism*. London: Routledge.

Morgan, D. H. J. (1992) *Discovering Men: Critical Studies on Men and Masculinities*. London: Routledge.

Nava, M. (1992) *Changing Cultures: Feminism, Youth and Consumerism*. London: Sage.

Ozga, J. (1990) Policy research and policy theory: a comment on Fitz and Halpin, *Journal of Education Policy*, 5(4), 359–67.

Pajaczkowska, C. and Young, L. (1992) Racism, representation and psychoanalysis. In J. Donald and A. Rattansi (eds) *'Race', Culture and Difference*. London: Open University/Sage.

Race Today (1975) Who's afraid of ghetto schools?, 1(1), 8 January.

Rattansi, A. (1992) Changing the subject? Racism, culture and education. In J. Donald and A. Rattansi (eds) *'Race', Culture and Difference*. London: Open University/Sage.

Rowbotham, S. (1989) *The Past is Before Us: Feminism in Action Since the 1960s*. Harmondsworth: Penguin.

Rutherford, J. (1990) A place called home: identity and the cultural politics of difference. In J. Rutherford (ed.) *Identity: Community, Culture and Difference*. London: Lawrence and Wishart.

Simpson, M. (1992) Out of the closet, into the fire, *Guardian*, 19 August, p. 19.

Skeggs, B. (1991) The cultural production of 'Learning to Labour'. In M. Barker and A. Breezer (eds) *Readings in Culture*. London: Routledge.

Troupe, Q. (1989) *James Baldwin: The Legacy*. New York: Simon and Schuster/Touchstone.

Walkerdine, V. (1990) *Schoolgirl Fictions*. London: Verso.

Weeks, J. (1989) *Sexuality and Its Discontents: Meanings, Myths and Modern Sexualities*. London: Routledge.

Weeks, J. (1990) The value of difference. In J. Rutherford (ed.) *Identity: Community, Culture, Difference*. London: Lawrence and Wishart.

Westwood, S. (1990) Racism, black masculinity and the politics of space. In J. Hearn and D. Morgan (eds) *Men, Masculinities and Social Theory*. London: Hyman.

Williams, R. (1961) *The Long Revolution*. Harmondsworth: Penguin.

Williams, R. (1977) *Marxism and Literature*. Oxford: Oxford University Press.

Willis, P. (1985) *Youth Unemployment and the New Poverty: A Summary of Local Authorily Review and Framework for Policy Development on Youth and Youth Unemployment*. Wolverhampton: Wolverhampton Local Authority.

Wolpe, A. M. (1988) *Within School Walls: The Role of Discipline, Sexuality and the Curriculum*. London: Routledge.

PART III

Historical and Theoretical Issues

CHAPTER 12

Coming Out in the National Union of Teachers

GILLIAN SPRAGGS

To 'come out', to identify oneself openly as lesbian or gay, is an odd experience. For people who have never questioned their heterosexuality, it is probably quite difficult to imagine. It is about taking loaded words, dangerous words, words that are widely pronounced with embarrassment and fear and distaste, and claiming them, with passion and defiance, as names for oneself: first alone, and then with people whose response one trusts, and eventually in front of friends and family, colleagues and strangers. At each stage, it is terrifying; it is also exhilarating. It is a moment of vulnerability, but it is also an assertion of freedom, a bringing into the open of a part of the self and its experience that would otherwise be left submerged: a part that one has been taught by extreme sanctions to despise and conceal, but that is nevertheless felt to be intensely precious, a source of meaning and power.

The risks are real: from cooling of friendships to harassment at work, public insult, and even physical assault. For many people, a gay man or a lesbian who is open about himself or herself is a repulsive and terrifying figure. In their eyes, when one identifies oneself as lesbian or gay, one is primarily making a statement about one's personal sexual behaviour; coming out is felt as a form of indecent exposure, intruding that contaminating secret, sex, into the public view, in a context in which the familiar, sterilizing conventions of monogamous heterosexuality are flagrantly neglected. Moreover, those of us who are lesbian or gay are generally believed to reverse or reject the social and sexual roles that are considered to be appropriate to our respective genders, and so we are conceived of as dangerous subversives, disrupting rightful and natural order.

By coming out, one is, of course, making a statement about one's sexual desires and practice. And in one way and another, many lesbians and gay men do resist traditional gender roles. But when I say that I am a lesbian, I am opening a gate behind which lie a great many more very important things: the central relationship in my life, and much of my experience of love; my experiences as a co-parent, and my affection for my lover's children; several, though by no means all, of my closest friendships; quite a few of the books I read, and the films I watch, and the plays I go to see; a considerable part of the reasons for my wariness towards policemen and fundamentalist Christians. So long as I remain 'in the closet', my sexual preference discreetly hidden, all these things and much more remain unspoken, almost entirely invisible. I conduct my interactions with the people around me through a deliberately constructed self-presentation that is not merely asexual but excludes or drastically distorts almost every aspect of my daily life, affectional, intellectual, political and aesthetic.

But when I choose to move out of the closet, I have to recognize that there is still no guarantee that I shall be able to speak my life and be heard. For many people, the imagined figure of that predatory, man-aping, man-hating, sex-obsessed monster, the evil lezzie, will still shout much louder than anything I myself might say or do. Yet it is only when lesbians come out that the two-dimensional, hostile stereotypes can be seriously challenged, and the rich, variety of ways in which a lesbian life may be lived begins to be more widely understood.

Coming out is a process, never a once for all time act. Many, perhaps most of us move in and out of the closet several times a day, depending on where we are and who we are with: at home, at work, with family, with trusted friends. There are longer term patterns, too: it is not uncommon for gay people to move from a situation in which they have been relatively open about themselves to one in which they have felt constrained to silence. School teaching is a profession in which the pressures against speaking out are generally very strong indeed. Like other people I have met, I experienced the move into teaching, after several years of student life, as a sudden plunge into a closet of almost stifling airlessness.

Successful teaching in any subject is a kind of performance art. As with all artists, your basic material is yourself and your experience: what you have learned and tested and explored. It is an interpretative art; you are offering your students ways of setting about the task of interpreting and reinventing the world they find around them. To hide what you have learned, about yourself, about possible ways of living, in contexts where it is relevant to what students wish to know, need to know – that feels deeply irresponsible. I am not just talking here about homosexuality, although that is a subject about which most teenagers are curious and very ignorant. I am talking about matters such as love and parenthood, and relations with one's own parents. My experiences of all these things and much else are so intricately involved with my sexual identity as to be virtually impossible for me to talk about in any situation where that remains obscure. I was an English teacher. Much of the time, I taught my subject in a mode of rigid and safe academicism. That was not the kind of teaching that fired my own enthusiasm as a teenager. I think that my pupils were cheated.

As for me: like many lesbians and gay men in the teaching profession, I was always aware of a provisional quality to my professional life, a sense of uncertainty and risk. Most of us know a few stories: the deputy head who was forced to agree to a change of schools because of staffroom hostility, the head of RE who resigned after repeatedly being jeered in the class-room, the games teacher compulsorily transferred to careers (one can't allow a lesbian among all those half-dressed girls). Not even the most cautious of closeted teachers can be entirely sure that she or he will never be the focus of some such damaging scenario. In this atmosphere, the choice of a trade union becomes a major decision. Is there a teacher union that will offer sound legal advice, good advocacy, and unstinting support to a lesbian, gay or bisexual teacher caught up in the complex, punishing machinery of complaints or disciplinary procedures?

There are two Trades Union Congress-affiliated teacher unions. In the late 1970s, the General Secretary of the National Association of Schoolmasters/Union of Women Teachers,

Terry Casey, announced his support for the exclusion of homosexuals from the teaching profession in a widely reported statement. In 1980, therefore, as a student teacher, I saw no alternative but to join the National Union of Teachers. The official policy of the NUT at that time as regards homosexual teachers had been expressed several years earlier, in response to an inquiry on that subject from the National Council for Civil Liberties. The Union asserted that it was

> naturally . . . concerned about any form of discrimination or interference with members in the exercise of the [sic] professional duties, and we would provide the full resources of the Union to any member that required assistance.
>
> (NCCL n.d.: 20)

Well, you can't ask more than that. Or can you?

At around the time that it was sending this assurance to the NCCL, the National Union was taking up a far from supportive position in the case of John Warburton, a teacher who had recently been suspended from employment by the Inner London Education Authority. Seen by one of his pupils as he was taking part in a demonstration for gay rights, he had found himself faced by jeers and insults from several of his classes. He responded by acknowledging that he was gay, and engaging in short discussions with his students as to what this meant. In this way, he was able to restore order, and his classes returned to working normally. Six weeks later, a similar episode occurred with a different class. On this occasion, news of the incident reached one of his colleagues, who reported it to the head. Subsequently, he was asked by the ILEA to sign an agreement that he would never again discuss his homosexuality with pupils. Warburton's refusal to do so was based on his beliefs, firstly, that it is never right for a teacher to allow perceived prejudice to pass without comment in the classroom, and secondly, that he would no longer be able to maintain order and teach effectively in a situation in which he was prevented from defending himself against taunts from pupils.

The NUT's advice to Warburton, in a letter from Doug McAvoy, at that time the Union's Deputy General Secretary, was that he should be prepared to sign the required statement, on the grounds that 'Teachers (including homosexual teachers) do not . . . have a basic right to instigate classroom discussion on sexual topics' (Gay Teachers' Group 1978: 37). In subsequent letters, McAvoy conceded that Warburton had never initiated the discussions that had so appalled the ILEA, but argued that he had nevertheless been responsible for allowing them to take place. But the crucial point in the Union's position here is that homosexuality is understood to be purely to do with sex. The fact that, like heterosexuality, it is also a social and cultural phenomenon is ignored. And the fact that teachers regularly discuss sexuality with their classes, particularly in its social and cultural aspects, is conveniently ignored also. Literature teachers may read *Jane Eyre* with their classes, or the love poems of Thomas Hardy, teachers of sociology or religious education may instigate debates on the institution of marriage, and no one reproaches them for discussing such matters outside a formal programme of sex education.

In one of his later letters, McAvoy made a further point, which requires examination:

> Most teachers endeavour to avoid a discussion of their own personal views and experiences, because to do otherwise would be to bring the teacher's personality into the discussion. The affirmation of a teacher's standpoint on religion, politics or sex or any other aspect of his [sic] personal life could alienate a class, or it could disturb a child whose inclinations were different from those of an admired or respected teacher.
>
> (Gay Teachers' Group 1978: 41)

It is not a teacher's business to emphasize continually her or his own opinions, let alone to press pupils to agree with them. But to assert that most teachers efface their own personalities when teaching is manifest nonsense, and to suggest that it is desirable that they should seek to do so is to disregard many of the realities of the classroom situation. An anecdote from life may drum home a point, whether of geography, grammar or ethics, far more effectively than any amount of impersonal exposition. Moreover, in a context in which pupils are pressured continually to expose their own experiences and thoughts, whether in classroom discussion, story writing or formal essay, the assumption by the teacher of self-protective silence and aloofness is neither pedagogically useful nor morally appealing. In practice, of course, most teachers, while maintaining personal privacy as it seems to them appropriate, continually make effective illustrative use of their own experiences; and all thoughtful teachers recognize the value of honesty, without which there can scarcely be mutual respect between class and teacher.

At the time I joined the NUT, I was aware of the Warburton case through the pamphlet *Open + Positive*, published by the London Gay Teachers' Group in 1978. As a result, I had no great confidence that the Union would offer any useful support to me as a lesbian. Still, to join a union that paid lip service to the idea of equal treatment was clearly preferable to joining one whose leaders wanted to see me hounded out of the teaching profession. For several years, like the majority of members, I paid my dues and stayed away from meetings.

In 1982, following a long campaign by London Gay Teachers' Group, the Chief Inspector of the ILEA formally lifted what was by then an eight year prohibition by the authority on the employment of John Warburton as a teacher. The right of gay teachers to come out to pupils was explicitly recognized. The following year, the Gay Teachers' Group pamphlet *School's Out* was launched at the National Conference of the NUT, and several members of the group came out publicly during debates. They argued that the Union should take up the issue of gay rights alongside its work on gender and race: that it should encourage teachers to challenge pupils when they used anti-gay insults to each other, seek to influence schools to include positive images of lesbians and gay men in the curriculum and support lesbian and gay teachers so that they could feel able to be as open and honest with their pupils as their heterosexual colleagues. In response, the conference was totally polarized: many delegates were moved and impressed by the courage shown by these gay men, while others jeered and booed (Gay Teachers' Group 1987: 96–105).

At some point during 1983, I bought a copy of *School's Out*. It was both heartening and terrifying to read statements by openly gay teachers, and impressive to hear about the pioneering educational work that was beginning to be carried out by the ILEA. None of it connected very much with my experience as an isolated, closeted lesbian teacher in a traditionally-run sixth form college in a Midland county. However, it confirmed my view that the NUT, in spite of the ambivalence of its leaders, had been the right teaching union for me to join.

In 1985, the NUT embarked on major strike action. The main objective was to restore teachers' pay, the level of which had been declining over many years, but for many of us the issues at stake were felt to be much wider. We believed that we were fighting a last-ditch battle in support of the state education service against a government that was already showing disturbing signs of a will to undermine and even abrogate the principle of a free, quality education for all. This was the atmosphere in which I became an active member of my local NUT association, City of Leicester, regularly attending meetings and acting as representative for my college. For nearly a year I kept silent about my sexuality. Then in the summer of 1986 a special equal opportunities meeting was announced, half of which was to be taken up specifically by a discussion of gay rights. I was shaken, elated, and scared. I knew that I could not attend such a meeting and contribute to the debate without coming out as a lesbian. I could not miss the meeting without acknowledging to myself that I was a coward, which would be intolerable. Moreover, there was a large part of me that was heartily sick of the closet. I had already settled in my own mind that if my students ever challenged or questioned me about my sexuality, I would be honest with them.

The session on gay rights opened with a report by two members of the association on the 'New Dimensions in Local Government' conference that they had recently attended in Nottingham. John Dryden, who introduced himself as a gay man, spoke of the revelation that he had found it to meet trade unionists from local authority unions that had already committed themselves to policies on gay and lesbian rights. He was followed by Lena Milosevic, who after coming out as a lesbian, threw out a challenging question: 'What is my union doing for me?' In the discussion that followed, the association officers made it clear that the answer, at that time, was 'not a lot'. They suggested setting up a working party to advise on a local code of practice and to develop ideas for campaigning within the National Union. I came out during that debate. What I remember most is my amazement and relief when no one, in a crowded meeting, expressed any hostility to gay people or even argued against the view that the issue was one that the Union needed to address. I also remember the extraordinary mixture of excitement, vulnerability and deep sense of purpose that I experienced afterwards, when the meeting had adjourned to the pub.

As it was set up originally, the Leicester working party was a mixed gay and heterosexual group, open to anyone who cared to come along. This was an important source of its strength. Those of us who were lesbian or gay had specific ideas about what we would like to see happen; we were less clear about how we might set about achieving these aims. Several of the hetero-sexual members of the association who regularly attended the working party were experienced union activists. To begin with, they knew little about gay issues, but they did know exactly how to use the communication channels and decision making structures of the NUT to influence national policy and put pressure on the Union's Executive. But first, we all had to learn to understand each other and work together.

The first meeting was nearly a fiasco. The association had booked a room in a local community college. Unfortunately, it turned out to be the library, and there were several pupils still working at one of the tables. John, Lena and I, at that point the only gay and lesbian members of the working party, were acutely aware of this, and reacted by becoming extremely guarded. The other people who had turned up grew increasingly baffled and impatient. With no useful input from us, they were at a loss as to how to proceed. At last, the school students packed up and left, and the talking seriously began. For a long time, our colleagues could not believe how wary and anxious the three of us were. After all, we had each of us come out publicly in a union meeting. We had to make it clear to them that a willingness to come out in one situation did not mean that we felt ready to be open about ourselves at any time, in front of any group of people. After a while, they began to under-stand that the depth of our anxiety reflected real experiences of oppression. Like many people who pride themselves on their own lack of prejudice, they had never fully recognized how pervasively anti-gay our society is, nor had they understood imaginatively what it is like to experience that hostility repeatedly in one's day-to-day life. It was a painful discussion, but valuable. Out of it came an agreement on the group's first principle: complete confidentiality. No one who came to the meetings should assume that he or she was free to reveal outside the group that one of its members was lesbian or gay unless they had that person's explicit agreement. After that first occasion, we always met in private houses, and though the dates of meetings were always publicized within the association, information about the venues could only be obtained by people who rang the group's contact numbers or directly approached the association secretary.

In that and later meetings we formulated our main aim: to see a resolution in support of gay rights passed by the Union's National Conference, and to press for such a policy, once adopted, to be translated into effective action. And so we embarked on several years of time-consuming, often tedious publicizing and procedural foot-slogging. First, we drafted a code of practice on lesbian and gay rights to put to the Leicester association. In formulating this code, we drew heavily on ideas contained in the Gay Teachers' Group pamphlet, *School's Out*, and in the Greater London Council publication, *Changing the World. A London Charter for Gay and Lesbian Rights*. Paragraph four of the code that we drew up reads:

> This association undertakes to support any gay, lesbian or bisexual members who encounter prejudice and discrimination in their professional life. This includes those members who choose to come out to other staff or to pupils.

A motion to adopt the code of practice was passed by City of Leicester NUT Association, and shortly afterwards it was also adopted by Mid-Leicestershire Association and Leicestershire Division. In addition, City of Leicester agreed to mail a copy of the code to each of the Union local associations, together with an appeal for support in piloting a motion on gay rights through the National Conference. This motion, which was closely based on the code of practice, now became the focus of our plans. However, early in 1987 we heard that it had failed to reach the conference agenda for that year.

One of the ideas that had been mooted at the very first meeting was that the group should put together a short book, along similar lines to *School's Out*. This was the germ of *Outlaws in the Classroom*, launched at the 1987 National Conference after several weeks of feverish last-minute effort, and written mainly by members of the working party and their friends. Indeed, we didn't only write it, we word-processed it, collated it, bound it, guillotined it, and organized the distribution – everything but actually print it. It was pilloried in the tabloids, blandly noticed in the quality press, and for the amateur publication it was, it sold extremely well, selling a thousand copies in a few months. And it brought us, in a small way, quite a lot of fame. Somewhat to our bemusement, we found that we were now reputed to be experts on all aspects of lesbian and gay educational issues. Members of the group were asked to run workshops, write articles, and facilitate meetings at conferences. A welcome sign that we were making an impression on the Union at a national level came in the form of an invitation to Leicestershire Division to run a workshop on lesbian and gay issues at the Equal Opportunities Conference in June. To any group with a cause to publicize, I would certainly recommend writing a book – with the warning that books themselves need publicity, they don't sell automatically.

Not all the attention we received at that time was positive. Alerted by the press reports, the right-wing Conservative MP, Peter Bruinvels, who sat for a Leicester constituency, announced his intention of demanding that our group be investigated by the education authority with a view to identifying and sacking its members. Fortunately, he lost interest when the electorate sacked him in the General Election a few weeks later. That same General Election, followed by the Conservative Party Conference later that year, saw the Conservatives and their supporters busily seeking to stir up anti-gay hatred and use it to political ends. They made a particular point of misrepresenting the pioneering work that a handful of Labour authorities, notably Haringey and the ILEA, had begun to carry out in education. A few months later the notorious Clause 28 was introduced, with government support, into what became the Local Government Act 1988.

The story of the campaign against Clause (now Section) 28, which forbids local authorities to 'intentionally promote homosexuality', has been told in other places (Sanders and Spraggs 1989). In common with all the other lesbian and gay groups in the country, the Leicester working party involved itself heavily in the campaign. Meanwhile, arrangements for the 1988 Easter Conference of the NUT were well under way. Initially, we had been pessimistic. Despite efforts to publicize our motion, far fewer associations than we had hoped had put it forward. Then, at the prioritization stage, in January, support surged. The motion came second in the Equal Opportunities Section, which meant that a debate was now a likelihood. There can be no doubt that what made the difference was Clause 28, and the vigorous campaign that so many lesbians and gays and their supporters were mounting against it.

A few weeks later, the National Union published a circular that condemned Clause 28 in the strongest terms. It not only affirmed the Union's support for the employment rights of lesbian and gay teachers, it also stated that 'a teacher's statement of personal position in classoom discussion, whether of sexual preference, religious or political affiliation, should never jeopardise that teacher's employment'. Moreover, it made the point that teachers have a responsibility to assist all pupils to achieve a positive self-image, and asserted that teachers should 'discourage prejudiced behaviour and attitudes by pupils towards homosexuals'.[1] In terms of NUT policy, this document was a landmark. Indeed, it marks a position to which subsequent public statements by the Union have never fully matched up. Certainly, the rival motion – technically a 'delete-all' amendment – that the Union's Executive added to the Conference agenda in response to our own was altogether more cautious in tone. In particular, although it committed the Union to reject 'all discrimination on grounds of sexual orientation', it made no specific reference to the right of lesbian and gay teachers to be open about their sexuality – and as events were to show, this was not an inadvertent omission.

At the NUT Conference, on the evening of Easter Sunday, City of Leicester Association held a fringe meeting on lesbian and gay rights in education. Between 200 and 250 conference delegates crowded in to hear a number of guest speakers, including the activist Peter Tatchell, Anne Matthews, leader of Southwark Council, and the comedian Simon Fanshawe. The following afternoon, the Conference reached the Equal Opportunities Section of the agenda.

We had always been clear in the Working Party that once our motion actually reached Conference, we wanted to see the proposing speech made by a lesbian or gay teacher, and not by one of our heterosexual supporters. Politically, our instincts were sound. When Lena Milosevic addressed the Conference about her personal experiences of oppression as

a lesbian teacher, she held the attention of the delegates riveted
– a rare event. After she had finished, well over half of those
present stood to applaud her, and if a vote had been taken
that afternoon, it seems likely that our original motion would
have been passed without amendment. Unfortunately, the time
allocated to the Equal Opportunities Section was too short, and
the debate had to be adjourned until unfinished business could
be taken on the Wednesday.

Lena's speech made the television news that evening, and
the national papers next day. The *Guardian* described it as
'a courageous plea', the *Yorkshire Post* called it 'moving'. Other
reports were not so positive, but most acknowledged her
remarkable impact on the conference delegates. Altogether,
the coverage was much less savage than we had feared. However, although the Leicester delegation had anticipated press
attention, they were appalled by the really aggressive treatment to which Lena was subjected by a small handful of photo-
graphers and journalists, who over the next two days followed
her around, tried to force their way into the hotel, and so on.
Their activities placed her under a considerable strain. More
cheeringly, during this time she received numerous messages of
personal encouragement from individuals and delegations at the
conference.

Meanwhile, the Union's Executive, rattled by the unexpected
depth of support for the Leicester motion, appeared to be
seeking to do a deal. One Executive member cornered Lena and
tried to bully her into accepting the 'delete-all' amendment as
'friendly', on the interesting grounds that the Union could not
be expected to find the money to defend all the 'out' lesbian and
gay members who in the Executive's pessimistic view were likely
to face harassment and unfair dismissal as soon as Clause 28
had passed into law. Years later, I am still stunned at the
arrogance and insensitivity here, at the bizarre concept that is
implied of the Union's responsibilities to its members, and the
brutality of such an approach to a teacher who had just come
out in front of the entire nation.

When the debate resumed on the Wednesday, the main
criticism levelled by members of the Executive against the
Leicester motion was precisely this: it would have committed
the Union explicitly to support teachers who were open about
their homosexuality. Sickeningly, it was even argued that our

motion would put lesbian and gay teachers at risk, by encouraging them to come out. Much scaremongering play was made with vague and inaccurate references to Clause 28. The vote, when it was taken, was very close; the President had to make his count twice, before he announced, to some open incredulity, that the main motion was lost. At this point the Executive amendment became the main motion. No speeches were made against it, and it was passed with only two dissenting voices. For the first time, the NUT was formally committed to a policy of support for lesbian and gay rights. We felt, on the whole, that it was a victory worth celebrating, though we also wrote immediately to Fred Jarvis, at that time the Union's General Secretary, and *The Teacher*, the NUT newspaper, to point out that if, as the Executive apparently believed, the motion had only committed the Union to defending those teachers whose sexual identity remained concealed, and who therefore were not under personal threat of unfair treatment, it was no sort of basis for a coherent gay rights policy.[2]

For two years we had hardly looked beyond our goal of getting a resolution through Conference; what the next stage would be, we had only a hazy idea. On the whole, we hoped it would be nothing to do with us. We all felt burned out. However, in early summer, I was told by Mary Hufford, now Deputy General Secretary of the Union, but at that time Executive Member for Leicestershire and Northamptonshire, that she had proposed me for co-option as a lay – that is, non-Executive – member on the Working Party being set up by the National Union to advise on implementing the new policy. I thanked her through gritted teeth. I had been seriously ill for months, and was beginning to understand that I would have to plan to leave teaching. However, it was already becoming clear that the Conference motion meant nothing unless the Executive and the establishment at the Union's headquarters could be persuaded, cajoled, shamed and bullied into taking effective action. I didn't want the job. On the other hand, I'd put in a lot of time and thought already; I wanted a victory that was more than hollow.

The National Working Party on Lesbian and Gay Issues in Education met very irregularly between the summer of 1988 and the end of 1990. Our initial task was to advise on adding a clause to the Union's code of professional conduct, in accordance with the motion that had been passed at the Conference. It is is now a disciplinary matter for any member of the Union to discriminate against or harass anyone, colleague or pupil, because of that person's sexual identity. Also at the first meeting, Tim Lucas, the other co-opted member, and myself, arguing that we did not wish to be seen as representative of the Union's lesbian and gay membership, or as speaking in their place, pressed for a National Conference on Lesbian and Gay Issues in Education, to enable the views of a spectrum of members to reach the Executive. That took place in June 1989, and was by turns tedious, thought-provoking, turbulent, and affirming – or so I found it. Others, no doubt, have their own recollections. A contentious issue was the publicity for the conference, which many of those attending thought should have appeared in the national press. They didn't think much of the argument, put forward by a member of the Executive, that the restrictions on the way in which the Conference had been publicized had been intended for their own protection. Paul Patrick, an out gay teacher, who addressed the conference on the work of the ILEA 'Relationships and Sexuality' project, memorably accused the NUT of trying to confine its lesbian and gay members in a new and slightly larger closet.

The recommendations of the Conference on Lesbian and Gay Issues provided useful support for our attempts to move the Union to action. Some of the things we pressed for are gradually, it seems, being put into effect. We asked for the consideration of lesbian and gay issues to be included in the programmes for the Union's many training courses. In 1992, or so I was given to understand, the first steps were taken in that direction. But there is a reluctance to commit the Union's resources, which means that everything is implemented in a slow and piecemeal way, by overworked officials with far too many other responsibilities. Only sustained pressure from the Union's grass roots will change this.

One of the most important achievements of the National Working Party was the development of the initial draft of the Union's pamphlet *Lesbians and Gays in Schools* (NUT 1991). At the first meeting, Tim and I had urged that the NUT should publish a range of materials dealing in depth with lesbian and gay issues in education and employment. Perhaps, one day, this will happen. Meanwhile, within the limits of its short length,

the pamphlet, which finally appeared in July 1991, is in most
respects a reasonable stopgap. It states that all Union members
have a responsibility to counter prejudice and discrimination
against lesbian and gay people, that lesbian and gay pupils
have a right to proper pastoral support and an education that
helps them 'to achieve a positive self-image', and that 'all young
people have a right to an education that prepares them to live
in a society where many of the people they meet will be lesbian,
gay or bisexual'. In effect, it commits the Union to a fairly
radical position on the contentious matter of so-called 'gay
lessons', that well-known bugbear of the 'moral' right. In addition, it offers ordinary members specific advice on how they
can support their lesbian and gay colleagues and pupils.

The original draft of the pamphlet, as drawn up by the
National Working Party, also asserted that in situations where
teachers, as sometimes happens, are asked whether they themselves are lesbian or gay, 'choice of response is a personal
matter'. When the published pamphlet reached me in the post,
it should have surprised me less than it then did to find inserted
at this point a whole new passage of nervous paltering, elabo-
rating the theme that 'ordinarily personal sexuality is not a
matter for discussion with pupils', and advising that in such
a situation, a teacher should seek 'to draw the questioner into
a more general consideration of relationships'. I felt betrayed.

The NUT has moved some distance over the last few years.
The change to the rules for professional conduct is of obvious
importance; and on curriculum and pastoral matters the Union's
advice to members is sensible and useful. Nowadays, too, there
is an explicit acknowledgement, as there was not in the mid-
1970s, that teachers who are lesbian or gay are for that reason
particularly at risk of facing unfair treatment, and the Union
has expressed a general commitment to combating this. Nevertheless, the NUT's position on lesbian and gay issues remains
disturbingly incoherent. First of all, the Union cannot proclaim
that lesbians and gays are entitled to equal opportunities in
education and society and in the same breath say that so long
as they are teachers, they must keep quiet about their sexual
identity. Not, at the very least, until it bans its other members
from wearing wedding rings and telling classroom anecdotes
about their spouses. If no one on the staff dares to be openly
gay, pupils will draw conclusions about the status of gays in

society that no amount of liberal rhetoric in relationships modules or social studies is going to erase.

Nor can the Union distinguish, as it seems to want, between teachers who are 'discreet' about their homosexuality, and those who 'flaunt' it and get into trouble. Any lesbian or gay teacher, no matter how hard they may try to conceal their sexual identity, is vulnerable to being exposed. All the time, one is aware that one is making risky choices: to visit the gay pub, to go to the gay film, to go on a demonstration, even to take one's partner to the local supermarket. And if pupils choose to mount a challenge, equivocation will not then protect one from a class that has scented blood. John Warburton's instinct was sound: in such a situation, a teacher's control over his or her students depends entirely on honesty rooted in self-respect.

The warning against coming out in *Lesbians and Gays in Schools* is intended to protect the Union's gay membership, or so I have been given to understand. In reality, it is quite unworkable, and leaves them dangerously exposed. Any lesbian or gay teacher who takes off the mask of 'normality', or inadvertently allows it to slip, will now be potentially vulnerable to being abandoned by their union, on the grounds that they have ignored its plain advice. I do not think it is unfair of me to suspect that this is the point. Certainly, the National Union remains haunted by the fantasy terror that the slightest encouragement will lead to lesbian and gay members coming out to their pupils in classrooms all over the country, resulting in a spate of disciplinary cases, and a consequent drain on the Union's resources.

The NUT's position on coming out, as expressed in the leaflet, *Lesbians and Gays in Schools*, is cowardly and dishonest. It ignores the fact, well known to the Executive and the officials, that some teachers have been open about their sexual identity for years, and, weathering the difficulties, have greatly enriched their colleagues' and pupils' understanding of human diversity. It spits on the lesbians and gay men who have risked misrepresentation, personal insult, even their careers to speak out publicly at the National Conference and in the other forums of the Union.

For a lesbian or a gay man to campaign for gay rights is, inevitably, to come out, and when people come out, as this narrative shows, they have a powerful impact. In the end, this is the most important thing: the shifts in consciousness that began to take place when John Warburton gave honest answers to his pupils' questions, when members of the Gay Teachers' Group challenged the Union's indifference at the 1983 Conference on Jersey, when Lena Milosevic talked about her experiences as a lesbian teacher at the Conference in 1988, and on the numerous other less publicized occasions when lesbian and gay teachers have spoken out, in staffrooms, in classrooms, in union meetings.

Whatever the context, to come out is to be involved in educating people, in correcting the lies and hostile folklore that some of our social institutions – the right-wing press, most sections of the Church – are actively engaged in promulgating, and that many others, including much the greater part of the education service, prefer to leave unexamined. It is also to begin a process of personal growth; for most of us, far from easy or smooth, but nevertheless rewarding. In the end, for some of us, to live outside the closet comes to seem a necessity, as basic as air.

Notes

1 *Local Government Bill Clause 28* (NUT ref. no. 72/88).
2 Letter, *The Teacher*, 2 May 1988.

References

City of Leicester Teachers' Association (1987) *Outlaws in the Classroom. Lesbians and Gays in the School System*. Leicester: City of Leicester Teachers' Association (NUT).

Gay Teachers' Group (1978) *Open + Positive. An Account of How John Warburton Came Out at School and the Consequences*. London: Gay Teachers' Group.

Gay Teachers' Group (1987) *School's Out. Lesbian and Gay Rights in Education*, 2nd edn. London: Gay Teachers' Group.

Greater London Council (n.d.) *Changing the World. A London Charter for Gay and Lesbian Rights*. London: GLC.

National Council for Civil Liberties (n.d.) *Homosexuality and the Teaching Profession, NCCL Report No. 8*. London: NCCL.

National Union of Teachers (1991) *Lesbians and Gays in Schools. An Issue for Every Teacher. NUT Guidance on Lesbian and Gay Issues in Education*. London: NUT.

Sanders, S. and Spraggs, G. (1989) Section 28 and education. In C. Jones and P. Mahony (eds) *Learning Our Lines. Sexuality and Social Control in Education*. London: Women's Press.

CHAPTER 13

On the Straight and the Narrow: The Heterosexual Presumption, Homophobias and Schools

DEBBIE EPSTEIN and RICHARD JOHNSON

In this chapter we focus on the different formations of homophobia and heterosexism of a kind which have been illustrated throughout the book. We insist on this focus because we wish to make 'heterosexuality' the problematic term of our analysis.[1] Usually heterosexuality is the silent term – unspoken and unremarked – when sexualities are spoken of. It is just this silence and the presumption of heterosexuality which we term 'heterosexism'. In contrast, we use the term 'homophobia' to refer to active and explicit attacks on lesbians and gays, often fuelled by unacknowledged motives and/or panic. Just as research on racism has tended to concentrate (for understandable reasons) on the problems experienced by black people, so too writing about sexuality has tended to focus on problems experienced by lesbians and gays.[2] In this volume, also, the problems experienced by lesbians and gays and the ways in which lesbians and gay men have developed strategies of resistance have been the focus of many of the articles. However, we did not wish to leave matters at that point. We wish to ask as well, 'How do these problems arise in the first place?'

Our interest in these issues arises, in large part, from our personal histories: one of us identifies as a Jewish lesbian and feminist who became lesbian after many years of marriage;

the other identifies himself as a heterosexual white man, who has been led to question heterosexuality in struggles and dialogues with feminists, lesbians and gay men. We draw on both the evidence from this book and on a research project on which we are currently engaged, with a number of other people, on the experiences of lesbians and gays in the school system.[3] The ways in which different forms of homophobia (including, specifically, anti-lesbianism) and heterosexism are played out in the cultural institutions of society can be illustrated by an examination of the institutions of education in general and schools in particular. However this is not simply illustration, for schools are very particular places with characteristic processes of their own, organized, for example, around age. There are differences, of course, between individual schools, but those differences are contained within the general features of schooling and of widespread homophobia and heterosexism.

The heterosexual presumption

All the articles in this book have demonstrated the pervasiveness of different forms of homophobia and heterosexism. At its most general level, there is a presumption of heterosexuality which is encoded in language, in institutional practices and the encounters of everyday life. Hence the experience, recounted over and over again in these pages, of having to account for yourself as lesbian or gay against the pressure of this expression of heterosexuality, compulsory in its insistent taken-for-grantedness (see KOLA; Rogers; Sanders and Burke, all in this volume).

It is not necessary for homophobia to be expressed for heterosexism as a cultural structure to be active in a particular moment. It operates through silences and absences as well as through verbal and physical abuse or through overt discrimination. Indeed, one form of heterosexism discriminates by failing to recognize differences. It posits a totally and unambiguously heterosexual world in much the same way as certain forms of racism posit the universality of whiteness. In this way, the dominant form is made to appear 'normal' and 'natural' and the subordinate form perverse, remarkable or dangerous. Recognition of this general structure throws a flood of light on everyday experiences. First, the sheer work of establishing a gay or lesbian identity in forms that others will recognize is testimony to the pervasiveness of heterosexism. This labour of coming out is often matched by the strength of denial on the part of recipients of significant messages. Homosexuality seems so impossible that it is immediately ignored or repressed (see Alistair *et al.*; Rogers; Akanke, all in this volume).

Second, the processes involved in 'coming out' or 'staying in' the closet say much about the ubiquity of heterosexism. As Gill Spraggs (this volume: 180) says:

> Coming out is a process, never a once for all time act. Many, perhaps most of us move in and out of the closet several times a day, depending on where we are and who we are with: at home, at work, with family, with trusted friends. There are longer term patterns too: it is not uncommon for gay people to move from a situation in which they have been relatively open about themselves to one in which they have felt constrained to silence.

The decision about whether to be out or not is made at several levels. There is a general decision to be made about whether to live in or out of the closet. For example, Debbie, like Gill Spraggs and Sue Sanders (this volume), has made a general decision to be out, which has involved appearing on national television as a lesbian and writing both in the lesbian and gay press and in more general contexts about herself. She made this decision in the context of the Stop the Clause campaign, when lesbian and gay politics were very strong and supportive and when her children were in their middle to late teens, by which time she was no longer afraid of losing custody of them. However, she had previously spent several years, after first becoming involved with other women, when she was so closeted that even women in her women's group did not know about these relationships. Similarly Akanke (this volume), with younger children and in the face of pervasive racism, has made the decision to remain in the closet in most of her social contexts.

In addition, there are decisions to be made on a continuous, day-to-day basis – often several times a day. Decisions like these involve a careful scrutiny of each context. Each such decision is accompanied by a risk and a wide range of possible effects: people may or may not accept the authenticity of such a statement (how many lesbians and gay men have been greeted with the response 'Are you sure?'); the legitimacy of one's views in general may be thrown into question, particularly, and ironically, in relation to issues of gender and/or sexuality; one may face overt, even violent, abuse and harassment; in some contexts, you may find your 'confession' [sic] spread across the pages of the tabloid press.

Of course, remaining in the closet has profound consequences and tells us much about heterosexism too. The feeling which many people experience of having an 'authentic' inner self and an 'inauthentic' public persona is enormously heightened by remaining in the closet. Thus, for example, Andrea, in *What a Lesbian Looks Like* (National Lesbian and Gay Survey 1992: 85) writes:

> Coming out is my way of bringing the two halves of my world together so that I can stay sane. If I don't try, they'll go spinning off in opposite directions, tearing me apart as they do so.

As Andrea suggests, staying in the closet involves a difficult double life, a splitting of the self between 'essential me' and what is 'acceptable' in the 'outside' world. This construction for the purposes of defence never escapes vulnerability. There is always the fear of being 'outed'. For example, Neville, one of our interviewees, said:

> So there are various overlaps. I have to be quite careful, no matter how far away I think I am from work . . . So there are all these links, this great sort of web in the area and not even in the immediate area . . . and it could easily filter back to where I work.

There is often an intensification of homophobia at points of coming out on the part of the person doing so and/or on the part of the 'audience'. Moments of coming out involve facing up to and overcoming homophobia in an acute form. Even in the process of coming out to oneself there is no free or neutral space in which heterosexism is not active. Thus, for example, in 'So the Theory was Fine' (this volume: 23), Alistair comments:

> . . . about the time when *Gay's the Word* was raided at the beginning of the '80s, I remember being at a YS [Young Socialist] event and somebody asked me to sign a petition about *Gay's*

the Word. Although being gay was on my mind, when there was a gay man asking me to sign this thing, suddenly I was really terrified, really scared. I felt quite guilty about being scared about things for a long time. I went to a lesbian and gay Young Socialist fringe meeting at this conference and sat at the back. It wasn't really a 'backs to the wall' situation, but I was asking myself, 'Are all these people really gay?'

What was the terror that Alistair experienced? In the context of being asked by a gay man to sign a petition, he clearly did not expect either verbal or physical abuse to ensue. Rather, it was a matter of making a long-considered private identity more public through an identification with other gay men. The later question 'Are all these people really gay?' is not really an expression of disbelief that there could be so many gays around, but rather expresses a moment of doubt about whether he *wanted* to make the identification with gays which was the logic of being at a lesbian and gay fringe meeting. This fear of lesbian or gay sexuality at the very moment of self-identification has been noted over and over again, not only in 'So the Theory Was Fine', but also in the interviews we have carried out in the course of our research and in published autobiographical material (see, for example, Hall-Carpenter Archives 1989). A clear indication of the embedded and ever-present nature of homophobic forms is the fact that there are no words for lesbian or gay sexuality which do not bear a hostile charge. Even those words which have been affirmed as a focus of positive identity and pride – such as 'gay', 'lesbian' and, more recently, 'queer' – represent a terrain of struggle rather than a simple affirmation. As Rachel puts it (this volume: 14), 'There was the word 'lesbian', which I found a very ugly word for a long time as well.'

It is always possible to find apparent exceptions to the pervasiveness of heterosexism. In some families, professional contexts or cultural milieus, sexuality is spoken of with unusual openness, often in connection with liberal or radical politics. Thus Rachel says:

My family is middle-class, trendy lefty, so I've always had an awareness of these things and when I was 13 or 14, I was in the Anti-Nazi League and thought Tom Robinson's Band were great. So the *theory* of everything was fine.

(this volume: 14)

Nevertheless, Rachel was not immune from the general stigmatization of lesbian identity and found the adoption of such
an identity problematic. Similarly, the Hall-Carpenter Archives
(1989) collection, *Inventing Ourselves*, contains several examples of women growing up in radical, left-wing (and often
Jewish) families where sexualities were openly discussed, but
lines drawn when it came to the daughters' own futures (see,
for example, the chapters by Myrtle Solomon, Sharley McLean
and Susan Lee).

There is further confirmation of the pervasiveness of the
heterosexual presumption in the relative absence of public versions of what it means to be gay or, even more, lesbian. Hence
the importance, historically, of a limited number of particular images such as those of Oscar Wilde and the character of
Stephen in Radclyffe Hall's *The Well of Loneliness*. Both of
these widely available images are of highly stigmatized, 'guilty'
characters. Not only are the quantity and 'quality' of available
points of recognition important, but also the diversity and
range. Thus, for example, Dave (in the discussion from which
Alistair *et al.*, this volume, is abstracted) talked about his wish
that Barry or Damon Grant (from the soap opera *Brookside*)
had been gay, and Epstein (1988: 33) wrote of her situation:

> I did not know any out lesbians and knew only one openly gay
> man . . . Reading [*The Well of Loneliness*], my sympathy and
> identification with Stephen did not stop me from seeing that she
> was a misfit and that lesbianism was clearly calculated to make
> a woman miserable.

In other words, it is not simply the availability of 'positive'
(however defined) images or role models that matters, but the
possibility for individuals to find *appropriate* forms according to their own particular biographies, which vary greatly,
producing differing needs. This means that diversity of versions
of being lesbian or gay is important. The contemporary pro-
liferation of publicly visible forms of lesbianism and gay masculinity (in, for example, television programmes such as Channel
4's *Out*, popular lesbian detective fiction and the enormous
popularity and exposure of gay author, Armistead Maupin) is,
perhaps, a flamboyant response to the historical paucity of
forms.

Heterosexism and gender difference

So far, we have discussed heterosexism as a general and per-vasive feature of the culture, but the ways in which the hetero-sexual presumption affects people's lives varies according to the gender relationship involved, the ways in which particular situations are racialized and a wide range of other contingent factors (for example, Alistair *et al.*; Rogers; KOLA; Bartell; Akanke; Mac an Ghaill, all this volume). This complexity of interactions is clear from Rachel's account of her own fears for her relationship with her mother in the light of her parents' history. Similarly, Roy Bartell's story is one of complex rela-tionships, involving the punitive homophobia embodied by various (presumably heterosexual) men in positions of power; the specificity of education; political and personal support from (mainly) lesbian friends; support from male and female col-leagues; and support from and costs to his wife. Akanke's story and those told by members of KOLA are very much about interactions of racism and heterosexism in their own lives. The interactions detailed in Mac an Ghaill's ethnography (for exam-ple, between young gay Asian men and their teachers) are equally complex. Of the range of differences, we focus here on those of gender and race.

There are differences between the ways in which men and women are positioned within homophobic discourses. Anti-lesbianism, within heterosexual masculinities, is almost always framed within a more general misogyny. For example, in the film *Basic Instinct* (which deals with the paranoias typical of some forms of straight masculine sexuality) fear and hatred of powerful women is expressed in relation to the sinister threat of a widespread lesbian conspiracy. However, despite demonstrations by Queer Nation, most mainstream film critics refused to see the homophobia of the film, regarding it as misogynist while denying any anti-lesbian content. The con-nection between lesbianism and women-as-threat is made extraordinarily blatantly in the film. Its denial, therefore, seems strong evidence for the operation of unconscious processes. The anti-lesbianism of *Basic Instinct* can also be seen as a version of the common conflation of the terms 'lesbian' and 'feminist'. Thus, in our experience, one of the fears most frequently expressed by women beginning Women's Studies courses is that they will be taken for lesbians and, for the same reason, many women, particularly young women, evade the label feminist even when they hold feminist opinions.

In strongly homosocial situations, such as boys' schools and school-based cultures of masculinity, homophobia is often a vehicle for policing heterosexual masculinities. Men habitually use terms of homophobic abuse against peers who deviate from hegemonic masculinities. In the course of our research, we have found repeatedly that terms like 'poof' and 'queer' may be deployed against any young man who does not conform. Ironically, however, conformity can be more apparent than real: for example, one of our interviewees who identified as gay from an early age reported that he 'had no problem with abuse, because [he] was captain of rugby'. On the other hand, young men who saw themselves as academic in orientation and had good relations with teachers, were often positioned by their classmates as gay, regardless of their heterosexual relationships. One of the reasons why we may wish to retain the awkward term 'homophobia' (see Plummer 1992: 16–17) is to catch that mixture of embarrassment, fear and homoerotic desire characteristic of contexts like sporting changing rooms, pub sociability and boys' boarding schools. Mixed feelings, here, are often expelled through verbal and physical violence and/or their 'humorous' or 'playful' acting out.

In these two different ways (as a misogynistic anti-lesbianism and as a policing of male heterosexuality and homosociality) homophobia can be seen as a constitutive part of heterosexual masculinities. It is not some incidental feature. Heterosexual masculinities are actually produced through different forms of homophobia, and this involves the expulsion or denial of homoerotic desire. The place of homophobia in school cultures testifies to this connection between the formation of heterosexual identities and the stigmatization of homosexual identities and gender ambivalence. In the early years of schooling, for example, boys who are perceived as 'sissy' or 'girlish' are liable to be punished through teasing and bullying in a variety of ways. It is demanded of them that they become more like 'real boys' (and later 'real men'). In critical accounts (see, for example, Walker and Barton 1983; Arnot and Weiner 1987; Flintoff 1993; Sikes 1993) these behaviours are usually seen as an important part of the socialization of girls and boys into stereotypical gender roles. We argue that there are at least three other dynamics involved:

1 The processes are more active than the term 'socialization' implies. Children are both acted upon and are active in making their own meanings (see Walkerdine 1981, 1985; Urwin 1984; Steedman 1986).
2 It is not only gender identities which are involved when 'boys will be boys', but also sexual ones. The policing of masculinities and femininities assumes the inevitability of heterosexual relations.
3 These processes are charged with emotion, as can be seen from the vehemence with which young children act out gendered and sexualized roles (like heterosexual mummies and daddies) and stigmatize behaviour which runs counter to those expected. This vehemence is one starting point for arguing that there is an unconscious or psychic dimension to the process of forming identities.

For girls and women, too, this process of becoming heterosexual, in part through the repression of homoerotic desire, is invested with considerable emotional energy. Sexual desire for other women may become virtually inconceivable, even where there is no overt hostility to homosexuality. As Tracy told us in an interview:

Tracy: . . . My cousin. He's gay . . .
DE: So does that make a difference to how you get on with him?
Tracy: No [I] just treat him as a normal cousin. Like, he takes me out places, he buys me things and gives me money . . . I mean, I'm not really gonna treat him nastily just because he fancies men instead of women. I mean, it's nature, innit? He fancies men instead of women. No big deal.
DE: . . . So you think it's something that people are either 'like that' or 'not like that'. It's not about deciding to be like something?
Tracy: I couldn't, I couldn't imagine myself like that you know. I mean, I'm saying this now and when I'm 20 I could be one, I could be a lesbian!
DE: Mm.
Tracy: But I can't imagine myself being a lesbian. I seriously can't.

DE: Mm.
Tracy: I dunno why, I just can't . . . I don't think anybody could
   really.

Tracy returns over and again to the issue of whether *she* (or
anybody?) could be a lesbian, with little prompting from the
interviewer. Her repeated denials are evidence of a certain
fascination with the problem and there is clearly a certain
ambivalence at work ('when I'm 20 I could be one, I could be
a lesbian!').

As our earlier example of Women's Studies courses suggested,
homophobia among women may often be derivative in part
from the power of men in heterosexual relations. The fear of
being taken for a 'man-hating lesbian' is the fear of being placed
outside 'normal' heterosexual relations. Within patriarchal
societies women suffer from inequalities (from lack of control
over their own bodies to discrimination and unequal rewards
at work) in a number of historically specific ways. Heterosexual
relations can be seen as a part of these patterns of inequality
and are experienced by many women, some of the time, as a
kind of 'solution', however unsatisfactory (see, for example,
Hollway 1987). For example, women often feel that they cannot
go out at night for fear of sexual assault, but having a male
partner makes going out possible despite the fact that most
sexual assaults occur within existing relationships. More generally, there are considerable rewards for heterosexuality. Heterosexual women are more likely to be able to be dependent on a
male 'breadwinner' and, if they work, are less likely to lose their
job as a result of discrimination. Marriage is an option available
to heterosexual women and may bring many material advantages: for example, inheritance and pension rights, wedding
gifts, and all that is involved in being the legal spouse and next
of kin. Heterosexuality may also bring fuller acceptance from
family members and recognition of the right and duty to bear
and bring up children.

The rewards and solutions constructed within heterosexual
power relations may all be threatened by the assumption of a
lesbian identity. This is a threat both to the woman who identifies as lesbian and to the heterosexual presumption and the
privileges that go with it. Adrienne Rich (1980), in arguing
for the existence of a 'lesbian continuum', includes all women

within it. We would rather argue that women are contradictorily and ambiguously placed within heterosexual relations but in ways dependent upon their other social positions. As a result, they tend not to have the same investment in the denial of the possibility of homosocial intimacies of all kinds as do heterosexual men. Women's friendships, therefore, are often extremely close, intensely emotional, and include touching and physical contact in ways that, at least in the English context, seem difficult within the hegemonic masculinities (see Faderman 1981).

Heterosexism and racism

The general context of racism is important in the responses of 'white' society, including the lesbian and gay communities, and shapes the responses of minorities in many ways, putting a premium on internal solidarities and making it difficult to express and recognize internal differences. But there are more specific interactions between racism and heterosexism, which we might refer to as the racialization of heterosexism. This process must be seen in the context of the differential racist sexualization of African-Caribbean men and women and South and South-East Asian men and women (hereafter 'black' and 'Asian'). Sexual relations are constructed in part through long histories of representations of Others from a white western standpoint. We have in mind, here, discourses, both overlapping and differing around the 'Orient', 'India' and 'Africa'. As Said (1978) and others have argued, these constructions are a kind of imaginary geography, which have more to do with the creation of Western identities and the controlling impulses of colonialism than with any actual place, period or people.[4]

Both racism in general and the racialization of heterosexism create particular problems for lesbians and gay men within black and Asian communities. Racism, especially in the context of migration, creates the necessity for internal solidarities within minority and majority communities. This demand goes many ways. Black and Asian lesbians and gays have often expressed the need for support from their own communities (see, for example, KOLA and Akanke, in this volume). Equally, these communities may reject lesbian and gay sexuality as being a product of 'western' society. At the same time, unconditional belonging is sometimes demanded by the white gay and lesbian communities themselves, overlooking the particular pressures on black and Asian people. Such demands are often focused on precisely those areas central to sexual difference: the family, marriage, procreation, inheritance, obedience to parents, religiously sanctioned moralities in general, and even the survival of the 'race' (see Akanke, this volume: 103). The ways in which these demands are made are very different in the different communities, but the consequence is to create extreme contradictions and choices for black and Asian lesbians and gays forced to work across the differences between strongly bounded cultural identities and their images of each other. For example, Lily, one of our interviewees,[5] remembered that:

> I felt very lonely, I mean, I mean, thinking back to when . . . to that time in my life, I thought I was the only Asian lesbian in the world. I thought I was *the* Asian lesbian and I was put on this earth to sort of start this revolution amongst Asian lesbians . . . for, about, about being gay. And that was my purpose in life . . . My image of the lesbianism was like this short-haired, really butch white dykes, bovver boot style, and here was me, this little Panjabi woman . . . this Panjabi girl you know, at that point, who you know, loved long earrings and long hair and . . . used to love Asian clothes.

A similar contradiction was expressed by Robert:[6]

> It wouldn't have been the same for a white gay man as it is for a black gay man. I mean . . . for me personally, it's more highlighted as a black gay man, it's very, that I *know* that I need my black community because I know I'm in the minority and because I know I'm being oppressed. I need the support of my black community in order to fight the racism that I face. So, and I know that, very often, like you say, that support doesn't come . . . A white person who's gay isn't in that same situation . . . I don't think a lot of white gay people realize that.

So, in coming out, for instance, blacks and Asians face a double dilemma. Can they risk marginalization within or even expulsion from their own community and be defenceless in a racist world? If they risk this, will they find an alternative community within a lesbian and gay scene dominated by white people? This second resource cannot be relied upon. Within the lesbian and gay communities there is a racist eroticization of black men and women, caught in the phrase 'dinge queen' used within the gay community to describe white gay men who are attracted to black and Asian men.[7] Besides, the lesbian and gay communities are by no means immune from the generalized racism of the society at large and contain within them both overtly racist and anti-racist currents. Thus the black or Asian person entering the lesbian or gay scene may face racist jokes in pubs and clubs and the obliteration of difference in the assumption that 'we are all gay together' on the one hand, and signs of solidarity on the other, which may, none the less, be difficult to read and respond to.

Not to come out, however, involves different costs. These are explored in this volume by Akanke when she records the isolation of her 'semi-closeted position' and her uneasiness about referring to herself as a single mother in relation to her children's schooling, thus 'actively denying [her] partner's existence and the part she plays in [their] lives', helping, for example, with the children's homework. Akanke has made the clear choice to prioritize her identification as black over her lesbianism, but this choice carries the risk, all the time, of rejection by those whose support she most prizes. As she says, 'over the last six years I have lost a few black friends whose friendship and support I had come to rely on'. She encapsulates her dilemma and her choice when she says that:

> I feel that being black is essentially more important to me than being a lesbian – a label which I choose to wear only when it is convenient, whereas being black is not a choice. This is in no way meant to undermine the strength or the importance of the relationship I share with Terri, but merely points to the fact that I/we would prefer to have the support of other black people while denying our sexuality, rather than the support of some white people and feel alienated from black people.
>
> (this volume: 104)

Very similar dilemmas are faced by Asian men and women obliged to become married but gay or lesbian in their sexual orientation. Khan (n.d.: 18), for example, quotes an Asian married man:

> I can't tell my wife about myself. It would destroy my family and her. I can't have a divorce because of the effect it would

have on my family as well as her. What would happen to her?
I go out maybe once a month, pick up some guy and stay the
night at his place. Or maybe drop by the cruising place on my
way home from work in the evening . . . I don't form relationships; that would be too dangerous. And now with the children
and all that, I just can't take the risk. I really would love to live
with a man, you know, have the proper thing, but that is not
possible.

In the accumulation of problematic situations, coming out
may seem to be just another source of damage to intimate
friends and relations and peril to the self. As Pratibha Parmar
(interviewed by Shruti Tanna) put it:

When I first came out my family didn't know. It was a part of
my life that I could not speak about and neither did I want to,
because I felt that at that time, my family had gone through so
many life changes that it wasn't really worth telling them about
it . . . And I just felt that particularly in the case of my mother,
she had gone through so many absolute life changes . . . with
moving from one continent to another and then coming to live
in England, into a kind of hostile climate, coming to accept the
fact that (a) I wasn't going to have an arranged marriage and
(b) that I was going to have a career, that was enough in itself.
I didn't really want to push those boundaries any further.

The sheer complexity of all these interactions and their connection with our earlier accounts of homophobia are caught
in Rajinder's analysis (Mac an Ghaill, this volume: 159) of
straight–gay relations:

Thinking about it, it's very complex. Straight men don't really
have a problem with gays, they have a problem with themselves.
Straight men seem to fear and love women, but fear and hate
gay men. Then whites, especially white men, have that fear and
hatred for Asians and Afro-Caribbeans. So black gay men are
a real threat to white straight men. Like James Baldwin says,
they act out their fears on our bodies . . .

Current contexts

The formations we have been discussing are not, of course,
transhistorical or unchanging, as is amply demonstrated by
recent debates within lesbian and gay history (see, for example,
Duberman *et al.* 1990). The 1980s and 90s have seen particu-

lar developments which have been influenced by lesbian and gay politics (and latterly Queer Politics), the women's movement, the epidemic of HIV and the conservative backlash against perceived gains made by lesbians and gays. One of the key consequences of this has been the heightened visibility of lesbians and gays, particularly within the popular media, dance and male fashion. Thus we see the contradictory developments of increased anti-gay and lesbian legislation and the existence of highly visible and popular, usually gay male, and almost invariably camp, figures such as Julian Clary and Andy Bell of the pop group Erasure. Athough there may be some real gains here, we are far from arguing that these appearances mark the end of homophobia. They may be precisely positioned, indeed, as licensed characters, similar in function for the mainstream to the court jester. As Stallybrass and White (1986) have argued in another context, the socially marginal becomes culturally central precisely because it can then become the object of ridicule and disgust, only to be re-expelled to a marginal position. This process is one which can take the sting out of the subversiveness of a character like Clary's. Such advances may be recuperated in another way: by the adoption of elements, say, of camp style, outside the context in which they initially signified as subversive (a similar process can be seen in the adoption of black music and styles by white youth and performers).

Institutional heterosexism

Although heterosexism has a general cultural presence, it is produced and reproduced through particular institutions where it takes specific forms. These institutional sites are both separate and linked. For example, the law and education can be seen both as institutions in their own right and as having combined consequences and reciprocal effects. In Roy Bartell's story, for example, it is the law which first intervenes to position him as 'deviant', differentiating his behaviour from the heterosexual norm. The immediate consequences of the law, in this particular case, however, were relatively limited compared with the panicked reaction within the educational institutions: his subsequent exclusion from employment within the school and the LEA. In Gill Spraggs' discussion of the debate on Section 28 at

NUT conference, it is clear that it was the popular media that exacted a price from Lena Milosevic for her role in opposing the unjust legislation (this volume: 190). In the event, the NUT passed a watered down version of the Leicester Association's original motion. Each institution in both these cases played its part in constructing a heterosexist outcome in which overt homophobia played a part.

We are particularly interested here in considering those institutions and institutional moments where homophobia is actively deployed. We have already mentioned the prosecution of gay men and Section 28 of the Local Government Act 1988. Our research also highlights the central role of familial expectations about the destinies of sons and daughters in regulating sexuality in general and promoting heterosexism in particular. The influence of Christian traditions in Western culture, although dispersed and secularized in the case of the United Kingdom, remains a major regulative discourse in familial and sexual matters (see Foucault 1978). Government circulars about sex education, for example, often rest upon an assumed Christian framework in which procreative sex, within traditional marriage, is privileged. This should not be taken to imply that Christianity provides an uncontested space within which conservative definitions prevail. There are liberal and conservative tendencies on sexual issues within most Christian churches, resulting in, for example, the conflict within the Church of England over homosexuality within the priesthood and the ordination of women. This may well be true of the Catholic Church too, but in its public face and in the evidence we have from interviews with lesbians and gays brought up as Catholics, this Church's line on sexual matters is severe in its (not always successful) demand for conformity.

Within Islam and Hinduism in Britain, religion forms part of a pattern of communal solidarities, transgression of whose governing norms, including, in many cases, 'arranged' marriage, may be felt to amount to dishonour to the community and to parents and extended family (Khan n.d.). Within the Jewish community, whether secular or religious, there seems often to be a feeling that 'deviance' (of any kind) is likely to engender anti-Semitism (DE, personal experience; Beck 1982). Within the 'sciences' and expert knowledges, biology, sexology, psychoanalysis and developmental psychology have often provided explanations of same sex desire and practice that have rendered them abnormal and deviant, while at the same time producing homosexuality as a social category (see Foucault 1978; Weeks 1981, 1985, 1986, 1991).

In exploring particular social spaces like schools, we have to be attentive both to the particular features of the institution (the salience of child–adult relations, for example) and the deployment of discourses which occur in other contexts as well. For example, within 'sex education', discourses of marriage and romantic love are presented as desirable, inevitable and natural, while, at the same time, discourses about the urgency and immutability of the male sex drive are present as the major danger against which girls should guard themselves and be protected from (see Hollway 1987 for further discussion of these discourses in the context of adult heterosexual relationships).

Schools

For the purposes of this volume, the most important site is, obviously, the school. However, it is impossible to understand the specific formations of schooling apart from the pervasiveness of the heterosexual presumption and the work of other institutions as sites of active homophobia. It is also necessary to explore the features of schools as a type of institution, but recognize that individual schools vary greatly. One way of understanding the individuality of schools is through the idea of a 'micro-politics', as developed by Ball (1987), and how such local conditions affect possibilities for change in particular cases.[8]

General features of schools

One of the most striking features of schools is that they are organized around relationships between adults-as-teachers and non-adults-as-pupils. This is so taken for granted that it is rarely mentioned in discussions about schooling. The age relationships of schooling are relations of power in which adult judgements are, in general, decisive, whether through the authority of the individual teacher or through the school and its institutional supports. Examples of such powers are the compulsion to attend school and the whole gamut of school rules. The elaborate dress codes enforced through school rules, but so often experienced as arbitrary by school students (who, of course, also have their own dress codes) are relevant examples here because they are so often specifically about the control of pupils' expressions of sexuality. Black stockings, for example, have particular sexual resonances. Sally and Tracy, in our interview with them, expressed their frustration clearly:

> *Sally*: There are loads of rules and stuff like that. You know, like, and they're not even like rules that are to, like, protect us from getting hurt, I'd understand that, it's like stupid little things like
> *Tracy*: It's like tights.
> *DE*: Sorry?
> *Tracy*: We're not allowed to wear black tights.
> *DE*: Why not?
> *Sally*: I don't know.
> *Tracy*: Well, like, I heard that
> *Sally*: They change the rules quite a lot, because when I first come you was allowed to wear black tights, socks and, um, white ones or blue ones, but they keep changing it and then people who aren't informed properly get into trouble.
> *Tracy*: You're only supposed to wear navy blue tights or white socks now . . .
> *Sally*: They don't even explain it to us. They just set down the rules and we have to follow them.
> *Tracy*: Exactly. I mean, I've been expelled from too many schools. Don't wanna be expelled from this one as well!

Like other relations of power, adult–child relations in schools are continually contested, complicated by other social relationships and always ambivalently experienced. Walkerdine (1981: 15–16), for example, draws attention to the complex interplay of gender and age between boys in nursery schools and their female teachers. In her study she quotes from a transcript in which two three-year-old boys use sexualized language (such as 'cunt', 'show your bum off', 'take all your clothes off') to position the female teacher as 'woman as sex-object'. As well as showing how pupils can use sexuality as oppositional to schooling (to which we shall return), this case illustrates more general processes in which teacher power is qualified or reinforced by discourses from other sources upon which both pupils and teachers are able to draw.

Childhood in western industrial countries is, in large measure, constructed through schooling. This has been the case since the institution of compulsory public education, especially with the introduction of age-related grades or progressions. These centre on notions of the natural development of the child, in which sexual categories play a part. Notions like 'latency period', 'puberty' and 'adolescence' carry the idea that age stages are distinguished, in part, by the person's relationship to the sexual. Thus, for example, early childhood is seen as a period of 'innocence',[9] while adolescence is seen as a period of heightened sexual awareness and danger.

This model of childhood and adolescence is problematic in several ways, one of which is that it ignores and denies the active engagement of children and young adults with the formation of their own identities. The different stages of schooling provide a key site for this engagement. Identities are formed in school in relation to the formal curriculum and its categories, for example, the academic/vocational split, the arts/science division and the academic/sporting polarity. They are also worked up from models and anti-models offered through everyday life social intercourse within the school between teachers, ancillary staff and pupils, among teachers and among pupils. Teachers, daily formed by the routines, are by no means immune from these more informal processes either. Rajinder, in Mac an Ghaill (this volume: 159) points out that:

> Like at our school, you could see some of the white teachers, the men, they really admired the Caribbeans and not just in sport and music, where it was really homoerotic, though of course they could never admit it to themselves. I think for a lot of teachers there, who felt trapped in their jobs, the macho black kids represented freedom from the system. There were anti-school macho whites and Asians but the teachers with their stereotypes fantasized about the Caribbean kids, who they saw as anti-authority, more physical and athletic, everything they couldn't be but greatly admired.

It is a condition of good teaching, perhaps, for teachers to recognize that they are involved in the daily work of identity formation: their own and that of their pupils. From this point of view, we could understand school in terms of shifting and reciprocal relationships in which both teacher and pupil identities are formed. Teachers need to be aware of these dynamics and reflexive about what is at stake for themselves in these transactions. As Gill Spraggs (this volume: 181) points out: 'Successful teaching in any subject is a kind of performance art. As with all artists, your basic material is yourself and your experience: what you have learned and tested and explored.'

Depending on domestic circumstances, schools mark, for many children, an entry into a world more public than that of the household or even of the peer group. Schools offer a very different social space for the work of identity formation than most domestic contexts. An early task for young children is to learn to be a pupil (see, for example, Willes 1983), work which involves both learning the externally given rules and discovering their own relation to being a pupil or student. This also involves negotiating the differences and tensions between the expectations and preferred identities of home and school. In this dichotomy, one commonly experienced but contradictory split is between the school as the public domain and the home as private. Children are often very aware of these splits and negotiate them actively. Akanke (this volume: 102), for example, recounts how her daughter was faced with a dilemma when making and addressing a Mother's Day card at school:

> She handed me an envelope and, beaming from ear to ear, she demanded that I open it and read what she had written inside. To my horror, it read, 'Happy Mother's Day to mummy and Terri'. Fearing the worst, I said to her, 'Did your teacher see this card?' 'Yes', she said, 'my teacher said it was a lovely card'.
> By this time I must have aged about 20 years. With much difficulty and as much calm as I could muster, I asked her what her teacher said when she saw Terri's name. In a most conspiratorial manner, my daughter replied, 'I added her name in the bus on the way home. That's why it's written in a different colour crayon'. The sense of relief that came over me was so obvious that we both started to laugh.

In this example, the form of the Mother's Day card, as originating and embedded in religious and commercial practices, is itself an institution of presumed heterosexuality. The little girl in this story is well aware that some kind of transgression is implied by pairing her mother's name with that of another woman. Her skill in resolving the conflict of expectations is impressive and recognized in the shared laughter and her mother's evident relief. The child learns important lessons here: that there is, indeed, a conflict of social identities, that being an acceptable pupil and a loving daughter are not the same, and that it is possible to occupy both of these conflicting positions without denying or expelling either, while, at the same time, expressing loyalty and a moral preference.

Schools and sexuality

When we consider the complexity of our last example, it becomes clear that the common-sense assumption that children are 'innocent' about sexual norms and relationships is very misleading. Yet prevailing notions of innocence in early childhood, in the context of child-as-pupil/adult-as-teacher power relations, nurture a certain apparent desexualization of schools as institutions. Paradoxically, sexual constructions are all-pervasive in the school context, while, at the same time, sexuality is specifically and vehemently excluded from the formal curriculum or confined to very specific and heavily guarded spaces. Sex education is a separate category, somewhat removed from the rest of the curriculum, and often devalued in relation to both vocational and academic subjects. In most cases, moreover, sex education is not about sexuality at all. It focuses on certain biological, procreative functions (and their 'plumbing') and on sex as danger, a constraint reinforced in the National Curriculum. There is little space, within this context, for a wider sexual agenda which includes pupils' own 'sexual cultures' (see Redman, this volume).

In particular, as Redman argues, key issues of pleasure and desire, of sexual identities and sexuality as power, autonomy and dependence are usually present only as conspicuous absences. During our participant observation of Personal and Social Education (PSE) lessons for a term, even in 'Heathland Girls' School' which we had chosen specifically for its good practice (and the teachers' practice in this area was, indeed resourceful, creative and innovative), the idea that sex or sexuality could be a source of pleasure was raised only very tentatively, gay sexuality was discussed only in relation to the spread of HIV, while lesbianism did not figure at all, and power imbalances were not discussed in any depth. In this all girls' school, it seemed that the girls were to be responsible not only for their own sexuality, but also for the sexuality of boys in (inevitable?) heterosexual relationships.

One of the problems which sexuality educators face in opening up 'serious' discussion about sexuality in PSE lessons is, precisely, the desexualization of schooling and the closeting of sexuality into this particular space. One consequence of this is that talking about sexuality, or sex, becomes either embarrassing or a form of oppositional student culture. In our observation at Heathlands School, a lesson about different methods of contraception during which various devices were passed round, was one which most of the girls found both embarrassing and, in their words, 'disgusting'. On the other hand, the repertoire of overt sexualization as student resistance is immense, including: sexual jokes and 'talking dirty'; the use of sexual categories such as 'poof', 'lezzie' or 'slag'; the deliberate, but covert, sexualization of teachers and texts; the finding of double (and sexual) meanings in everything; fantasies about the famous; and gossip about the relationships, desirability and reputations of peers.[10] Such cultural forms are not confined to the secondary school or the culture of older pupils. Sex play is well established from an early age, and finds expression both in pupil talk and 'pretend' games. Even as young as six, however, children are often well aware that such play is transgressive within the school context (see Sealey 1993: 6–7). The transition from what can be seen as mainly 'sex play' to 'sex talk' is a gradual one, as pupils adapt to what is seen to be appropriate to their age. However, 'sex talk' remains playful and the pleasure derived from it is, at least in part, to do with the feeling that it is very different from the formal discourses of sexuality in schools and hence oppositional. In this way, pupils' sexual cultures may emphasize playfulness in sexual exchange, the pleasures of which are expelled from the formal curriculum.[11]

In this situation, it is not surprising that attempts to open up class discussion about sexuality are often met with silence, giggles or 'messing about' (Wolpe 1988: Redman, and Sanders and Burke, this volume). It is interesting that the common element between expressions of embarrassment and disgust and the Rabelaisian humour which pupils often use or generate is the emphatic release of emotion – which is precisely what is ruled out of order by the serious lesson and the general school context. This difficulty in engaging in serious and emotionally literate discussion about sexuality is not created only by teachers. Pupils also split off the informational work around 'sexual problems' from emotionally charged 'sex talk'.

Reflection on the conditions required for two adults, even in the context of intimate relations, to communicate openly and effectively about sexuality may help us to understand some of the dimensions of the problem for the sexuality educator. The ability to discuss and to recognize the reality of the other's experience depends upon a mutual struggle to subvert existing power relations. But sex education in schools occurs within the context of grossly unequal relations. Furthermore, in our society, sexuality is seen as the most private aspect of the 'inner self'. According to Pattman (1991), even within the 'liberal sex education paradigm' it is unusual for teachers to refer to their own experience of sexuality, yet liberal methods prescribe that the students' own experience is, at least, a starting point. Students are likely to resist such one-sided revelations. For example, at Heathland we observed one lesson on the subject of 'love', which was a follow-up to a lesson on 'friendship'. The teacher, 'Lorna Dixon', in discussion about girls' brainstorms on 'love', asked them about the difference between loving members of the family and loving one other person:

> *LD*: Let's be bold and talk about one-to-one relationships. How is that love different from love in the family?
> *Asma*: I feel it'll be stronger.
> *LD*: Have any of you felt love for a boy or a man?
> *Tracy*: [nods]
> *LD*: Thanks for being honest. Why has this group put here 'love is a sexual relationship'?
> *Diana*: You wouldn't have sex with someone you didn't love.
> *Asma*: Prostitutes do.
> *Tracy*: It's a job to them – like you're a teacher.
> *LD*: Let's explore that.
> *Tracy*: You can still have sex without loving someone. You might be pressured by your boyfriend.
> *Tasneem*: You could be raped.

In this interchange, the girls distance themselves from the teacher's 'preferred honesty'. The only moment of overtly personal revelation is Tracy's nod, and Lorna acknowledges that this is courageous (an acknowledgement which is a feature of her style). It is interesting that in this formal context, the girls themselves expel the pleasures and focus on dangers of sex.

Heterosexism and the sexual cultures of school

Many stories told by lesbians and gays focus on the difficulties involved in coming out. However, the accumulated evidence of this volume is that coming out is especially difficult in schools.

> I had heard the term 'shock horror' of course, but I had never witnessed it until the day, several years ago, when I said 'yes' to a student who asked the question, 'Are you a lesbian?'. The scene has been replayed many times since and my response is always the same – grave concern for both of us.
>
>   (Sanders, this volume: 65–66)

> Like other people I have met, I experienced the move into teaching, after several years of student life, as a sudden plunge into a closet of almost stifling airlessness.
>
>   (Spraggs, this volume: 180–81)

> Most of my respondents . . . kept very quiet about their sexuality during their schooldays. Of the few who were open, the majority experienced hostility. Diane, for example, told me the following story: 'My form tutor . . . once took me out of the classroom after registration and asked me if I could stop talking about my sexuality in front of the other girls because apparently it was upsetting some of them!'
>
>   (Rogers, this volume: 35)

> My friend, another teacher, told me that I'd recently been seen snogging a woman at a bus stop. 'Oh shit!' I said, 'what shall I do?' I'd only been teaching a year and a half in this school that's not very supportive generally. For my department lesbians and gays don't exist and the rest of the school was worse. Well, what on earth was I going to do?
>
>   (Rachel, this volume: 28)

> One of the students, Denton Purcell, confided in his best friend that he was confused about his sexuality. 'The next day when some of our mates were around, my friend said, "your mom must be proud of you, that means she has two washing powders, Persil [Purcell] and Omo [homosexual]". They all started laughing. They all got the message, as they already thought I was

effeminate. It was one of the worst things that ever happened to me. I felt so violated.'

(Mac an Ghaill, this volume: 164)

Why might coming out in schools be so difficult and the costs of doing so willingly or being 'outed' so high?

Earlier in this chapter, we discussed what we termed the 'heterosexual presumption'. Schools as institutions and the individuals within them are in no way immune from this general cultural feature. Whether 'straight' or 'queer', everyone lives, daily, a relation to the heterosexual norm both within and outside the school. These relations vary hugely according both to social position and the particularities of individual biographies. As we have demonstrated above, the boundaries are by no means fixed and individuals may experience moments of confusion, ambivalence and the need to declare a sexuality and draw tight boundaries around it. It is precisely because of these ambivalences and contradictions that those who patrol moral categories attempt to enforce their own psychic 'resolutions' on others. In this way, we see the psychic processes of individuals paralleled, and indeed, activated in the sphere of public policy. The crucial condition, here, is who has, or acquires, the power to install their own criteria into legislative or other institutional frameworks. Even then, the results of such interventions are unpredictable and may be highly contradictory.

Such rules or laws have an 'educative' as well as a coercive force. Section 28 of the Local Government Act 1988 prohibited the 'promotion' of homosexuality by local authorities, but, ironically, failed to apply to schools. It both legitimated and encouraged heterosexism and homophobia and, at the same time, promoted homosexuality in the shape of a massive agitation against the (then) clause (see Stacey 1991). Section 28, then, had massively contradictory effects. By heightening awareness of the issues, it both increased self-censorship among teachers and, in some contexts, enabled teachers to take on board the issues for the first time. Partly because of the poor drafting of the original clause and the contradiction between it and the Education (No. 2) Act 1986 which made sex education the remit of school governors rather than local authorities, Section 28 has been, legally, a dead letter.

However, the New Right maintains its influence on educational policy and, as part of the constant struggle to reinforce sexual boundaries, the Department for Education (DfE) (with John Patten, a Conservative Catholic, as Secretary of State) has issued new draft guidelines on sex education (22 April 1993), paragraph 25 of which states:

> There is no place in any school in any circumstances for teaching which advocates homosexual behaviour, presents it as the norm, or which encourages homosexual experimentation by pupils . . . Although it does not impose any responsibilities upon them, school staff and governors should also be aware that section 2 of the Local Government Act 1986 (as amended by Section 28 of the Local Government Act 1988) prohibits Local Authorities from intentionally promoting homosexuality or from promoting in maintained schools 'teaching . . . of the acceptability of homosexuality as a pretended family relationship'.

This is a tighter and more restrictive formulation than earlier circulars, though the reference to Section 28 is best read as bluff, with the implication that schools have to obey the section, even though this is not the case in law. The Education Act 1993 has, again, confused the issue of sex education. It has made three major changes in the law:

1 Secondary schools and special schools with secondary age pupils must provide sex education which includes education about HIV/AIDS.
2 Parents have been given the right to withdraw their children from sex education other than those aspects which are a statutory obligation imposed by the National Curriculum.
3 The Secretary of State is required to redraft the statutory orders for the Science curriculum so that it includes only education about biological reproduction.

Thus, the Act simultaneously recognizes that (secondary age) children need to receive sex education and makes it possible for parents to withdraw them from it. Despite the contradictions of the whole process of legal regulation, the overall ideological effect, depending on local circumstances, is to make the act of coming out still more risky.

Heterosexism in schools themselves operates in a number of different ways. Like all other social institutions, schools are suffused with the heterosexual presumption. In every area of the formal curriculum heterosexuality is the norm. For example, PSE lessons about sex, by focusing on contraception, the biological facts of penetrative sex and the expectation of heterosexual relationships and marriage, construct a framework which is all too straight and narrow. In English, with the possible exception of William Shakespeare, it might be hard going to 'out' any of the prescribed list of authors for Key Stage 3! These are two areas of the formal curriculum in which the appearance of lesbian and gay sexuality is relatively likely (and relatively likely to be positive). An examination of other curriculum areas would show the same general pattern.

More important, in our view, are the larger cultural dynamics around sexuality in schools. This embraces the informal cultures of teachers and taught as well as the formal curriculum. We have already noted the general illicit nature of sexuality and, especially, personal revelation about sexuality in the school context. If (hetero) sex is difficult to talk about seriously and pleasurably at the same time, such discussion about lesbian and gay sex will be even more unapproachable and unspeakable given the heterosexual presumption of the general culture. Moreover, the terms of discourse on sexuality in schools limit the acceptable appearance and framing of homosexualities. Gay and lesbian sexualities may appear as problems, as phases, perversions, deviances and as sources of disease. Their affirmation or 'promotion' was extremely difficult long before Section 28 existed. These exclusions are particularly impoverishing for the educational context, since the theory and practice of sexuality within lesbian and gay cultures often centre upon the wider dimensions of sexuality – matters of pleasure, identity and alternative ways of living (see Kerr 1991).

Students' oppositions to school are equally inhospitable to openness. As we have seen, stigmatization of gay and lesbian identities is a routine feature of student/pupil life (see also Alistair *et al.*; Mac an Ghaill, both this volume). In this respect, as in others, the sexual culture of school pupils, although always a resistance to schooling, is not necessarily transformative. It may, indeed, be very conservative, policing boundaries even more effectively than government decrees or school rules. This places students identifying as lesbian or gay in an almost impossible position (see also Trenchard 1984; Trenchard and

Warren 1984; Warren 1984). They cannot appeal to the school hierarchy against the abuses of the informal culture with any certainty of support or understanding. They cannot depend on the solidarities of the pupil culture against the heterosexism of teachers. Young gay and lesbian students may identify strongly with other subordinated groups. Being out as lesbian or gay, or even seeming to be lesbian or gay, may well lead to alienation from peer groups because of homophobia, enforced through the culture of the school as a whole. Given the strategic place of schooling in constructing public identities and the importance of sexual identity, there is a strong pressure to identify some pupils as sexually 'deviant'.

Teachers, too, often find themselves in an almost impossible position. On the one side, they cannot depend on support from the school hierarchy, from their fellow professionals, or even from teacher unions (for example, Bartell, this volume). Lesbian and gay teachers may well find it difficult to 'fit in' with the 'ordinary' sociability in and around the staffroom, which, like other workplaces, often revolves around gossip about (presumed to be heterosexual) relationships and lifestyles. Moreover, the widespread mythology of lesbian and gay sexuality as dangerous to children has resulted in classically homophobic responses in which panic has been allied to the demand for protection. Industrial tribunals, for example, will not uphold the claims of unfair dismissal by lesbian or gay adults working with children who have lost their jobs on account of their sexuality alone. The restatement of Section 28 feeds the myth that educating the young and homosexuality are incompatible. As we have found, even the presence of lesbian or gay researchers in the classroom can be seen as 'dangerous' by New Right campaigners actively seeking out targets. In this context, 'paranoia' on the part of lesbian and gay teachers, and a consequent unwillingness to come out, is quite rational.

In relation to pupils, lesbian and gay teachers have to negotiate a difficult dilemma between being available to support lesbian and gay students and putting themselves at risk. In an impassioned and painful article, Clare Sullivan (1993: 97) explores this dilemma:

> I have many lesbian friends who are teachers, and like me none
> of them are completely 'out' at work. I feel that as a lesbian I

am letting down those young lesbians at my school. I know that they need support from lesbians, information, advice and role models. I do feel guilty about it. On the other hand young lesbians do find me . . . I always try as far as possible to support those young lesbians who turn to me without compromising them or myself.

The double binds of pupils and teachers are, inevitably, inter-active. A great deal of student energy goes into assessing (or imagining) the sexual proclivities of teachers, while a lot of teacher energy seems to be devoted to damping down the sexual proclivities of (especially) adolescent pupils. The possibilities of misrecognition across and within these boundaries are endless but so too are the possibilities of creative teaching despite (or because of?) the perils (see Sanders and Burke, and Patrick and Sanders, both in this volume; Sullivan 1993).

On the turn?

In this chapter we have pointed to problems created by hetero-sexism, not only for lesbians and gays, but for everyone. We have also stressed the contradictoriness of sexual identities and attempts to police them. It is these contradictions which pro-vide the space for turning situations around in ways which both challenge lesbian and gay inequalities and untie the double binds around heterosexual identities.

We have argued throughout that the contradictions of hetero-sexuality lie at the heart of discrimination against lesbians and gays. It is because, in our society, heterosexuality is culturally and psychically enforced that homosexualities are stigmatized and expelled. As we said at the beginning of this chapter, 'heterosexuality is the silent term – unspoken and unremarked – when sexualities are spoken of'. Its invisibility is part of its power. But as the dominant form, preferred in a thousand different ways, it is also the term which must be made visible and challenged if some measure of equality is to be achieved. Because of this, the burden of challenge and change cannot be left only to lesbians and gays. Heterosexuality and homo-sexuality are mutually dependent categories. Change in the subordinated form alone, however out and proud, cannot altogether change the balance of forces. So those who identify as heterosexual must also share the load. Although the conditions we described are general, cultural and structural, there is a responsibility which can only take an individual form. It is through people's actions in micro-political contexts and in both individual and collective ways, that general structures are reproduced or transformed. In this sense, among others, the personal is indeed political.

Contradictions show up best in what we earlier termed 'the micro-politics of the school'. By this term we understand the ways in which power relationships, conflicts and resolutions are negotiated within the context of individual schools. These intensely local conditions and their outcomes are unpredictable without a detailed knowledge of the actual school, though they inflect larger processes of the kind we have discussed in particular ways. Clearly, the advances made in the south London comprehensive discussed in this volume (Patrick and Sanders, this volume) were made in the face of a generally hostile climate and depended on the particularities of the school and area. We want to insist, however, that there are *always* particularities of this kind.[12] Attention to these particularities is an absolute condition of positive change.

There are two or three levels of action open to teachers and their allies: the institutional, the departmental (except in the smallest schools) and the classroom. In each of these levels individual teachers, especially if they organize with others, can make a difference. Some of the ways in which this has happened or can happen have been explored in this volume (see Introduction, Rogers, Sanders and Burke, Patrick and Sanders). Such possibilities are not fixed or predictable, but can be opened up through creative teaching and the use of micro-political insights to shift individuals and, eventually, school structures.

Notes

1 See also Kitzinger *et al.* (1992) in their introduction to the special issue of *Feminism and Psychology* on heterosexuality.
2 There is also a body of literature discussing representations of black sexualities, particularly in the context of the study of racism

(see, for example, hooks 1991, 1992, Pajaczkowska and Young 1992, Hill Collins 1990).

3 The people who have worked or are working on this project besides ourselves are Louise Curry, Mary Kehily, Gurjit Minhas, Anoop Nayak, Peter Redman and Shruti Tanna.

4 See, for example, Gates (1987) and Mercer and Julien (1988) on the sexualization of 'Africa' and of African-Caribbean men, bell hooks (1991, 1992) on the sexualization of African-American men and women, Pratibha Parmar (1987) on sexualized representations Asian women, David Parker (1993) and David Smith (1994) on representations of China and Chinese people.

5 Asian women quoted here were interviewed by Shruti Tanna.

6 We would like to thank KOLA, the Birmingham Black Lesbian and Gay Group, who, in addition to providing a transcript for publication in this book, have also allowed us access to a taped discussion held in 1991, from which this extract is drawn.

7 Gay culture includes a detailed categorization of different 'kinds' of gay men and, to a lesser extent, lesbians. So 'dinge queens' take their place alongside 'leather queens', 'opera queens', 'drama queens', 'lipstick lesbians' and so on.

8 The practical value of Ball's concept can be seen in analyses of school change based on case studies (e.g. Epstein 1993) and in the application of the ideas of Michel Foucault on the 'micro-physics of power' to education (Ball 1991).

9 See Jenny Kitzinger (1990) for detailed discussion of ideologies of innocence and protection and the damage they may cause in relation to dealing with child sexual abuse.

10 For elaborated examples of mythic sexual tales in school, see Kehily (1993).

11 Note, however, that pleasure and danger are often closely connected (see Vance 1984, Kerr 1991).

12 For a discussion of how such particularities can be used to develop anti-racist education in predominantly white schools, see Epstein (1993).

References

Arnot, M. and Weiner, G. (eds) (1987) *Gender and the Politics of Schooling*. London: Hutchinson in association with the Open University.

Ball, S. J. (1987) *The Micro-Politics of the School. Towards a Theory of School Organization*. London: Methuen (republished by Routledge).

Ball, S. J. (ed.) (1991) *Foucault and Education: Disciplines and Knowledge*. London: Routledge.

Beck, E. T. (ed.) (1982) *Nice Jewish Girls: A Lesbian Anthology*. Watertown, MA: Persephone Press.

Department for Education (1993) *Draft Circular to replace Circular 11/87: Sex Education in Maintained Schools*. London: DfE.

Duberman, M., Vicinus, M. and Chauncey, G., Jr. (eds) (1990) *Hidden from History: Reclaiming the Gay and Lesbian Past*. Harmondsworth: Penguin.

Epstein, D. (1988) The well of loneliness: review, *Lesbian and Gay Socialist*, 15, 32–33.

Epstein, D. (1993) *Changing Classroom Cultures: Anti-Racism, Politics and Schools*. Stoke-on-Trent: Trentham Books.

Faderman, L. (1981) *Surpassing the Love of Men: Romantic Friendship and Love between Women from the Renaissance to the Present*. London: Women's Press.

Flintoff, A. (1993) One of the boys? Gender identities in physical education initial teacher education. In I. Siraj-Blatchford (ed.) *'Race', Gender and the Education of Teachers*. Buckingham: Open University Press.

Foucault, M. (1978) *The History of Sexuality, Volume 1, an Introduction* (trans. R. Hurley). Harmondsworth: Penguin (first published 1976 as *La Volonté de Savoir*).

Gates, H. L. (1987) *Race, Writing and Difference*. Chicago: Chicago University Press.

Hall-Carpenter Archives, Oral History Group (1989) *Inventing Ourselves. Lesbian Life Stories*. London: Routledge.

Hall, R. (1982) *The Well of Loneliness*. London: Virago (first published 1928, Jonathan Cape).

Hill Collins, P. (1990) *Black Feminist Thought: Knowledge, Consciousness and the Politics of Empowerment*. London: Unwin Hyman.

Hollway, W. (1987) *Subjectivity and Method in Psychology*. London: Sage.

hooks, b. (1991) *Yearning*. Boston: Turnaround Press.

hooks, b. (1992) *Black Looks: Race and Representation*. Boston: Turnaround Press.

Kehily, M. (1993) 'Tales we heard in school: sexuality and symbolic boundaries', unpublished MSocSci thesis. University of Birmingham.

Kerr, L. (1991) 'Perversion and subversion: a study of lesbian and gay strategies of resistance', unpublished M Soc Sci dissertation. Department of Cultural Studies, University of Birmingham.

Khan, S. (n.d.) *Khush: A Shakti Report*. London: Shakti.

Kitzinger, C., Wilkinson, S. and Perkins, R. (1992) Theorizing heterosexuality, *Feminism and Psychology, Special Issue on Heterosexuality*, 2(3), 293–324.

Kitzinger, J. (1990) 'Who are you kidding?' Children, power and sexual assault. In A. James and A. Prout (eds) *Constructing and Reconstructing Childhood*. London: Falmer Press.

Mercer, K. and Julien, I. (1988) Race, sexuality and black masculinity: a dossier. In R. Chapman and J. Rutherford (eds) *Male Order: Unwrapping Masculinity*. London: Lawrence and Wishart.

National Lesbian and Gay Survey (1992) *What a Lesbian Looks Like*. London: Routledge.

Pajaczkowska, C. and Young, L. (1992) Racism, representation, psychoanalysis. In J. Donald and A. Rattansi (eds) *'Race', Culture and Difference*, London: Sage.

Parker, D. (1993) 'The cultural identities of young people of Chinese origin in Britain', unpublished PhD thesis. University of Birmingham.

Parmar, P. (1987) Hateful contraries: media images of Asian women. In R. Betterton (ed.) *Looking On: Images of Femininity in the Visual Arts and the Media*. London: Pandora.

Pattman, R. (1991) 'Sex education and the liberal paradigm', PhD research, Department of Cultural Studies, University of Birmingham.

Plummer, K. (ed.) (1992) *Modern Homosexualities: Fragments of Lesbian and Gay Existence*. London: Routledge.

Rich, A. (1980) Compulsory heterosexuality and lesbian existence, *Signs*, 5(4), 631–60.

Said, E. (1978) *Orientalism*. London: RKP.

Sealey, A. (1993) 'Making up stories: the constraints of discourse in research with children'. Paper presented at British Sociological Association Conference, University of Essex.

Smith, D. (1994) 'Representations of China in the west', unpublished PhD thesis in progress. University of Birmingham.

Stacey, J. (1991) Promoting normality: Section 28 and the regulation of sexuality. In S. Franklin, C. Lury and J. Stacey (eds) *Off-Centre: Feminism and Cultural Studies*. London: Harper Collins Academic.

Stallybrass, P. and White, A. (1986) *The Politics and Poetics of Transgression*. London: Methuen.

Steedman, C. (1986) *Landscape for a Good Woman*. London: Virago.

Sullivan, C. (1993) Oppression: the experiences of a lesbian teacher in an inner-city comprehensive school in the United Kingdom, *Gender and Education*, 5(1), 93–101.

Trenchard, L. (1984) *Talking about Young Lesbians*. London: Gay Teenagers' Group.

Trenchard, L. and Warren, H. (1984) *Something to Tell You*. London: Gay Teenagers' Group.

Urwin, C. (1984) Power relations and the emergence of language. In J. Henriques, W. Hollway, C. Urwin, C. Venn and V. Walkerdine, *Changing the Subject. Psychology, Social Regulation and Subjectivity*. London: Methuen.

Vance, C. (1984) *Pleasure and Danger: Exploring Female Sexuality*. London: Routledge & Kegan Paul.

Walker, S. and Barton, L. (eds) (1983) *Gender, Class and Education*. London: Falmer Press.

Walkerdine, V. (1981) Sex, power and pedagogy, *Screen Education*, 38, 14–21.

Walkerdine, V. (1985) On the regulation of speaking and silence: subjectivity, class and gender in contemporary schooling. In C. Steedman, C. Urwin and V. Walkerdine (eds) *Language, Gender and Childhood*. London: RKP.

Warren, H. (1984) *Talking about School*. London: Gay Teenagers' Group.

Weeks, J. (1981) *Sex, Politics and Society: The Regulation of Sexuality since 1800*. London: Longman.

Weeks, J. (1985) *Sexuality and Its Discontents: Meaning, Myths and Modern Sexualities*. London: Routledge.

Weeks, J. (1986) *Sexuality*. London: Tavistock.

Weeks, J. (1991) *Against Nature: Essays on History, Sexuality and Identity*. London: Rivers Oram Press.

Willes, M. (1983) *Children into Pupils: A Study of Language and Using Language to Learn*. London: Routledge.

Wolpe, A. M. (1988) *Within School Walls: The Role of Discipline, Sexuality and the Curriculum*. London: Routledge.

Index

LESBIAN AND GAY ISSUES IN THE ENGLISH CLASSROOM
THE IMPORTANCE OF BEING HONEST

Simon Harris

This book aims to examine aspects of sexuality as they pertain to contemporary English teaching. It begins by examining how it is that sexuality has found its way onto the educational agenda, concentrating particularly on the impact of Section 28 of the Local Government Act 1988 and the advent of health education relating to HIV and AIDS.

The book then looks at how lesbian and gay students currently fare in our schools before turning to the amenability of the subject English as a means of integrating issues of sexuality into the curriculum. This is then developed by an examination of how each level of the education system could best deal with the issue, paying particular note to the proposals for the National Curriculum and taking in the role of both Media Studies and Drama.

There then follow two schemes of work, one relating to Timothy Ireland's *Who Lies Inside* and the other to *Annie on my Mind* by Nancy Garden. Each consists of a six week unit suitable for GCSE course work based around the novel, making use of a range of additional materials.

The final section examines the role of the individual teacher dealing with the issue in isolation, a department acting on their own and the place of whole school policies. There is then a discussion of the rights and responsibilities of lesbian and gay teachers and the usefulness of positive images.

The appendix to the book consists of an annotated list of novels, plays and poems which might be of use in raising the issue.

Contents

160pp   0 335 15194 9 (Paperback)

CONTEMPORARY LESBIAN WRITING
DREAMS, DESIRE, DIFFERENCE

Paulina Palmer

In exploring the development of Anglo-American lesbian writing since the early 1970s, this study contextualizes and re-evaluates certain key works of theory and fiction by relating them to the political and cultural movements of the period. These include the Lesbian Feminist Movement, the writing of the lesbian sexual radicals and Queer politics. As well as discussing fiction and theory separately, Palmer also explores the interaction between the two. She examines the way writers as different as Caeia March, Sally Miller Gearhart and Sarah Schulman rework in fictional form ideas from lesbian and/or Queer discourses. The study explores the contradiction and interaction between popular forms of lesbian writing such as the thriller and the comic novel, which appropriate and revise mainstream genres, and academic approaches based on psychoanalysis and poststructuralism. Theorists who are discussed include Radicalesbians, Adrienne Rich, Audre Lorde, Monique Wittig, Luce Irigaray and Judith Butler. Political fictional genre such as the Coming Out novel are considered, and the study concludes with a discussion of the treatment of fantasy, narrativity and sex in the fiction of Jeanette Winterson, Ellen Galford, Jane DeLynn and Sarah Schulman.

Contents

Introduction – Theoretical perspectives – Political fictions – Genre fiction: the thriller – Genre fiction: the comic novel – New developments in fiction: fantasy and sex – Bibliography – Index.

c.160pp   0 335 09038 9 (Paperback)   0 335 09039 7 (Hardback)

THE MAKING OF MEN
MASCULINITIES, SEXUALITIES AND SCHOOLING
Máirtín Mac an Ghaill

Wayne: 'You can't trust girls because of what they expect from you . . . And you can't be honest with your mates because they'll probably tell other people.'

Rajinder: 'There's a lot of sexuality . . . African Caribbeans are seen as better at football . . . and dancing . . . the white kids and Asians are jealous because they think the girls will really prefer the black kids.'

Richard: 'OK sharing the housework and things like that are fair. But it's all the stuff not making girls sex objects. It's ridiculous. What are you supposed to do. Become gay?'

William: 'We wanked each other one night when we were really drunk. Then later on when I saw him, he said he had a girlfriend. I knew he hadn't. We just had to move apart because we got too close.'

Gilroy: 'It's the girls who have all the power. Like they have the choice and can make you look a prat in front of your mates.'

Joanne: 'You lot are obsessed with your knobs . . . all your talk is crap. It's just to prove you're better than your mates. Why don't you all get together and measure your little plonkers?'

Frank: 'My dad spends all his time in the pub with his mates. Why doesn't he want to be with me? Why doesn't he say he loves me? . . . It does my head in.'

Máirtín Mac an Ghaill explores how boys learn to be men in schools whilst policing their own and others' sexualities. He focuses upon the students' confusions and contradictions in their gendered experiences; and upon how schools actively produce, through the official and hidden curriculum, a range of masculinities which young men come to inhabit. He does full justice to the complex phenomenon of male heterosexual subjectivities and to the role of schooling in forming sexual identities.

Contents

224pp   0 335 15781 5 (Paperback)   0 335 15782 3 (Hardback)